Heaven and Earth in the Middle Ages

The Physical World before Columbus

Heaven and Earth in the Middle Ages

The Physical World before Columbus

RUDOLF SIMEK

Translated by ANGELA HALL

THE BOYDELL PRESS

© C. H. Beck'sche Verlagsbuchhandlung, München 1992
Translation © Boydell & Brewer Ltd, Woodbridge 1996

First published 1992
by Verlag C. H. Beck, München
as *Erde und Kosmos im Mittelalter: Das Weltbild vor Kolumbus*

Translation first published 1996
The Boydell Press, Woodbridge

ISBN 0 85115 608 8

The Boydell Press is an imprint of Boydell & Brewer Ltd
PO Box 9, Woodbridge, Suffolk IP12 3DF, UK
and of Boydell & Brewer Inc.
PO Box 41026, Rochester, NY 14604–4126, USA

A catalogue record for this book is available
from the British Library

Library of Congress Cataloging-in-Publication Data
Simek, Rudolf, 1954–
  [Erde und Kosmos im Mittelalter, English]
  Heaven and earth in the Middle Ages : the physical world
before Columbus / Rudolf Simek ; translated by Angela Hall.
      p. cm.
  Includes bibliographical references and index.
  ISBN 0–85115–608–8 (alk. paper)
  1. Cosmology, Medieval. I. Title.
BD495.5.S5513 1996
523.1'09'02–dc20   96–33259

This publication is printed on acid-free paper

Printed in Great Britain by
St Edmundsbury Press Ltd, Bury St Edmunds, Suffolk

CONTENTS

Contents

ILLUSTRATIONS

Figures

Maps

PREFACE

For people today the Middle Ages have a particular fascination because they were clearly so different in many ways from our own time. However, this fascination has made a dark period into one of the most researched and thus illuminated periods in the history of mankind. Yet despite all the apparent and obvious differences there is a striking modernity in those times, a likeness of spirit with man today which attracts us. From this point of view, the Middle Ages not only saved the rich legacy handed down from Classical times through the confusion of the Migration period, the horrors of wars and plagues, but were also an epoch in which national languages and national states in the modern sense hardly played a role. Consequently, the Middle Ages might be seen as an exemplary period for us who live in a time during which petty nationalism is breaking out once more just when it seemed to have been overcome. Not only that, today's pluralistic society with its diversity of co-existing religious and politico-economic ideologies is stirring a longing for a united, closed system of thought.

It is therefore not surprising that there is a remarkable number of books not only dealing with detailed questions about the Middle Ages, but which also consider the *Weltbild* of medieval man, his view of the world,[1] in an attempt to bring this – fictitious – medieval man closer to us and to make him more comprehensible.[2] These works are trying to convey the religious, professional, political, private, and even intimate feelings and thoughts of men who lived and died in the thirty or forty generations between the collapse of the Roman Empire and the discovery of America, a period which, for want of any better definition, has been called retrospectively the *Medium Aevum*, 'middle age'.

The people of the Middle Ages, like those of all other times, were not only determined by their own way of thought and action, but also by their environment and their ability to cope with it successfully. To cope they had to understand it and explain it. Explanations of the physical environment are very different in each stage of human development. They run from the demonised environment of archaic cultures via the pantheistic Hellenism and monotheistic-monistic culture of the Middle Ages up to today's rationalised and materialistic understanding of the universe. Nowadays we have no place for either god or demon on a physical level; both are ousted to a purely transcendental level. This division between spiritual and material spheres is not a development exclusive to the 20th century but in the Middle Ages a monistic, or a holistic, *Weltbild* was an everyday reality. Spirit and matter still permeated each other despite a distinct external dualism, even if the spiritual side was consistently given precedence. A certain disdain of material concerns, which originated in Neo-platoism, can be perceived all too frequently.[3] This did not contradict the fact that people in the Middle Ages had a scientific interest in the physical world. A Latin treatise written in southern Germany in the 11th or 12th century which explicitly deals with heaven and earth begins with the words *Mundus sensibilis* 'the world experienced by the senses'. This it subsequently sets out to explain.[4]

The purpose of this book is to describe medieval notions of the physical world. Beginning with concepts concerning the structure of the cosmos, I shall move on to the shape of the earth and the continents before turning to geographical and ethnographical matters as well as questions of natural science. Not only will such principal questions as man's quest to understand the universe be dealt with, but also his understanding of his environment and its functions.

There is no chapter in this book concerned with society, the estate system, or popular religion. These aspects of the human condition are variables which have exhibited substantial, if not revolutionary, changes during the long period between the fall of the Roman Empire and the beginning of the Reformation in Europe, quite apart from regional differences. So, the social environment has been deliberately excluded in order to be able to depict more clearly the impression of the inanimate creation; this world of the first four days of creation, before men and animals came into being, was something over which man had hardly any influence in a pre-scientific age.[5]

In the title of this book Columbus is used to signify the end of the Middle Ages. His geographical discoveries, as well as those made by Copernicus and Kepler in mathematics and astronomy, destroyed the coherent *Weltbild* of the Middle Ages more drastically than any other change in the last millennium. The physical *Weltbild* described here is therefore justifiably referred to as being 'before Columbus'; however, it could equally well be referred to as 'the *Weltbild* before Copernicus'. Thus the final chapter predominantly deals with these discoveries and their part in the disintegration of the medieval world.

The representation of the complete physical view of the world is an artificially constructed house of cards for two reasons. On the one hand the four centuries from the beginning of the 12th century to the end of the 15th century, with which this book is concerned, was such a long period of time that, even if one considers the slow progress made by medieval scholarship, a cross-section of the many different, constantly developing, regionally distinct theories concerning the physical world, can never do justice to all of them.

On the other hand, the view of the world presented here is clearly a scholarly *Weltbild*, characterised by the tradition of Classical culture in the monasteries, and from the 13th century increasingly strongly influenced by the universities. It would therefore not be wrong either, to speak about a scholarly ecclesiastical *Weltbild*, because the universities remained dominated by the knowledge collected and protected by the Church well into modern times. The seven liberal arts, especially the subjects of the *quadrivium* (astronomy, geometry, mathematics, and music) which are the basis of this inquiry, were the servants of the other subjects, in particular theology, for a long time. This, at least, was the theory, but ever since the 9th century independent research has been made in these subjects which today would be called the natural sciences. It should be noted in this that the attitude of a particular religious order towards the study of natural science was more important than the basic attitude of the church hierarchy.[6] The *Weltbild* described here in detail was therefore not that of any one individual scholar or of any one religious order or university, but instead it represents the theoretical sum total of concepts of the physical world in the Middle Ages. It is virtually impossible for one individual scholar to have known all these theories. As to the question of how medieval people outside the universities, monasteries, and episcopal courts tried to explain their environment, we can only speculate despite the occasional illumination provided by some discourses or popular treatises.

FOREWORD TO THE ENGLISH EDITION

This volume, discussing how medieval man understood matters relating to the physical heaven and the earth, is the translation of my *Erde und Kosmos im Mittlelalter. Das physische Weltbilt vor Kolumbus,* first published in German in 1992. It has been revised and altered for its English edition, with some bibliographical updating, as a result of help gained from a large number of reviews of the German edition.

The book is aimed at both the educated layman and the interested scholar and tries to give a readable account of concepts held in the Middle Ages as well as ample material for further reading in the notes. It is obvious that a relatively small volume cannot nearly cover this field completely, and I have not attempted to do justice to all the scholars in Europe throughout the 1000 years from the fall of the Roman Empire to the Reformation. The presentation is therefore selective with a tendency towards both the symptomatic and the idiosyncratic, rather than attempting the impossible and filling several tomes with all the available evidence.

The English public is served better than any other with books on the natural sciences in the Middle Ages, but most of these concentrate on the findings of a small group of medieval scholars in those sciences, rather than presenting popular views. This book should therefore be seen as the first attempt at a broader view of the physical world as understood by medieval man, leaving scope for other scholars to pursue the subject further.

R. Simek
Gmunden, summer 1996

CHAPTER ONE

Christopher Columbus and his Achievement

When Christopher Columbus set off westward from the small Spanish port of Palos on his first voyage of discovery in August 1492, the greatest problems concerning his voyage were already in the past. Political, organisational, and financial problems were only a few of the things which had dogged him during the eighteen years since he first conceived the idea of this voyage. The question uppermost in the minds of those involved, particularly the Spanish crown which was to bear over 7/8 of the costs of the enterprise, was whether such a voyage to the west was a physically possible way of reaching the easternmost countries of the world.

The modern belief is that Columbus was rejected or even mocked[1] for believing that the earth was a sphere and that a journey to the west would result in the discovery of a direct route to the riches beckoning in India and East Asia. This is a fallacious opinion and has been disputed by scholars since the mid-19th century. Columbus's problem was not the shape of the earth but determining its size and circumference and consequently the duration of the voyage from Spain or Portugal to Asia. In the 15th century journeys lasting several weeks, let alone sea voyages of several months, were generally considered to be difficult and dangerous, if not impossible.

In order to be able to convince the Spanish king of the feasibility of such a voyage, the so-called Talavera commission was called in Salamanca at the end of 1486. According to Columbus's biographers Las Casas and Fernando Colón (Christopher Columbus's son), the commission was made up of astronomers, cosmographers, sea-farers and philosophers.[2] The chairman was a cleric called Hernando de Talavera, father confessor to the Queen (and later Bishop of Avila)[3]. Despite certain doubts about its very existence, it appears that a commission was indeed called upon, in some form or other, to discuss the enterprise.[4] However, the idea that Columbus had to appear before it like an accused, to be interrogated and cross-examined, and be called to defend his supposedly innovatory thoughts about the sphericity of the earth, belong to a popular but totally erroneous mythology about Columbus.[5] Similarly, Columbus was not confronted by conservative clerics with quotations from the Church Fathers in order to refute his belief in the spherical shape of the earth.[6]

This would have been absurd at a university where one of the greatest contemporary astronomers, Abramo Zacuto, was teaching and propounding in his lectures the teachings of John Regiomontanus (1436–1476). These teachings were later developed and perfected into the Copernican system at the beginning of the 16th century. It would also have been difficult to find the supposed profusion of quotations from the Bible or the Church Fathers. The only possibly useable passage comes from the doctrinal teachings (*Divinae institutiones*) of the African Church Father Firmianus Lactantius (from around AD 300).[7] Lactantius repudiates the sphere-shape of the earth, together with existence of the Antipodes and the concept of gravity on supposedly biblical grounds.[8] A second passage which theoretically could be considered to refute the global shape of the earth comes from the confused *Topographia Christiana* written in c. 545 by the Alexandrinian monk Cosmas who called himself Indikopleustes, 'Indian traveller'. He believed that the Bible professed the world was shaped like an altar and refuted all the teachings of Classical astronomers. However, this work was never translated into Latin. It was only printed in Paris in 1706 and was virtually unknown in Europe beforehand (with only three Greek manuscripts extant);[9] the members of the Talavera commission had certainly never heard of this particular passage.

The state of astronomical knowledge in the late 15th century means that we may assume that the spherical shape of the world was taken for granted by all the members of the commission.[10] It is also by no means certain whether this commission ever indeed met formally or if Columbus only had the opportunity to speak privately with Talavera and other members.[11] It is quite easy to reconstruct what would actually have been discussed there because of the state of geographical knowledge and of expeditions at the time. The main question no doubt concerned the distance between western Spain and the east coast of Asia, or rather the Japanese islands lying off that coast. Their quest would be aided by the work of the scholarly doctor and astronomer from Florence, Paolo Dai Pozzo Toscanelli (1397–1482), whose correspondents included not only Columbus but also Regiomontanus and Nicolas of Kues.

One matter which needed discussion would have been the absolute distances for the degrees of latitude. It is possible that due to his interest in getting his plan passed Columbus tried to falsify the results here so that the distance appeared to be less. As a result a shorter journey than he privately believed to be necessary would be anticipated.

The discussions of the Talavera commission would probably also have covered the less important problem already suggested by Toscanelli: would a voyage discover other islands apart from Cipangu (Japan) on the way to Asia? Scholars have frequently pointed out that Columbus seems to have been convinced that he would sight land relatively soon after setting out on his chosen route. His peculiar falsification of the distances and degrees of longitude found in his logbook suggests this. However, he could hardly have deceived the other two captains who would surely have been tracing the course themselves. It is, of course, impossible to discover whether the basis of his expectations in this respect was a result of knowledge of the Scandinavian discovery of Vinland[12]

(Newfoundland) or a hypothetical, but not completely impossible, Portuguese discovery of the New World by Dualmo as early as 1485. Dualmo, a Fleming living on the Azores, had discovered that there was a land barrier to the west. This discovery was, at the time, maintained as a matter of extreme secrecy by King John of Portugal. He wanted to keep from the Spaniards the information that the only possible sea-route to India was round the southern cape of Africa.[13]

The third problem which beset Columbus and was equally important to the money-lenders, the crown, and seafarers alike, was the technical feasibility of such a long sea crossing. There was nothing new about this; the Portuguese had initially had to conquer the problem of travelling great distances in their voyages along the coast of Africa. For his part Columbus was able to draw on his own experiences made on his voyage to Guinea in 1482 or 1483. The Portuguese solution to the question of supplies had been to set up a series of forts along the coast, a solution hardly suitable for sailing across the Atlantic. However, Columbus had probably learned on his trip to Guinea that it was quite possible to be at sea for far longer than the average sailor of his time thought possible. Columbus knew that it was possible to be on board for one or even two months without fresh water or fresh food, but he was also well aware of the pyschological resistance from conservative and notoriously superstitious sailors which he would have to overcome.

The greatest uncertainty of all was probably the islands which they expected to encounter on their passage west (as Columbus's experience was to prove). On the medieval maps of the world and in cosmographies there were hardly any islands marked between Ireland in the west and Cipangu (Japan) in the east. Those which were drawn in were not known from any direct personal experience. Consequently the explorers were partly reliant on fables and mythology.[14] On the other hand the discoveries of Madeira in 1420, the Azores in around 1430, and the Cape Verdes islands by Cadamosta in 1455[15] had drawn attention to the fact that there were more islands in the Atlantic than had been known to the medieval cosmographers. Fabulous islands such as the remains of the legendary submerged island of Atlantis or Antiglia which was mentioned by Toscanelli,[16] must surely have had a place in the discussion about the length and possibility of such a voyage to the west. What we do not know is whether Columbus knew about other, real, islands in the Atlantic.

The main question, however, was the distance between Europe and East Asia. Here it was easily possible to refer to the authority of Classical and clerical medieval scholars (see Chapter 3), although the problem was more one of mathematics than of theology. It is quite plausible that St Augustine was quoted as denying the existence of the Antipodes[17] but as Columbus wanted to go to Asia and not to the Antipodes (that is, to people living on the opposite side of the globe to Europe), this argument is unlikely to have been considered significant.

The commission of Salamanca came to no decision despite Columbus's indisputable eloquence and his deep conviction of the aim of the enterprise.

This is not surprising since a scholarly ecclesiastical gathering in the 15th century (or any other preceding century for that matter) could hardly arrive at a clear recommendation to their 'Catholic Majesties'[18] about the practical possibility of sailing round the earth when there was the further question of hefty investment. Comments made in the Bible and by the Church Fathers, or indeed by the Classical authorities and the scholars from the High Middle Ages, are too vague to have given a clear picture of the shape, size, and nature of the earth and the universe. Columbus's enthusiasm alone, together with some very speculative calculations and a little support from the Dominicans at the University of Salamanca (among them Prior Diego Deza, with whom Columbus enjoyed a life-long friendship)[19] could hardly justify such an investment according to the view of an impartial commission, but one which was nonetheless responsible to the crown.

Only six years later, in the wave of enthusiasm following the fall of Granada on the 2nd January 1492 and the final expulsion of the Moslems from the Iberian peninsula which resulted, Columbus found that the Spanish court suddenly had far greater interest in his plans than hitherto. Now he was offered frugal, but adequate financing for his project.

Our interest in the 'six or seven years of great worries', which Columbus spent waiting for his voyage to receive royal approval[20] and what makes the discussion of the Talavera commission particularly fascinating for us, is the preoccupation of Columbus and his contemporaries with the essential questions of cosmography in the late Middle Ages, a matter which was of practical relevance during Columbus's first voyage.

These questions of cosmography concerned the basic principles of our world. These were the physical structure and the elements of the universe, the role of the earth in this cosmic structure, and the property of the surface of our globe. They also included the appearance and characteristics of far-off countries and islands and their role in divine providence, and the nature and origin of their inhabitants. There was also the question of various natural phenomena and what caused them.

Man's questions about his physical environment will be dealt with systematically in the following chapters. Of course medieval man was far more distant from the explanations than his modern counterpart. The answers to these questions had changed far less in the five centuries before Columbus's first expedition, that is from the early Middle Ages, than they have since Columbus's discovery of the West Indian islands.

There were indeed traditional answers to these questions. Until the 14th and 15th centuries these were accepted much in the same way as we accept modern research or hypotheses. The modern layman tends to view contemporary findings with respect to the basic principles of astronomy, physics, geography, and geology as virtually definitive. However, a 13th-century scholarly clerical astronomer who had managed to combine the knowledge of Classical times handed down by Arabian scholars, with his own Christian learning to form a closed system might well have believed, despite unexplained details, in the principle invariability and correctness of his *Weltbild* just as we believe in ours. His beliefs might have been considered correct not only from the point of view of theological doctrine, which is often extraordinarily open in physical questions, but also from the point of view of the scientific research of his time.

CHAPTER TWO

The Earth as the Protected Centre of a Finite Universe and the Earth as the Yolk in the Cosmic Egg

The Spherical Shape of the World

The *Weltbild* of Christopher Columbus and man before him was a finite system. This has nothing whatsoever to do with the 20th-century concept of the constantly expanding universe, but refers to a far more tangible limitation than one of definite and permanent dimensions. The earth was believed to be surrounded by the universe in a very real sense because it was the centre of concentric spheres. Even the outermost of these spheres, though at an immense distance from the earth, and the furthest physical shell of this gigantic, but not infinite 'cosmic onion' built from planetary orbits, was secure in God's hands since God surrounded all of the spheres in his infinite magnitude.

Besides the purely physical aspect, the limitation of the universe also concerned two basic philosophical assumptions. The first in particular led to controversies due to the rediscovery of the works of Aristotle in the 12th and 13th centuries. Aristotelians believed that the world was eternal, a belief that contradicted the Christian teaching that God had created the world and it was therefore finite. The Aristotelian belief in an eternal world was therefore repeatedly and strictly condemned, especially by the bishop of Paris in 1270 and 1277.

The second assumption was less open to dispute since there was unanimous agreement on the premise that the world was unique. There was an enormous body of evidence from both Classical philosophers and Christian theologians[1] which stated this. However, the theoretical possibility that other worlds might exist was treated as valid because of the limitations otherwise posed for God's omnipotence.

The concept of the earth as the centre of the planetary system and thus the universe derives from Greek astronomy. Since the 4th-century BC Greek astronomers had developed two somewhat different geocentric systems. By late Classical times, and particularly in the Middle Ages, these had been homogenised into a not always consistent but nonethless comprehensible and generally accepted view of the cosmos. The older of these two models (by Eudoxus and Aristotle) was the model of homocentric spheres which assumed fully concentric physical spheres moving round the earth. The other was the model of excentric epicycles which attempted to explain the irregularities of the orbits of the planets by eccentric spheres and the epicycle theory (see p. 18f and Figure 6). From the 12th century onwards and especially in the late Middle Ages this second model began to supplement the previously accepted model of the spheres as devised by Ptolemy.

The spheric model had already been outlined by Eudoxus of Cnidos (about 408–350 BC), said to have been the first to teach the concept of planetary motion. His works are no longer extant but the model was extended by Aristotle to incorporate 27 crystalline spheres. The Greek astronomer Hipparchus of Nicaea (Bithynia) in the 2nd century BC and especially the mathematician Ptolemy four hundred years later developed it from a predominantly symbolic to an astronomical system[2] and made it generally accepted.[3] This geocentric cosmic model of planets which moved in exact circular orbits around the earth remained valid for one and a half millennia until the work of Copernicus. But even from the 12th century onwards attempts were made to correct the obvious errors of the system.[4]

In this model devised and refined over the centuries by Eudoxus, Hipparchus, and Ptolemy the immense but not infinite cosmos was built of concentric physical spheres. These were based on the orbits of the seven 'planets' known at the time, including the sun and the moon, and the firmament formed by the extra (assumed) sphere of the fixed stars. There can hardly have been any scholar in the Middle Ages who still thought of these spheres as really being crystalline, as Ptolemy is supposed to have done. Rather, they were perceived as mathematical quantities which were determined by the length of time it took the planets to orbit the earth. The orbits of the planets were presented in the armillary spheres of the late Middle Ages as arcs divided into degrees. (Armillary spheres are metal models of the universe, in which the spheres are represented by thin metal arcs rather than by solid spheres).

On each of the seven spheres between the earth and the firmament one of the seven 'planets' (the moon, Mercury, Venus, the sun, Mars, Jupiter and Saturn) was moving. The sun was the middle, and most important planet. It was also considered to be the largest (either seven to eight times bigger or even 160 times as big as the earth[5]). The seven planetary orbits were confined within an eighth sphere, called the firmament, or sphere of fixed stars. Hipparchus of Nicaea catalogued 1026 fixed stars,[6] and there can be few more than this number visible to the naked eye.[7] The firmament turned fastest and completed a whole revolution round the earth every 24 hours. Outside the firmament lay the mobile and multifarious crystalline heavens (*coelum cristallinum*) which were transparent like crystal. Beyond this there was only the empyrean heavens (*empyreum*), thought to be an immobile homogeneous light.

The earth was the centre of the universe, not because of its importance but strangely enough because of its inconsequence in the cosmic system as perceived from the medieval point of view. This attitude, which appears to us today to be totally contradictory, could be explained primarily by the fact that the earth, as the heaviest element, was located furthest *down*. This meant that seen from the centre all the other spheres were further *up* and therefore were more important. Secondly the size of the earth was in so far correctly estimated in that it was considered to be tiny in comparison to the entire *mundus*, a mere 'indivisible dot',[8] compared with which all the stars in the firmament were larger. Thirdly and finally, the importance of the *momentum* was decisive for the earth to be on the bottom of the heavenly hierarchy. The momentum within the universe had its source outside the firmament whereas the earth, apparently untouched by it, lay immobile at its centre.

The firmament rotated round the earth quickest (exactly once in 24 hours) whilst the planets had varying orbital times (now called 'sidereal periods'). Thus, the conclusion could easily be drawn that the power causing the movement of the firmament (and of all the planets) lay outside the firmament. This 'first mover' (*primum movens*) was either identified as an invisible ninth or tenth sphere or else as God himself. God's divine love caused him to impart this cosmic momentum[9] to the universe by bringing the *primum mobile* (the 'first movable'), the most outer physical sphere, into motion. The movement of the outermost sphere transferred itself to the whole planetary systrem through the friction between the spheres.

The visible planetary motion indicated, however, that the lowest planets which were furthest away from the *primum movens*, namely the moon, Venus, and Mercury, by no means had the most irregular orbits and longest sidereal periods as might have been expected in the strictly hierarchical structure of the universe according to Aristotle. Curiously (from the medieval point of view), the planets which were furthest away, and thus nearer to the *primum movens*, had the longest orbital times. Aristotle had considered the *primum mobile* to be the origin of the regular planetary orbits and hence given the outer planets (Jupiter, Saturn) a higher rank than the lower ones (Mercury, Venus), thus reflecting the hierarchy of the respective ancient gods.

In the Middle Ages a further problem was added by the attempt made by scholars to evaluate God's function in the *primum movens*. The discrepancy between the actually visible planetary motion and Aristotelian theory led to a new classification of the spheres in scholastic cosmography. In this new system they were now rated not according to their situation (or mythological rank), but rather according to the function of the middle 'planet', the sun. The sun was considered to be the most distinguished celestial body and even surpassed the firmament in its importance.[10]

The Ptolemaeic system of the universe in its simple form (with eight spheres) was valid throughout the entire Middle Ages. The diagram of his model of the cosmos was probably the most common astronomical illustration in medieval manuscripts (see Figures 1 and 2). The Venerable Bede's work, *De natura rerum*, written in the early eighth century, already includes it, as does the metric *Calendarium* composed by Wandalbert of Prüm in the 9th century.

This illustration of the universe usually had a symbolic depiction of the earth at the centre. This might be either a T drawn into a circle, as an abbreviation of

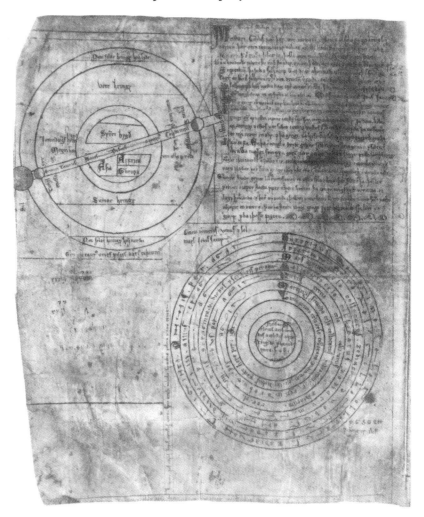

Figure 1. Simple diagram of the universe. Copenhagen, Arnamagnaean Institute, AM 736 I, 4 to, f.IV (c. 1400).

the word *terra*, simultaneously representing the medieval *mappae mundi*:[11] the word *terra* in a small circle; or else a diagrammatic drawing of a scene on earth (often complete with towns and harbours) surrounded by the hydrosphere.[12] This abbreviation for our planet, or in medieval understanding the centre of the universe, is surrounded in these diagrams by eight concentric circles which bear the names of the seven planets and the firmament. In this simple form the illustration of the universe itself serves as a pictorial contraction for the physical cosmos. For this very reason it is included in nearly all works which deal with astronomical or cosmographic questions,[13] and not only these. Illustrations of

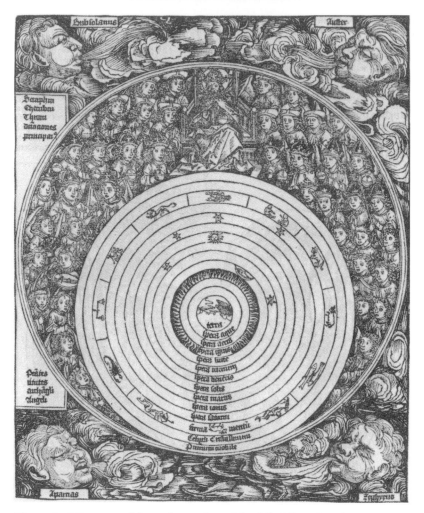

*Figure 2. Diagram of the universe from Schedel's Liber chronicarum
from 1493. From the copy in Vienna, Österreichische Nationalbibliothek,
Ink.25. A.6,f.Vv.*

the universe are also found in manuscripts of works which deal with the creation
of the world from commentaries on Genesis to Hildegard of Bingen's mystical
view of the world.[14]

Depictions of the universe such as these usually illustrate an additional one
to three concentric circles beyond the firmament, representing the spiritual
heavens. According to medieval opinion, the crystalline heaven (often identified
with the *primum mobile*), an empyrean heaven (*empyreum*) and then finally
God or the *primum movens* were to be found outside the firmament. The
empyrean heaven which lay between the two was, to some extent, thought to be

immobile. As a result there was a constantly renewing terminological and factual confusion in the Middle Ages about the relative positions of the crystalline heaven, empyrean heaven, and *primum movens*. Scholars in the Middle Ages were aware of this confusion. Thomas Aquinus stated that there are, apart from a symbolic, two other meanings of the word 'heaven'; on one hand there was the physical heaven to which everything from the lunar sphere to the empyrean heaven belonged, and on the other was the so-called third heaven (*tertium coelum*) which lay outside the physical heaven and was where the saints, angels, and God lived.[15]

Popular medieval treatises went even further and simplified the matter by differentiating between three heavens: a physical (*coelum corporale*), a spiritual (*coelum spirituale*) and an 'intellectual' (or rather 'transcendental': *coelum intellectuale*).[16] The first of these heavens encompassed the physical spheres including the firmament and the empyrean heaven. The spiritual heaven was the home of the angels and the Trinity was enthroned in the intellectual.

The spiritual heaven as the home of the angels could be further subdivided into its own (spiritual) spheres which served as domiciles for the nine hierarchies of angels.[17] This kind of sub-division was illustrated in detailed illustrations of the universe such as Hartmann Schedel's famous *Liber Chronicarum* (in the German edition called *Weltchronik* 'World Chronicle') where two (physical) spheres, the crystalline heaven and the *primum mobile*, were included outside the firmament. Even further outside this lay a large circle in which the Trinity, surrounded by angelic hosts had their place.[18]

Consequently, in high and late medieval texts the number of heavenly spheres varied. There were either eight or nine (the latter in particular in astronomy texts), ten or even fourteen spheres included,[19] the latter not only by extending the heavens beyond the firmament into different spiritual spheres, but sometimes also by the subdivision of the sublunar sphere into the four elements (see Chapter 8).

Theological elaborations of this kind fulfilled the need for a homogenisation of theological doctrine with the astronomical *Weltbild*, and they are manifest in attempts to explain matters like the one mentioned by Thomas Aquinas. This finite *Weltbild* then shows in a quite concrete way how God holds all creation in his hands. In medieval theological manuscripts, especially in the so-called *bibles moralisées* (biblical manuscripts with commentaries and illustrations), a beautifully executed iconography was developed to depict this idea of God holding the world in his hands. In one of the two famous illustrations of Genesis in two Viennese biblical manuscripts God the Creator holds the world before him, represented by an artistic illustration of the universe. In the other version he supports the earth and compasses in each hand to symbolise his responsibility for the plan of creation. Although in the example shown in Figure 4 and other rich illuminations, the individual spheres are not shown, some of the numerous smaller illustrations of the Creator with the cosmos[20] include them. Despite the free, non-astronomic style of illustration and the tendency to

Figure 3. Diagram of the universe in the prose version of Walter of Metz's Image du monde (c. 1245). London, The British Library, MS Royal 19. A. IX., f. 149r (15th century).

emphasise the elements rather than the spheres they are clearly recognisable as illustrations of the universe.

The universe included the planetary spheres, the firmament, the crystalline and empyrean heavens, and the so-called spiritual spheres. But beyond the

Figure 4. Diagram of the universe with God the Creator from a **bible
moralisée** *(13th century). Vienna, Österreichische Nationalbibliothek,
MS 1179, 1v.*

universe was an infinite void which, since God is infinite, was thought to be
filled by God. The concept of an empty infinity, which does not take into account
God's omnipresence, was derived from Aristotle's *De coelo* (which naturally
enough does not mention God's omnipresence). This text was made accessible
to medieval scholars in 1271 by William of Moerbeke's translation of Simplicius'
6th-century commentary on Aristotle's work. However it was brought into line

with Christian doctrine by medieval scholars of the 14th century, such as Nicolas Oresme or Thomas Bradwardine.[21] Since 1277 the theoretical possibility of other universes had been stated in writing,[22] but the discovery of their existence in the space assumed to be empty remained to be dicovered by modern man.[23]

No matter how detailed the model of the spheres was, the firmament was always the outermost visible sphere. It seems that in comparison to Arabian or Chinese astronomers,[24] the Europeans in the Middle Ages apparently took very little notice of celestial events such as novae, although there are at least two references to supernovae (in 1006 and 1054).[25] One permanent phenomenon, the Milky Way, was not only the subject of popular interpretation but also generated serious interpretations. It was in fact correctly interpreted as a mass of stars.[26]

The spheres were not only illustrated in scholarly manuscript illustrations and in the iconographically simplified diagrams of the universe. They were also presented as visual metaphors which explained the movement of the planets to a wider public. Honorius of Autun described a planet revolving round the earth like a fly sitting on a rotating mill-stone (*Imago mundi* I, 67). An Old Icelandic text even speaks of two flies.[27] The so-called *Mainauer Naturlehre* ('School-Book on Nature from Mainau'), an interesting but uninfluential Middle High German book on nature, compared the planet to a midge on a wheel while in his *Deutschen Sphaera* Konrad of Megenberg talks of an ant on a mill-stone. The prettiest image of all is that suggested by Vitruvius who compared the system of spheres with a potter's wheel into which concentric grooves have been chiselled for the ants to run in.[28]

The system of spherical planetary orbits was extremely useful. It explained the most important characteristics of the geocentric structure of the universe, and the diagram of the spheric model provided an iconographic abbreviation for 'world' (that is, universe) for the identification of the contents in astronomical manuscripts. Nevertheless the inadequacies of this *Weltbild* are all too clear. A dissatisfaction with its shortcomings found expression in the discussions between theologians and astronomers concerning the number of heavenly spheres. This was shown in a woodcut in the printed version of Pierre d'Ailly's *Concordancia Astronomie cum Theologica*, where an astronomer and a theologian hotly discuss the number of spheres shown above them.[29]

The first striking inconsistency of the spherical model was the discrepancy between the actual orbiting time of the planets and the theory of the *primum movens* as the impetus of all planetary movement. This in turn led to the already mentioned theory of the sun's exceptional position as the middle one of the seven 'planets'. However this conflict is hardly mentioned in astronomical literature, probably because the astronomers, as a result of the clear physical flaws, also avoided a detailed interpretation of the planetary momentum.

There was a more serious problem. In Classical antiquity the observation had been made that Venus and Mercury were only ever seen as evening and

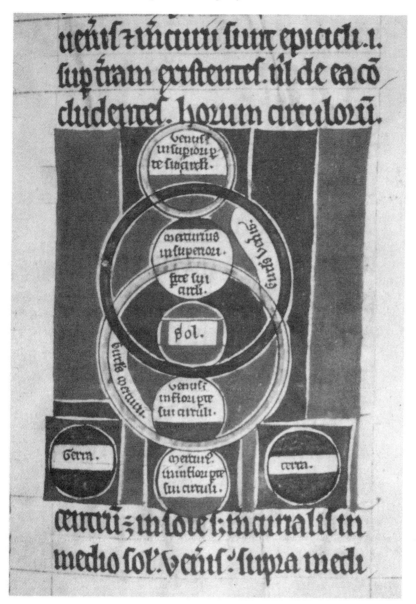

Figure 5. Heliocentric orbits of Mercury and Venus (top) and the heliocentric epicycles of Venus (bottom) by Daniel of Morley, Liber de naturis inferiorum et superiorum. London, The British Library, MS Arundel 377, f. 119r (13th century).

morning stars. That is, they were seen to be only at a slight angular distance from the sun whereas the larger, outer planets could take on any angular distance to the sun. Nowadays we know that is because both planets are closer to the sun than the earth. They therefore appear to follow the sun across the sky but are normally made invisible by the solar glare. Only when they rise before, or set after, the sun are they visible and then only at dawn or dusk.

In the 4th century BC Heraclides of Pontos supplied the quite logical explanation that both these planets did not revolve round the earth, but round the sun, which in turn revolved round the earth.[30] This explanation from Heraclides' lost works was included in the early Middle Ages in the works of several encyclopedists, among them Martianus Capella (5th century AD) and Macrobius (around AD 400), both of whom were well known in the Middle Ages. The theory was made more widely known later by the medieval encyclopedists who copied it for use in their own compilations. Heraclides' theory was only taken up again at the beginning of the 12th century by William of Conches from the Chartres School (teacher in Paris and tutor to Henry II of England) in his *Philosophia mundi*. Daniel of Morley, in his *Liber de naturis inferiorum et superiorum* composed after his astronomy studies in Toledo and at the instigation of John of Oxford (bishop of Norwich 1175–1200), also discussed in detail the heliocentric orbit of Mercury and Venus. Like William he illustrated this theory with a diagram (Figure 5).[31]

Daniel's handbook was far less widespread (with only two manuscripts still extant)[32] than William's. The explanation given above for the peculiarities in the orbits of Mercury and Venus were interestingly enough not taken up in the most widely known astronomy handbook of the Middle Ages, John of Sarobosco's (also known as John Holywood or Halifax, fl. 1230) *Liber de sphaera*, written at the beginning of the 13th century, nor in its subsequent German translations. There was similarly no sign of it in Robert Grosseteste's less-successful handbook of the same title.

From the 13th century onwards these books were prescribed texts at the universities. As a result they contributed enormously to the popularisation of knowledge about astronomy. The first product seems to have been John of Sacrobosco's *Liber de sphaera* (or *De sphaera mundi*) which the northern English scholar wrote at the beginning of the 13th century (before 1220) when he was teaching at the university of Paris. In his relatively short handbook he dealt in four sections with the spheric structure of the universe according to Ptolemy's system, the astronomical circles, the rise and fall of the celestial bodies with regard to the climatic zones, and finally planetary motion.

Despite, or perhaps just because of, the brevity of the presentation which ignored several important astronomical questions, this little book was one of the bestsellers of medieval non-fiction. There are probably several hundred Latin manuscripts still extant. In the days of early printing, when its content was already slightly out-of-date, it was printed in sixty-five editions between 1472 and 1647 alone. There are around eighty Latin commentaries known[33] and the work was either completely or else partially translated into several vernacular languages. It was translated into Middle High German in three different versions. The first was produced between 1347 and 1350 by the scholarly and energetic canon Konrad of Megenberg (1309–1374), when he was head of the school of St Stephan in Vienna. He called his free translation the *Deutsche Sphaera*.[34] An anonymous translation entitled *Puechlein von der Spera*[35] ('Booklet on the Sphere') came into existence, likewise in Vienna, in the second half of the 14th century. Finally another translation was made at the beginning of the 16th century by the mathematician and astronomer Konrad Heinfogel, a cleric from Nuremberg (c. 1455–1517) whose version was printed as *Sphaera materialis* between 1516 and 1539 in four different editions.[36]

If John of Sacrobosco's textbook was the most influential work on astronomy of the Middle Ages, it was by no means the only one which was conceived as a handbook. There seems to have been a tendency for the individual religious orders to have their own textbooks written. At almost the same time that John of Sacrobosco was writing his work, his fellow countryman, the Franciscan Robert Grosseteste (c. 1175–1253), from 1235 bishop of Lincoln, was composing an even shorter work. It had nearly the same content which he quite obviously adjusted to the needs of his order. The five chapters of *De sphaera* even contain illustrations which are closely related to those in Sacrobosco's work, but it did not gain acceptance at the universities and it probably remained limited to use within the Franciscan order.[37] Another English cleric and author of another textbook on astronomy was the Franciscan John Peckham (c. 1220–1292) who composed his *Tractatus sphaerae* long before becoming archbishop of Canterbury in 1279, and likewise adjusted this for practical usage in the order's schools.[38] Soon afterwards in the mid-13th century Campanus of Novara, Pope Urban VI's chaplain (pontificate 1261–1265), wrote his *Tractatus de Sphaera*. It had fifty-four very short chapters and was largely based on John of Sacrobosco. In a few cases it goes beyond the *Liber de sphaera*, for example in a description of the continents and also in the above mentioned problem of the relationship between the sun's orbit and the orbits of Mercury and Venus.[39] This question was admittedly sporadically mentioned in the commentaries to John of Sacrobosco's work,[40] but none of these texts insisted on the heliocentricity of the two planets.

The third and most striking irregularity of Ptolemy's teaching is described in all these works in great detail. Mars, Jupiter and Saturn had all been observed to appear to stop at the point in their orbits when the Earth lay between them and the Sun, and then move backwards (known now as 'retrograde motion') before continuing their normal course but this was hardly ever recorded in the diagrams of the spherical model of the universe. Venus and Mercury were observed to exhibit a different form of retrograde motion. Either could rise before the sun ('morning stars') or set after it ('evening stars'), but never moved very far from the sun. Each appeared to move away from the sun, slowing as it

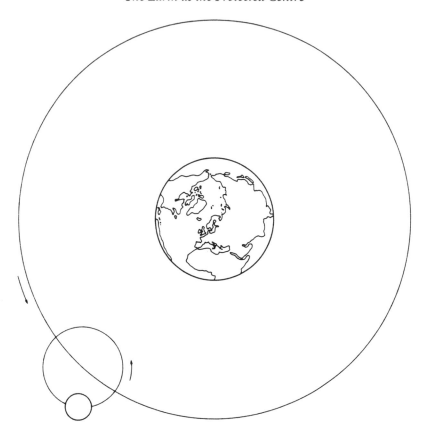

Figure 6. Schematic illustration of the epicycle theory.

did before apparently pausing and moving backwards until it reappeared some time later on the other side of the sun when the pattern was repeated.

These irregularities had puzzled astronomers and philosophers since Classical times and caused them to come up with new theories to explain it. Usually they tried to explain the standstills and retrograde motion by assuming new spheres.[41] The different speeds and directions of rotation of the intermediary spheres were supposed to allow a logical interpretation of the irregularities observed from earth. In order to do so Aristotle came to the conclusion that there were twenty-seven spheres in all which were later increased to up to fifty-five, and even then not all the irregularities of the planetary orbits could be explained;[42] these remained problematic right up to Kepler's theories at the turn from the 16th to the 17th century (see Chapter 9 below).

The solution which was finally widely accepted in the high Middle Ages was Ptolemy's epicycle theory[43] based on preliminary work by Apollonius of Pergae (around 200 BC). This epicycle theory interpreted the actual orbits of the planets as smaller circles (the so-called epicycles) whose centres moved on the large spheres, the so-called deferentials (see Figures 5 and 6).

This theory, propagated by the *Almagest* and Sacrobosco's *Liber de sphaera* as well as the other astronomy handbooks above, became the valid explanation for the planetary orbits from the 13th–16th centuries. However, it was only recorded in specialised astronomy literature. The generally accepted explanations in encyclopedic literature remained uninfluenced by this complex theory and continued to present the spherical heavens without detailed explanations as simple concentric circles. Only since the work of the philosopher John Scotus Eriugena, an Irish scholar at the court of Charles the Bald (grandson of Charlemagne), in the 9th century had there been sporadic attempts to modify the traditional iconography of the diagram of the universe according to the epicycle theory. This modification meant that variations of the heliocentric theory for Venus and Mercury were depicted.[44] This theory had led Aristarchus of Samos in the third century BC to come up with the first heliocentric concept of the world (which is usually but incorrectly credited to Heraclides of Pontos in the 4th century BC).[45]. This so-called geo-heliocentric solution, according to which Mercury and Venus revolved round the sun, whilst the sun and all the other planets revolved round the earth, was occasionally assimilated into other works in the Middle Ages (in particular by William of Conches and Daniel of Morley, see Figure 5). Only in the 16th century did Tycho Brahe extend it to create a more complex system in which all the planets moved around the sun. This whole system rotated round the earth.[46]

The spherical model, as represented in both diagrams and simple astronomy texts, stood in the Middle Ages as a symbol for the whole universe, the *mundus*. Consequently, besides such diagrams being found in astronomic-computistic collections, they also appeared in historiographic and even theological works and compendia. This was because world history not only included the *orbis terrarum* but the whole *mundus* as a result of the record of creation in *The Book of Genesis*. The fact that for medieval scholars the diagram of the universe symbolised the essence of the world, is shown by the legend given with a small copy of the diagram in the anonymous *Mainauer Naturlehre* (13th century):[47] *Diese figura betvtet die welt wenne die elementen und die himmele die hie getecket sint daz heizzet als die welt.*[48] ('This figure here *means* the world, because the elements and the heavens shown, all that (together), is called the world').

This simple diagram could, however, easily be developed in astronomy literature. By using the epicycles and the intricate orbits of Venus and Mercury, a very complex, but sometimes illogical, system of concentric and eccentric motion of the celestial bodies moving round the earth, the sun and certain supposed theoretical points, could be created. So it is easy to understand why Robert Grosseteste called – using Lucretius – a diagram of the universe such as this, a world machine: *Tale autem corpus est tota mundi macchina*[49] ('This body namely is the whole world machine').

19

Parallel to the scholarly explanation of the structure of the universe with the aid of increasingly complicated spheres there was also a more popular and, in particular, more symbolic variant, which compared the universe with an egg. (The comparison of the earth with a ball or an apple will be discussed in Chapter 3.)

The comparison with an egg is not based on the spherical *Weltbild* as suggested by Ptolemy, but on the medieval teaching about the elements (see Chapter 8). The comparison assigned the four elements to the four sections of the universe and this was then compared with the structure of an egg. One form of this egg-comparison is to be found in Honorius of Autun. In his *Imago mundi*, composed at the beginning of the 12th century, he compares (Figure 7b):

the sky (*coelum* = water) with the shell (*testa*),
the aether (*purus aether* = fire) with the albumen (*album*),
the air (*aer* = air) with the yolk (*vitellum*),
the earth (*terra* = earth) with the drop of fat (*gutta pinguedinis*).

Not all versions of this popular comparison followed this pattern. One of the reasons was clearly that assigning elementary parts of the cosmos to parts of a chicken's egg was very problematic. Equally, Honorius' division of parts of the universe and elements was too theoretical even for medieval thinking and was therefore usually replaced by the following simpler but also more logical pattern (Figure 7a):

sky for the shell,
air for the membrane,
water for the albumen,
earth for the yolk.

The comparison of the earth and the cosmos with the yolk in an egg was not a medieval invention.[50] It was based on ancient Greek cosmology where the idea of a cosmic egg or at least the idea of the egg shape of the vault of heaven had been common since Aristotle in the 4th century BC.[51] The great Roman scholar M. T. V. Varro (116–27 BC)[52] then varied the analogy by equating the shell with the sky and the albumen with the earth. The encyclopedists of late Classical times and of the early Middle Ages retained this image[53] and their views were popularised by the commentators of the Middle Ages, at least as much as through copies of the ancient works themselves. The former include the commentaries on Martianus, composed in 859/60[54] by John Scotus Eriugena and the grammarian and exegete Remigius of Auxerre in the 9th century.[55] Abelard aided the popularisation of the image by including it in his *Expositio in Hexaemeron*[56]. His source was probably a somewhat younger contemporary, William of Conches. For the latter there was obviously no contradiction between the comparison in question and a spheric *Weltbild*, which at the time was at the

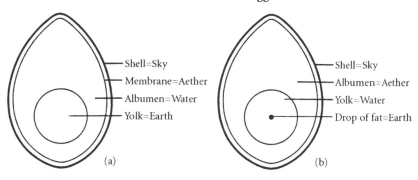

Figure 7. Diagrammatic illustrations of two versions of the cosmos-egg simile.

peak of its popularity, and which he discussed in great detail in his popular *Philosophia mundi*. The simile is also to be found in his (still unedited) commentary on Macrobius.[57] There is a continuity in this concept from the early to the high Middle Ages, up to Hildegard of Bingen. Manuscripts of her *Liber Scivias* even contain egg-shaped pictures of the universe, of which one (from Stuttgart) bears the legend: *Terra autem rotunda in celi medio sicut creato ex nihilo, sic pendet in nihilio, ut vitellum in ovo*[58] ('As the round earth in the middle of the heaven was created from nothing, so it floats in nothing, like the yolk in the egg'). In the *Otia imperialia* of Gervasius of Tilbury (c. 1152 – after 1220), composed as a textbook or encyclopedia for the German emperor Otto IV, the comparison also appears. With the exception of William of Conches the image was more widespread among authors interested in philosophical and theological questions than among cosmographers.[59]

The popularisation of this advanced *Weltbild* was promoted, among other ways, by sermons such as the one called *Saelic sint die reines Herzen sint* by the German Minorite friar Berthold of Regensburg (d. 1272). He said of the universe: *daz ist geschaffen als ein ei. Diu ûzer schale das ist der himel den wir dâ sehen. Daz wîze al umbe den tottern daz sint die lüfte. Sô ist der totter enmitten drinne, daz ist diu erde*[60] ('It is built like an egg. The outer shell is the heaven which we can see. The egg white around the yolk, that is the air, and the yolk in the middle, that is the earth'). Whereas the sermons in the Middle Ages were unquestionably the medium with the greatest public influence, it should not be overlooked that the preacher himself, as is true for most of the lower clerics, hardly ever had personal contact with astronomy or cosmographic works, even those as widespread as the work by William of Conches. Their education was influenced far more by simple didactic works used in monastic teaching. Such works were often the only source of scientific knowledge. These works were frequently composed in the form of dialogues which simplified the contents to suit the most frequently used teaching method, learning by rote. One of the most important was the already named *Elucidarius* by Honorius of Autun (composed around or after 1100), which was then translated into the vernacular.[61] The Middle High German *Lucidarius* (written around 1190) serves as an example for the reception in such vernacular didactic works. Similar passages are to be found, however, in the *Buch Sidrach*,[62] which was widely known in the whole of Europe and where the comparison is reduced to the three elements (shell = firmament, albumen = water, yolk = earth)[63] as it was in Berthold's sermon, and in the already-mentioned *Mainauer Naturlehre: dise welt ist sinewel, unde ist unbeslozen mit dem wendelmer. da inne suebet die erde alse der duter indem eige indem wisem*[64] ('this world is round, and is surrounded by the *wendelmer*, in which the earth floats like the yolk in the white of the egg'). The *wendelmer* (encircling sea, cf. German *Wendeltreppe*) can be equated with the ocean which forms the (incomplete) hydrosphere of the earth.

These simplifying texts unquestionably had a broader effect than the astronomy textbooks. However, their aim was to provide not an astronomic but a symbolic image of the world. The effect was not as different as might appear at first glance, for we have here a ball-shaped world made up of layers. The outer layer, which in the comparison with the egg is identified appropriately enough with the hard shell, and in the diagram of the universe is defined as the firmament, encompasses the physical world, the universe visible to man. This enclosed, finite universe rests in its entirety in God's hand and is enclosed in the shell which excludes the far-reaching (divine) infinity. The protected finiteness of the universe was taken for granted to such a degree in the Middle Ages that it was bordering on the visionary when Konrad of Megenberg, referring to actual observations, noted that it often appeared at night *als ob ain gruntlôs tiefen gê in den himel* or *wenn der himel den wahtern des nahts offen scheint.*[65] ('as if a bottomless depth goes into the sky' or 'when the sky seems to stand open to the nightwatchmen'). In keeping with astronomy teaching of his age, he of course explained away this feeling of the infinite depth by dismissing it as an illusion of perspective. The impression of this observation is nevertheless palpable, as is the fear of standing beneath such a bottomless open heaven.

The Structure of the Universe from the Four Elements

The comparison between the egg and the universe was not only a result of a genre-specific distribution of both world models, but also because as a consequence it was relatively easily compatible with the spherical model. Even with a purely astronomical view of the structure of the universe, the general opinion was that the universe was composed of four elements in physical layers according to their specific weight. The prevalent opinion was that between the lunar sphere, the lowest planetary sphere, and the immobile earth, located as it was at the centre of the universe, there were layers of fire, air and water which surrounded the earth. According to its nature as the heaviest element the earth lay deepest, that is, at the centre of the universe, from which there was no possible movement down.

Yet the hydrosphere was an incomplete one. Although most of the earth's surface is covered by water, the dry land protruded above it. Notker the German confirmed this in his 10th-century translation of Boethius: 'on the side of the earth that we know you can see the three continents above the water, but we don't know what it is like on the other side of the earth'.[66] The atmosphere lying above it was similarly thought to be immobile, but the medieval scholars could not find a concensus of agreement as to how far up it reached and whether the movement of the spheres also set the higher layers of air in motion. The disagreement, however, never reached the level of an outright dispute.

According to Aristotelian teaching only the area beneath the lunar sphere was composed of the four elements. Above the atmosphere of the earth there was a sphere of fire or rather ether but even this ended either on the lowest planetary sphere[67] or else on the firmament.

From the 12th century onward the image of the universe was divided differently, possibly influenced by the epicycle theory. The atmosphere was thought to reach up to the firmament whilst the heaven beyond it formed the empyrean heaven and was identified with the element of fire.[68] This division is clear, in particular, from the diagrams of the universe dating from the 12th–15th centuries, but clarity about the exact division of the elements in the universe was neither found in the works of astronomers nor of the encyclopedists, for the two attempts at explanation mentioned previously made generally valid statements impossible. Likewise, they were not aided by suppositions such as the one aired in the *Elucidarius* which assumed a hydro-heaven and an empyrean heaven. The reason for the relative situation of the elements in the universe not leading to open discussions was probably a result of the astronomer's awareness of the merely symbolic role of attempts at identification of the world's parts and the elements. They realised that these played no role in the observation of the planetary orbits and the attempts at their interpretation. Consequently, in the great revolution of the astronomical *Weltbild* in the late Middle Ages, and in early modern times, the teaching of the elements is not really a burning question.

CHAPTER THREE

The Shape of the Earth

Columbus and the Spherical Shape of the Earth

Columbus's idea or plan was the *practical* realisation of a journey to the west in order to reach East India and China. This plan carried with it the supposition of the earth as a globe. The prerequisites for this plan, the spherical shape of the earth and an area of open sea between Europe and the Indies (or China), were *theoretically* not a problem, either at the end of the fifteenth century or during the whole of the Middle Ages. What was shocking and revolutionary, however, was putting the theory to the test.

It should not surprise us (see Chapter 1) that the attacks on Columbus did not concern the question of the shape of the earth, despite the many books which say the opposite. There were remarkably few quotations from the Church Fathers which could be held against him – and even Columbus's clerical contemporaries no longer took these literally.[1] The concrete arguments against his plan were much more concerned with the dimensions of the globe rather than with the shape of the earth, and as a result dealt with the problems of distance, and the possibility that other inhabited continents might exist apart from Asia, Africa and Europe (see Chapter 4 for a discussion of the Antipodes problem). On the practical side there were the questions of imaginary or actual navigational problems of sailing over such an immense stretch of exposed water as the Atlantic Ocean.

The greatest problem for Columbus's adversaries appears not to have been centred on theoretical considerations but rather in 'the lack of will or capacity to think about the sphere-shape of the earth with all its consequences to a logical conclusion'.[2] In other words the concept of reaching the Indies and Cathay by navigating westwards across the supposedly immeasureable stretch of water between Europe and Asia was simply inconceivable for most of Columbus's contemporaries.

Such a mental inhibition becomes more comprehensible when compared with other contemporary ventures, such as the Portugese attempt to circum-navigate Africa. Here the problems were initially more of a psychological than logistical nature. Neither the geographers nor the sailors thought it feasible to sail round either the infamous Cabo de Não ('Cape No', roughly on the latitude of the Canary Isles) with its dangerous shoals and fogs, or Cape Bojador[3] ('Cape of Fear') which lies even further south. In fact, they both proved to be negligible obstacles for sea voyages in the following centuries despite minimal improvement in technical knowledge. As soon as these psychological hurdles were overcome, the distances conquered increased dramatically.[4] The problems of supplies and communication were quickly solved and even the self-confidence of the discoverers and their patrons soon grew. They showed this by setting up *Padrãos*, stone pillars with the cross, Portugese coats of arms and inscriptions as symbols of their presence on the west coast of Africa.[5]

Not only was it crystal clear to Columbus but it must surely also have been obvious to most of his reasonably educated contemporaries that, because the earth was the shape it was, it must be possible to reach China by sailing westwards. The spherical shape of the earth was taken for granted, and had been so since Aristotle. This fact had been an integral part of scholarly knowledge since the Carolingian renaissance of the 8th century. From the 12th century on astronomy handbooks and university teaching led to the Classical Ptolemaic view of the world being made known firstly to most clerics and subsequently to all university students. By the 13th century the spherical shape of the earth, and therefore also its theoretical circumnavigation, had found its way not only into scholarly but also into popular literature. This included one of the most widely read travel books of the age, *Travels* by Sir John Mandeville (see below). This extremely popular author had in fact never seen any of the countries described in it personally, and far less, as he claimed, had he circumnavigated the earth.

The rest of this chapter discusses the three main groups of sources which presented the medieval belief in a spherical earth: firstly the encyclopedias and compendia based on scholarly works of the Early Middle Ages and which preserved the clerical tradition of learning; secondly the astronomical handbooks of the High Middle Ages; and, finally, the literary and encyclopedic works of the High and Late Middle Ages which began to draw practical conclusions from a spherical earth. In addition reasons will be considered for the incorrect, but nevertheless commonly accepted opinion frequently held even today, that people in the Middle Ages thought that the earth was flat.

The Learned Clerical Tradition

The most influential collector and compiler of knowledge in the Middle Ages, the Spanish bishop Isidore of Seville (c. 570–636), only made vague comments on the shape of the earth. Perhaps the question was irrelevant to him, but it is more likely that his conceptual understanding, torn between the teachings of Classical authors, the Bible and the Church Fathers, was itself vague. Whatever the reason, Isidore's comments about the shape of the earth are not clear. In *De rerum natura* he seems to be describing the universe as sphere-shaped, but his concept of the five climatic zones as five circles arranged round the centre of the inhabited earth is so far from logical thinking that it has led many to believe that he thought of a disc-shaped earth.[6] This is supported, in particular, by a misinterpretation of the small world maps which accompany his work in the manuscripts. These only show the three known continents in a circle. Two centuries later Hrabanus Maurus (780–856), archbishop of Mainz from 847, who was given the title '*Praeceptor Germaniae*' ('Germany's teacher') in honour of his scholarly and didactic works, copied large chunks of Isidore's work with a commentary into his own encyclopedic work, *De Universo*. He likened the circular inhabited part of the earth (*orbis*) to a wheel. However, he is not referring to the entire globe when he says this, but rather only the inhabited part of it.

The circular maps that are included in all manuscripts of Isidore's works, and indirectly described by Hrabanus, were a common way of depicting the earth. The intention was not to show the whole earth, but only the known inhabited areas (Asia, Africa, and Europe) in a two-dimensional form, a circle, which would represent the whole sphere. As such they are not so very far removed from reality (Figures 13 and 14). They are clearly not, as has often been claimed,[7] evidence for the concept of a disc-shaped earth. The purpose of the maps was to show the inhabited earth and the relative size of the continents to each other: Asia takes the eastern half of the *orbis terrarum*, while Africa and Europe share the western half. The maps are known as wheel or rota maps because of their circular form, or T–O maps because of their diagrammatic nature (see the Appendix).

In order to re-evaluate their apparent disc-like shape, we need to consider the contexts in which the maps appear in relation to other illustrations and, perhaps more significantly, their association with texts discussing the earth's sphericity. Most of these maps occur in medieval astronomy manuscripts together with zone maps (Figure 8) or climatic maps (discussed further in Chapter 4). Such contexts do not presuppose the concept of a sphere-shaped earth but in most cases they were embedded in texts in which the sphere-shape was argued in detail. This had been the case ever since Bede's time in 7th and 8th century Britain. All zone maps, climatic maps, and the astronomical drawings mentioned are based on the concept of a spherical earth; so, there would be an inherent contradiction if we tried to evaluate the T-O maps which occur in the same manuscripts as evidence for a belief in a flat, disc-shaped earth.

There were also the so-called 'Noachid' maps. These rectangular maps, were supposed to depict the settling of the earth by Noah's three sons, Sem, Cham, and Japhet. No-one has ever used these maps to support the notion that the inhabited part of the earth was a rectangle. Why then should we assume a disc-shaped earth from the so-called rota-maps?

For the Church Fathers and the scholars of the Early Middle Ages the actual shape of the earth and the universe was less interesting than its symbolic form, as the idea of the cosmic egg suggests (Chapter 2 above). Just as the round yolk in the egg is at the centre, so is the earth at the centre of the universe, and from

Figure 8. Zone map from the Liber floridus by Lambert of St Omer (c. 1120) from the manuscript in Paris, Bibliothèque Genevive, MS 2200, f. 34v.

the analogy between universe and earth the sphericity of earth was deduced in the writings of such authors as Honorius of Autun.

The importance and influence of Honorius' encyclopedic and didactic works *Elucidarius* ('illuminator') and *Imago mundi* ('image of the world') during the 12th and 13th centuries cannot be over-emphasised. Probably born in southern Germany, Honorius spent most of his life as a monk in Siegburg and Regensburg. Besides the popularisation of the comparison of the universe with an egg, Honorius also gave more evidence to support the idea of a spherical universe. As early as c. 1120 he wrote (in his *Elucidarius,* I,11) of the creation of man from the four elements (earth, water, fire and air) considering that man is a microcosmos, representing the parts of the macrocosmos, the actual universe. For this reason the head of man is spherical because the whole world is spherical too. By world (*mundus* = the whole universe) Honorius meant the entire universe and not only the earth, but the analogy is correct here too. The concise *Elucidarius* was conceived as a popular handbook for lesser educated clerics. It was successful and had a considerable impact so that the ideas it contained became very widely known.

Two similar works were written in the vernacular German on the same lines as Honorius' Latin *Elucidarius*. One is the Middle High German *Ludicarius*, written around 1190. Despite a similar title it is not a translation of Honorius. The author used the *Elucidarius* as a model but creating his own individual work.[8] The other work is the *Book Sidrach* which was possibly originally written in southern France. The *Lucidarius* uses the egg comparison from Honorius' *Imago mundi*, but is more specific and decidedly calls the ocean-enclosed earth *sinewel* 'sphere-shaped'.[9]

The work, known by the name of *Book Sidrach*, and translated into Italian, French, Provençal, English, Dutch, Danish and German, is a religious-encyclo-pedic work composed in the 13th century which contained further and even more popular examples demonstrating the shape of the earth. The oldest Low-German manuscripts, which only date from the 15th century, appear to be dependent on a Dutch version dating from 1318 and were severely shortened. Nonetheless, they include a clear statement about the form of the earth: *see is ront also eyn appel*[10] ('she is as round as an apple'). This popular and clear comparison of the earth with the apple was certainly not limited to the quota-tion in the *Book Sidrach*, but was also found in all sorts of medieval texts. A Middle English cosmography from the second half of the 13th century used the comparison, as did the Norwegian *Kings' Mirror* from the mid-13th century, where the author compared the earth with an apple and the sun with a candle flame held closely to it.[11] By using this practical 'experiment' he explained both the different climatic zones via the angle of solar radiation and the proximity of the sun as well as the shape of astronomical shadows. These were discussed in all medieval astronomical works because of their significance for solar and lunar eclipses. However, it is not only these various extracts which prove that people in the High Middle Ages thought of the earth as being like an apple. The frequent illustrations were far more important. These showed secular rulers or even Christ as the ruler of the world with the orb in his right hand, on which the continents were drawn in so that there could be no doubt about it being the 'earth apple' (Figure 9).[12]

The early globe made by Martin Behaim (1459–1507), which was donated to his hometown of Nuremburg,[13] and unmistakably called an 'earth-apple', forms only a late piece of evidence for a wide-spread medieval tradition. But his was the first physically tangible example of this tradition from which the art of globe-making developed in the next century. Behaim's globe, a ball made out of papier-maché and plaster of Paris covered with parchment inscribed with a

Figure 9. The orb, shown as the earth with the continents. Norwegian carving (c. 1300).

considerable number of legends, was 54cm in diameter. Behaim had been in the service of the Portugese Crown since 1484 and in 1485–86 had taken part in one of the Portugese expeditions along the African west coast under Diego Cão. Therefore in 1492 he was able to impart his knowledge about the circumnavigation of the Cape of Good Hope. His knowledge was augmented by the Nuremburg scholarly cosmography of Hartmann Schedel, Conrad Celtis and Hieronymus Müntzer where the Ptolemaic geography, which had been rediscovered during the 15th century, was well documented.[14] In spite of the already well advanced cartography of Africa, Behaim's globe was still firmly anchored in medieval tradition by only showing three continents.

Considering all the medieval evidence for a spherical earth, one wonders why the German Carmelite Johannes of Hildesheim, writing his *Dreikönigslegende* ('Three Kings' Legend') in the mid-14th century, presents the comparison of the earth to an apple as a controversy. In this hagiographic text, which he first wrote in Latin and then translated himself into the vernacular German, he discussed the Nestorians, who whom he regarded as heretic Christians, apparently blaming them for discussing the question of an apple-shaped earth.[15] Yet, it is not clear whether Johannes really did not believe in a spherical earth or whether he disagreed with the comparison with an apple, or whether he blames the Nestorians for discussing the matter at all. As other passages of his imaginative *Dreikönigslegende* reveal, Johannes was not an expert in astronomy. In fact he appears to have been remarkably uneducated for his time. Over the preceding century the first European universities, including those in the German speaking world during his lifetime, had a relatively high degree of learning in astronomy.

Besides the comparison of the earth with the yolk of an egg and with an apple, another comparison which occurs mainly in vernacular texts, is that with a ball. It is of ancient origin and has numerous Classical parallels although the exact source, whether the philosophical writings of the younger Seneca,[16] Pliny,[17] or from other as yet unknown sources, is uncertain. As with the egg/yolk-comparison, the ball analogy reveals yet again that such a generally comprehensible and unquestionably popular interpretation of the shape of the world in no way need have led to a trivialisation or even falsification of the scholarly view of the world valid at the time. A sermon, *Saelic sint die reines Herzens sint* ('Blessed are the pure in heart') by the German Minorite monk Berthold of Regensburg (d. 1272) includes both the comparison of the cosmic egg and next to it the comment *diu erde ist rehte geschaffen alse ein bal* ('the earth is created quite like a ball').[18] It is quite clear from this that the Minorite brother could find himself on the same level of knowledge as his contemporaries who had been educated in astronomy. He could use this knowledge in his sermons without causing any offence at all.

In the 13th and 14th centuries the teaching of the quadrivium (the four 'scientific' subjects of astronomy, geometry, arithmetic and music) at the recently founded universities meant that a spherical earth was generally accepted at least in scholarly circles. In encyclopedic works, such as the one written by Thomas of Cantimpré, a Dominican scholar and pupil of Albertus Magnus (*Liber de natura rerum* Lib. XIX, 2), or by Vincent of Beauvais (*Speculum naturale* Lib. VI, Cap. 8–10 and 13), tutor to the French prince around the mid-13th century, the treatment of the shape of the earth was a thoroughly rhetorical question. It was always clearly answered by favouring the sphere. The question was similarly treated in the works of Robert Grosseteste. Authors such as these three belonged just as much to the social and scholarly establishment as the lay writer, Gervasius of Tilbury (fl. 1211), who wrote his *Otia Imperialia* in c. 1200 for the emperor Otto IV. He too regarded the earth as a ball and the egg comparison was just as familiar to him as to his scholarly contemporaries.

Considering these authorities alone ought to be enough to refute the idea, nevertheless still common, that the Church in the Middle Ages considered the idea of a spherical earth to be heretical and therefore systematically suppressed it. Consequently it is no surprise at all that the most popular astronomy handbook at medieval universities, the *Liber de sphaera* by John of Sacrobosco, not only presupposed a spherical earth, but also gives detailed evidence in support of it. He included all the astronomical knowlege of his age, for example the shape of the shadow of the earth during a lunar eclipse (when the earth's circular shadow passes across the moon, thereby suggesting that the earth must be round). This had long formed part of the European canon of knowledge. Bede knew of it by c. 700 and it was even exemplified in the *Liber floridus* by Lambertus of St. Omer (c. 1120) in numerous illustrations.

John of Sacrobosco also commented on the observation that the time at which the stars and planets rose in the east grew later each day as one travels west. He referred to the fact that as one travels south so the pole star was seen to move towards the horizon and the southern constellations rose higher in the sky. Evidence for this was readily available. Travellers from northern Europe to Jerusalem repeatedly commented that on the way south some northern constellations, particularly those close to the pole star, sank closer to the horizon. Even more elementary was another piece of evidence for the sphericity of the earth – and therefore also its seas – mentioned by John of Sacrobosco, which is accompanied in almost all the handbooks by an illustration. If a ship leaves the shore, then the ship's hull soon disappears over the horizon whereas the mast-top remains visible for longer. The disappearance of the ship is therefore not caused by the increasing distance but by the curvature of the surface of the sea.

Both pieces of evidence can already be found in Pliny,[19] writing in the 1st century AD, so that John of Sacrobosco was able to support his claim with the

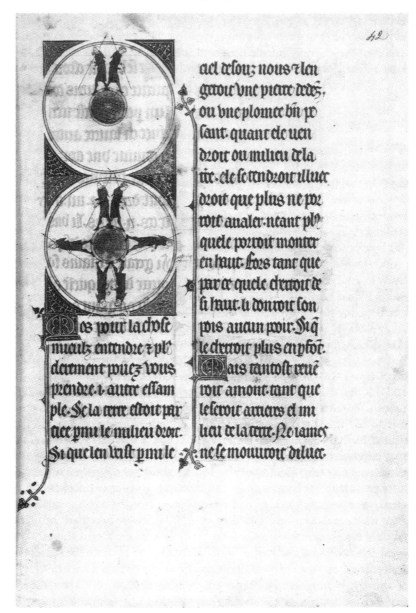

Figure 11. Illustration concerning the possible circumnavigation of the earth from the prose version of the L'image du monde by Walter of Metz (c. 1245). Paris, Bibliothéque National, MS fr. 574, f. 42r.

*Figure 12. Illustration concerning the
possible circumnavigation of the earth
from the prose version of the L'image du
monde by Walter von Metz (c. 1245).
London, The British Library, MS Royal
19. A. IX. f. 42r (15th century).*

Pierre d'Ailly (Petrus de Alliacus, 1350–1420), the French theologian and
later cardinal, also believed that the earth was a sphere. He cited Eratosthenes'
figure, whose computation he probably knew through John of Sacrobosco's
Liber de sphaera.[22] In his work *Ymago mundi*, which Columbus used and
annotated (this particular copy[23] belonging to Columbus and printed between
1480–1483 in Louvain still exists), he quoted various statements about the

relationship between water and land on earth,[24] before concurring with the opinion that more than a quarter of the earth's surface was inhabited.

Pierre d'Ailly's opinions, together with the fabulous tales by Sir John Mandeville, appear to have convinced Columbus that a circumnavigation was possible. Moreover, it seems most likely that Columbus had probably heard about Icelandic journeys to Greenland and 'Vinland' (Newfoundland?) in a roundabout way via English fishermen and merchants, and this would no doubt have strengthened his belief that the size of the Atlantic Ocean was relatively small.[25]

Whether one could actually sail round the entire earth is a question that Albertus Magnus did not mention, whereas Pierre d'Ailly only refers to the voyage westwards in connection with the size of the oceans and the inhabited earth. Sailing around the world is only mentioned for the first time in the manuscripts of the *Image du monde* by Walter of Metz, written in around 1245. Walter writes of how two men who set off in opposite directions will meet each other on the other side of the globe. This logical consequence of a spherical earth is furthermore illustrated in Walter's book. The illustration (Figures 11 and 12) did not fail to make an impression on contemporaries nor on later readers.

It would appear that Sir John Mandeville, writing a century after Walter, had this text in front of him when he wrote his almost entirely fictitious *Travels* (see below). Mandeville[26] copied great quantities from older journals and geographical passages in encyclopedias to make up for his own lack of experience. His description of foreign parts conformed totally with, and was well within, the bounds of medieval tradition. He placed great emphasis on miraculous and extraordinary things, but could, naturally enough, not speak from his own experience. Despite this – or perhaps because of this? – his work was a resounding success and it was translated into numerous European languages.[27]

For Mandeville the possibility of sailing around the earth was taken for granted to such a degree that at the beginning of his book he wrote impressively that anyone setting sail from England sailed 'uphill' to Jerusalem because Jerusalem was the centre of the inhabited world and therefore lay on top of the globe. From Jerusalem to India on the other hand it went 'downhill', that is to say down the other side of the globe. This concept of Jerusalem as the physical centre of the earth's surface was shared by the German translator of Marco Polo's journal,[28] who wrote that Japan lies 1000 miles away from China in the depth of the ocean.[29] If England, on the one hand, and Japan on the other hand were thought to be far from the centre of the earth, Jerusalem, which lay at the top of the globe, then the passage over the Atlantic must be round the bottom of the globe, not a very pleasant thought. This notion was further emphasised in Walter's illustration (Figure 11) by the picture of the people standing on their heads.

Towards the end of his fictitious journal, Mandeville mentions that he thought he could have returned by a shorter way from the East Asian islands if he had travelled further, but he did not do so. Some versions include here an anecdote of a man who by accident arrived back home having been round the earth, but did not recognise either the language or his home and therefore turned around and walked right round the earth again to return home the way he had come.[30] Such a fabulous tale was probably a product of the author's imagination, just like the rest of the book, but in the 14th century this was accepted as truth, as the whole work was. This means that the idea could have occured to Columbus after he had read Mandeville since it is one of the books which was so popular and so widely used, along with Pierre d'Ailly's *Ymago mundi* and Marco Polo's journals to China and India.

Disc or Sphere? The Background to the Concept of the Disc-shaped Earth

When all the evidence has been amassed which suggests that people during the entire Middle Ages had no difficulty in believing that the world was a sphere, the question naturally occurs as to why people in modern times could ever have hit upon the still very widespread idea that people in the Middle Ages believed that the world was a flat disc. It seems that there are three reasons for this[31]:

(1) the comments of a few late Classical Church Fathers who turned for religious reasons against the heathen Classical view of the sphericity;
(2) the modern misunderstanding concerning the medieval question of the Antipodes;
(3) the misleading disc or wheel shape of medieval world maps which probably were and still are the main reason for the disc theory.

Firstly, there are the comments of a few late Classical Church Fathers who turned for religious reasons against the heathen Classical view of the sphericity. In scholarly literature the medieval concept of the shape of the earth is still traced back to the Christian Egyptian merchant Cosmas (called Indikopleustes) who shortly after 500 AD travelled to India and East Africa and is said later to have become a monk in Alexandria. Basing his ideas on the Bible he rejected the Classial view of the world and replaced it in his description of the world with a view of his own which essentially consisted of a disc- or trapezium-shaped earth and heaven as a chest- or altar-shaped superstructure. Contrary to the beliefs of earlier scholarship, it should be noted that Cosmas' views were by no means typical of the medieval perception of the world or even influenced it significantly. His *Christian Topography*, written in Greek, was not even translated into Latin and consequently had virtually no effect in Europe before the 17th or 18th century (see Chapter 1). The case is similar for the writings of Firmianus Lactantius (c. 300) who likewise seems to have believed in the disc-shape of the earth. The writings of Cosmas were totally unknown in the Middle Ages so that his belief in a flat earth may be considered to be totally irrelevant in determining the medieval concept of the earth's shape. Yet despite playing little part in medieval thought the opinions of Cosmas and Lactantius have been decisive in determining modern man's belief concerning the medieval notions of the shape of the earth. It seems that these Church Fathers are to blame for the incorrect belief that medieval man thought of the earth as a disc.

Secondly there has been a modern misunderstanding concerning the medieval question of the Antipodes. From the time of St Augustine in the early Middle Ages up to Columbus's times there a debate constantly recurred about whether there was another continent on the far side of the globe and whether it was inhabited or not. This is pursued in greater detail in Chapter 4 (concerning the question of the Antipodes). It should be noted that in modern times the Church's rejection of the Antipodes as being inhabited by humans (following Augustine's teachings) has frequently been confused with the question of the existence of a continent in the Antipodes or the shape of the earth itself. Church doctrine with regard to the last two questions was almost always neutral.

Thirdly there is the problem of the misleading disc or wheel shape of medieval world maps which probably were and still are the main reason for the disc theory. The medieval world maps depict the inhabited earth drawn in a circle which is divided into the three continents by means of an inscribed T. The upper half depicts Asia, while Europe and Africa make up a quarter each. Such circular *mappae mundi* are widespread in medieval manuscripts from the time of Isidore and can be understood as *the* symbolic representation of the inhabited earth in the Middle Ages – but only the inhabited world (see Figure 16). This representation of the inhabited part of the earth concentrated onto a circle led to and still leads to misinterpretation and hence to the belief that people in the Middle Ages thought that the world was a disc. It is easy to forget that the circular shape of the map is a convention of projection. The intention was to show the most important part of the earth (the inhabited part) as plainly as possible and therefore no claims were made to depict the 'actual' appearance of the continents.

This inhabited part of the world was, however, comparatively small since the surface of the water in comparison to the dry surface was considered to be very large, a ratio of roughly four to one, partly also up to ten to one.[32] The T–O maps which were so popular in the Middle Ages thus only show the dry surface of the earth and a part of the water, and not the whole globe. They should not and cannot therefore be interpreted as evidence for the belief in a disc-shaped world (Figure 17).

CHAPTER FOUR

The Fascination of the World Down Under: the Fourth Continent and the Antipodes

The Three Continents and the Medieval Maps of the World

After five weeks of sailing westwards after having put into port on the Canary Islands Columbus and his small fleet finally sighted land again on the night of the 12th October 1492. He must have believed that he had arrived at his intended destination and was finally gazing at the coast of East Asia.

During those first weeks and months when he explored the northern coasts of Cuba and Hispaniola from the small island of San Salvador Columbus must have had a growing awareness that these islands were not part of legendary Cipangu with its gold-roofed palaces and rich towns which Sir John Mandeville and Marco Polo had described. No doubt his own increasing disappointment led him to leave his sailors and officers under the illusion that they had discovered the Indies (in the broadest medieval meaning of the term), even though he himself was certain that he would have to encounter Japan and China en route for India. Columbus thought the Caribbean islands he had discovered were a hitherto unknown archipelago in East Asia. However, by his third or fourth voyage at the latest, when his ships battled with the elements along the coast of Central America, he must have realised that he had discovered more than the direct way to Asia and a few islands inhabited by savages on the way there.

The exceptional nature of Columbus's discovery was never really appreciated during his lifetime. It was only during the first decades of the 16th century that the Europeans began to realise that Columbus's discoveries in the Caribbean during 1492 and 1504, the settlements of the Portugese in Brazil (from 1500),[1] and the landfalls made by John Cabot on Labrador (1497),[2] and his son, Sebastian in North America (1526–1530),[3] had all taken place on different parts of the same gigantic new continent.

It is not surprising that both Columbus and his contemporaries took a long time to recognise that the new found land was not an unknown region of Asia. The geographical knowledge of Europeans before the 16th century was limited to three continents in the whole northern hemisphere and whether there was any land at all in the southern hemisphere was the subject of scholarly discussion.

In Classical times the horizon of the (southern) European was limited to the area surrounding the Mediterranean, but by the last centuries before the birth of Christ news began to trickle in about countries far away. Merchants and other travellers brought back information about Arabia and the Indies,[4] from those areas of the Near East and East Africa already referred to in the Old Testament[5] and finally even from the Atlantic coasts of western and northern Europe.[6] Asia, Africa and Europe were the only continents known until the end of the Middle Ages. This tripartition of the known and inhabited world was lent additional weight in the whole of Christendom from its occurrence in the Old Testament. Furthermore, the three continents were said to have been settled after the flood by Noah's sons Sem, Cham, and Japhet, which led to a misunderstanding among many medieval scholars who believed that this meant that all possible continents had been accounted for in this list.[7]

Of the three continents Asia was the most important. This was not only because of its size, which, according to medieval cosmography, accounted for the whole of the eastern half of the inhabited world, but even more so because of the many places there known to every Christian through biblical history. The Garden of Eden as well as Mount Sinai and the Holy Land lay in Asia, reason enough for it to be the most important part of the world for Christians. However, its religious significance was augmented by a material importance: all the luxury goods which had arrived in Europe since the time that pilgrimages to Palestine had begun, and then increasingly throughout the Crusades (from the late 11th century), came from the east: spices,[8] oils and dyes, exotic fruits as well as cotton, silk or incense.

The third aspect of Asia's significance in the European mind was the legendary one: In literature, everything on earth which was considered to be fabulous came from Asia. These included the Four Rivers which flowed out of Paradise (itself surrounded by a wall of flames), to the fabulous animals which were known from bestiaries[9] and the fabulous peoples who had been described in the Alexander Romances from the times of Alexander the Great's campaign in India.[10] There were stories of legendary islands in the Indian Ocean such as 'Taprobana' (probably Ceylon or Sumatra). Isidore described the island as a place where all the plants bore fruit twice a year. Ptolemy mentioned a magnetic mountain which lay in the sound between India and the legendary southern continent. It was reputed to attract ships whose hulls contained iron nails so that they were shipwrecked on it.[11] These tales all originated in Arabian story-telling and thus made their way into European literature.

Whilst information of this kind could be found in the cosmographies, composed either in prose or verse,[12] and were only depicted on the largest of the world maps,[13] the smaller world maps or *mappae mundi* concentrated particularly on showing the supposed outline of the continents and the countries therein. Here, too, biblical sites played a significant role. The most important sites of biblical history are almost always included, and similarly places relevant to locally venerated saints at the map's place of origin.

Medieval world maps[14] were created with different intentions to those of modern maps and therefore should not be judged on today's criteria and theories on cartography. They have very little, and possibly nothing, to do with what we usually understand by 'maps'. These differences are not only found in the manner of illustration, and in the contents, but also in the function of the map. Medieval and modern cartography have one mutual aim: both attempt to show the world *as it is*, i.e. truthfully. Not surprisingly the way they did this was different, partly because their conception of what the truth amounted to was different.

A modern map of the world starts with the fiction that certain two-dimensional projections of the picture of the surface of the earth can make the physical view of this surface 'correctly' visible. Satellite photography and geographical projections can compensate for distortions to a certain degree so that in an oblong elliptical picture the whole of the surface of the world can be illustrated. Naturally, the whole impression of a spherical earth is lost. On the other hand, photos taken from space give us a good overall impression of the spherical planet Earth although they can only show half that sphere by grave distortion of details which would otherwise be compensated for by cartographical projections.

The medieval *mappae mundi* were based on a totally different concept. The intention was to depict the known surface of the earth diagrammatically. Simultaneously, they wanted to reproduce the curvature of the sphere in two-dimensional form on the parchment using the circle in which this diagrammatic illustration is given. The impression of the curvature of the spherical earth was maintained by reducing the visible surface of the earth (possibly including even the fourth southern continent) to what could be shown within the circle. It is a historical misconception of modern scholarship that the circular maps of the inhabited earth with their three or four continents presuppose that the medieval cartographers believed in a flat, disc-shaped earth. The fact is that the sole aim of these maps was to depict the three continents in the northern hemisphere. Likewise the so-called hemisphere maps, like the astronomy handbooks, show a whole hemisphere with relation to the main climatic zones and the sphere shape of earth (see Figure 19). It is therefore simply absurd to use these maps, many of which are found in astronomical manuscripts where the sphericity of earth is explicitly discussed, as proof that medieval man believed that the earth was a disc.

The distortions of the actual sizes and relative distances which occurred on the *mappae mundi* by the integration of three or four continents into the shape of a circle were irrelevant. So too were the relative distances between places on the map. Although one of the main objectives of modern maps is to determine the relative position of geographical points and to record these distances in scale, the creators of medieval world maps had no such intention whatsoever. The most important entries on medieval maps of the world were not limited to geographical and topographical detail but could include all areas of life and

history. Larger maps encompassed topography, ethnography and natural science, and also historiography with respect to to Christianity and even literary history, or at least legendary history.

The information included on the maps shows that practical considerations from today's point of view played only a very minor role on medieval world maps. In comparison to the late medieval sea-charts (the 'Portulan charts') which were used for navigational purposes along Europe's coasts and which were of good quality in southern Europe as early as the 13th and 14th centuries, such empirical construction and practical usage were completely irrelevant for the world maps.[15] Whereas the sailors used their Portulan charts like today's sea charts and therefore distances and coastline had to be as accurate as possible, it would have been thought quite bizarre to want to establish the distance between Rome and Jerusalem on a world map by scale. It 'is probably true to say that the great majority of these *mappae mundi* are to be regarded as works of art and not of information. Their authors [. . .] would have branded any man a fool who might have supposed that he could determine the distance from London to Jerusalem by putting a ruler across a map.'[16] Medieval world maps were not

Figure 14. Circular section of a satellite photo with the centre in Jerusalem, orientated now towards the east.

Figure 13. Hemisphere of the earth (taken from a satellite photo; the centre is roughly in Rome; orientated towards the north); a circle with the centre in Jerusalem clarifies the diagrammatic horizon of the inhabited earth in the Middle Ages.

conceived as an aid for travellers and neither pilgrims nor Crusaders used maps on their journeys, other than possibly the lists of places to be passed en route given in the itineraries.

Nonetheless, world maps were a geographical instrument of particular vividness as is clear from the prolific manner in which they were used to illustrate and clarify historiographical and astronomic literature. Primarily the map was a 'normative image of ideas which presents a "*Weltbild* in the head", the structural model of medieval education'.[17] This of course only applies in a limited sense to the many small world maps in medieval manuscripts, but even here the visual element is of primary importance with regards to the function of these maps. Thus, they become irreplaceable additions to the prose texts whilst making the physical world tangible, at one glance, without obliging a reader or listener to make sense of the text. These maps served as physical abbreviations of all reality, incorporating both the material and the spiritual world. *Mappae mundi* are representations of the *Weltbild* on parchment and not a practical aid for travellers. (A systematic interpretation of one of the largest medieval *mappae mundi*, the map from Hereford cathedral, can be found in the Appendix.)

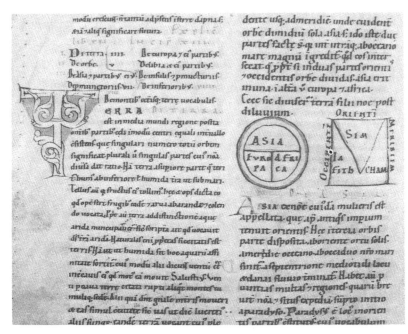

Figure 15. Diagrammatic T–O map from Isidor: Etymologiae. Vienna, Österreichische Nationalbibliothek, MS 67, f. 117r (12th century).

Whereas modern maps always have north at the top, the psychological orientation of the Middle Ages towards the geographic centre of Christianity in the east was reflected in medieval maps. They were almost always orientated towards the east (hence the word *orientation*) with their centre in Jerusalem. The extreme east of Asia was where Paradise was thought to be. Similarly it marked the furthest outreaches of the inhabited world although the entrance to Paradise was barred to all mortals by a wall of flames.[18] The geographical determination of paradise was not incompatible with its miraculous suspension at a safe distance from the ground (which meant that it was not reached by the Flood). On the other side of Paradise there only lay the large ocean. The only islands known in this direction were Cipangu (Japan) though the south-eastern coast of Asia was dotted with islands. These included the legendary island of Taprobana and the magnetic mountain, as well as the island of T(h)ile (frequently confused with the island of Thule which lay in the North Atlantic and may be identified as Iceland)[19] and the islands of Crysen and Agiren supposedly rich with gold and silver.[20] In the south-west Asia ended in the Red Sea. The Nile, the border between Africa and Asia, ran from there to the east of the Mediterranean where Jerusalem, the centre of the inhabited world, was situated at the intersection of the three continents.[21] From Palestine the border between Asia and Europe ran along the Dardanelles and the Black Sea to the river 'Tanais'

Figure 16. Mappa mundi from Hereford Cathedral, England (end of the 13th century) with elaborated T–O structure.

(the Don) and from there to its source in the far north amongst the Riphaean mountains on the shores of the northern ocean, the very limit of the inhabited world.

To the east lay the Hyrcanian Forests and the Caspian Sea which is shown on most of the world maps as a gulf in the northern ocean. To the north of Asia there are some islands which were believed to be even more fabulous than those in the Indian Ocean because, like the mysterious islands Bizes and Crisolida, they are taken from Alexander Romances and were generally reputed to be populated by fabulous peoples.[22] Even on the mainland, northern Asia was at least as well considered to be settled by fabulous races and beasts as the south-eastern part. The imaginations of the medieval cosmographers were fired in particular by the cannibal races of Gog and Magog, who were subjugated and immured by Alexander the Great in a valley at the other side of the Hyrcanian Forests on the Caspian Sea. This is possibly the case because they were the only fabulous races who were already mentioned in the Old Testament,[23] but here they were not referred to as being cannibals.

In the division of Asia into countries and provinces as well as in some sporadic topographical references, for example the rivers of Paradise, Nile (also known as Geon), Euphrates, Tigris and Ganges as well as Mounts Sinai, Horeb and Ararat, there are only slight differences between the medieval maps and cosmographies and their late Classical precursors. They are based for the most part on information contained in the Old Testament, Greek and Roman historiographers and the compendia made from older literature by earlier encyclopedists, in particular Pliny and Solinus.

The choice of the names of countries on the world maps was not completely whimsical, but were dependent on the size of the map, the main interests of the compiler and, in particular, by the medieval principles of universal cartography. Medieval cartography was, as we have already seen, not concerned with distances and topographical details, but with providing a historiographical aid. The places mentioned were those of historical importance or interest and therefore, and only for that reason, were they included on the map.[24]

On these maps Asia occupied the whole eastern half of the inhabited earth. Africa and Europe shared the western half. Europe had the north-west quarter and Africa lay to the south-west.

Africa, known as Libya in the oldest sources,[25] was the part of the Old World that was least known. Admittedly, the provinces on the north African Mediterranean coast, which had been converted to Christianity in late Classical times, were well known to the Classical and early medieval authors. However, the expansion of Islam from the 7th and 8th centuries on halted any European exploration of Africa for centuries. Knowledge about the 'dark continent' in the High Middle Ages was correspondingly meagre and antiquated. The land to the south of Libya and Ethiopia was thought to be inhabited only by fabulous peoples and beasts. Beyond there the continent was believed to be uninhabited, and indeed uninhabitable due to the extreme heat of the sun. Whether Africa continued south of the equator or whether there was a hot equatorial ocean there, and, if so, what was at the other side of this ocean, were questions discussed by medieval scholars (see below).

Europe was, naturally enough, the most familiar for Occidental geographers of the Middle Ages, but, despite detailed information about south, west[26] and central Europe, even the cosmographies which were compiled in Germany and England were confused and reticent when writing about northern or eastern Europe.[27]

Apart from Anglia, Scotia and Hibernia, only a few, vague, islands were depicted to the north of Germania, such as Dacia, Norvegia, Suecia and Thule before the Riphean mountains in the far north on the border with Asia were reached.[28] The area of mainland between Germania and the Don is usually called Scythia in the north and Russia in the south.

Whereas knowledge of Asia in the 13th and 14th centuries was constantly improving through the reports of travellers to Asia, the European cosmographers continued to be quite badly informed about their own continent. The Scandinavians were virtually the sole exception to this and they continued their interest in geography even after the decline of their extensive voyages of exploration in the 9th to 11th centuries. Knowledge of the discovery and settlement of Greenland and Vinland (Newfoundland) was kept alive at first orally and then at least since the early 12th century in writing. When finally as part of developing Christianisation the monks brought not only literacy but also the most important works of Occidental scholarship to Norway and Iceland, the native Scandinavian clerics set to work with enthusiasm. They merged the information from the Latin descriptions of the world in the manuscripts and the indigenous records of discovery to produce Old Norse descriptions of the world which were considerably more accurate than those of continental Europe. In these Old Norse compilations the usual descriptions of Asia, Africa and Europe are to be found alongside the number, location, population and ecclesiastical organisation of the northern Atlantic islands, such as the Orkneys, Shetlands and Faroes of whose existence the Central European monasteries and universities had probably never even heard,[29] as well as far more realistic geographic descriptions of Denmark, Norway, Sweden and Iceland than could be found in any Latin cosmography. The descriptions of the situation of Greenland, which was thought to be connected to Siberia by an Artic land-bridge, were even more significant, and so was the information about the distances to the islands of Helluland (Baffinland), Markland (Labrador) and Vinland (Newfoundland), let alone the supposition that Vinland was connected in the south with Africa.[30]

With the first crossing of the equator in about 1473,[31] two decades before Columbus's first voyage, the Portuguese had been able to prove that Africa extended far further to the south than anyone had ever thought possible. Even the Scandinavian theory about a land-bridge between Africa and a land in the west (North America), admittedly a virtually unknown idea in southern Europe, was disproved by this Portuguese venture. However, the Scandinavian belief in the North Atlantic as a sort of manageable inland sea between western Europe and the 'islands' south of Greenland seems nevertheless to have given Columbus's plan added impetus. It is unlikely that Columbus was ever in Iceland though this has been the subject of great speculation.[32] However, even the tales told by Scandinavian seafarers, with whom he could quite conceivably have been acquainted through the relatively lively trade links between Scandinavia and the English ports (probably Bristol),[33] must have been enough to strengthen his belief in the relatively short distance across the Atlantic ocean, despite the fact that this turned out to be wrong.

The Fourth Continent: Terra Australis Incognita and the Antipodes

In the 2nd century BC the grammarian Crates of Mallos developed a theory about the inhabited regions of the earth. He believed that the oceans divided the inhabitable land into four quarters and one part of these landmasses lay to the south of the equatorial ocean. Ever since this idea was propounded the notion that there was a fourth, hitherto unknown, continent existing on the other side of the earth seems to have been common among scholars. The usual explanation for this was that otherwise there would have been an imbalance in the distribution of weight on the earth's surface. This was something of a paradox considering the normal assumption at the time that the earth lay immobile at the centre of the universe. It is quite possible that speculation about the southern continent had originated from ancient knowledge of the Pacific islands or even Australia and South America, brought to the Near East and thence to Ancient Greece by traders. Any detail about the situation and kind of continent could then have been forgotten during the last few centuries BC and was only subsequently manifested in the theoretical speculations about the size of the inhabitable land on the earth and the recurrent speculations about a fourth continent.

It is clear from ancient texts still extant today that the ratio between the size of land and water on the earth had been the subject of on-going scholarly discussions ever since antiquity. The fourth book of *Esdras* in the Apocrypha (an apocalyptic vision, composed after the destruction of Jerusalem at the end of the first century AD), stated that after the creation of the world the water was gathered into one seventh of the surface of the earth, whilst the rest remained dry land.[34] This apocalyptic vision stood very much alone with this opinion since human experience was aware that a considerably larger part of the earth was covered by water than suggested by this visionary piece of writing.[35] Only one scholar concurred with this assumption and based his own reckonings that the ratio between water and land was six to one on this passage. This was Roger Bacon (c. 1210/14–c. 1292), an English Franciscan and a genius notorious for his non-conformity. He alone argued against the generally accepted tradition and in favour of the concept that the seas made up only a very small part the earth's surface. The knowledge and astuteness of Roger Bacon's works on the whole may have caused Columbus to place more trust than he need (or should) have in Bacon's comments, so that he may have been led further astray than necessary in his estimations of the distance between Spain and China. On the other hand, he may have regarded it as useful to have his own argument (when he had to argue the case to his patrons) about the feasibility of his undertaking supported by such a famous and accredited scholar as Bacon. Even if he was only too aware of the fallacy of Bacon's deliberations, this may have led him to emphasise the inaccurate ratio in his favour whilst still being conscious that the ratio must be greater the other way. Water covers, as we know today, over 70% of the earth's surface (Figure 17), hence the distance that Columbus had to cover in order to reach his intended destination was far greater than he had assumed.

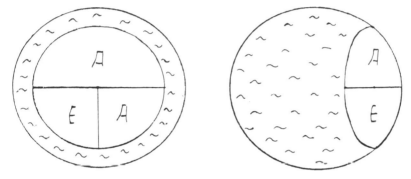

Figure 17. Diagrammatic illustration of the relationship of the inhabited world and the hydrosphere at a ratio of 4:1.

Ptolemy, writing a century after the composition of the *Esdras*-apocalypse, speaks at one point of a ratio of land to water of five to one and elsewhere of three to one. Moreover, he also quotes Aristotle who had also presumed the ratio to be three to one. The Arabic cosmographers of later centuries, whose works were known in western Europe from the 12th century onwards, assumed even more extreme ratios between water and land, for example four to one (Abulfeda) or even eleven to one (Al Battani),[36] possibly because of their knowledge of the Indian Ocean. Pierre d'Ailly, in his cosmographical encyclopedia, *Ymago mundi*, composed towards the end of the 14th century, reached his own conclusion that more than only a quarter of the surface of the earth must be inhabited. Whether his deliberations were meant for use at the university in Paris or the French court is uncertain, since he had an influential position at both,[37] being both a renowned scholar and cardinal, his work nevertheless contained references to all the above mentioned opinions of both antiquity and Middle Ages.[38] Following Aristotle (who on the other hand had overestimated the circumference of the earth) this implied for Pierre d'Ailly that the distance

Figure 18. The concept of the division of the landmasses on the earth (following Behaim's globe 1492; solid line) and the actual landmasses on the earth (dotted line).

between Gibraltar and the East Indies in a westerly direction could not be very great and consequently he declared that this small sea lying between the two should be easily navigable. Columbus must have been well acquainted with these views because we know that he owned a copy of the *Ymago mundi*.[39] Since one of his personal comments on the *Ymago mundi* refers to the ratio one to six described in the fourth book of *Esdras*, it used to be thought that Columbus believed in a proportion of one to six between water and land[40] and that he subsequently underestimated the distance between Portugal and China by assuming that it was a distance of only 130 degrees longitude. In fact it is about 230 degrees. However, it is far more likely that he himself agreed with the prevalent opinion of the ratio three to one and only took the ideas given in *Esdras* and Pierre d'Ailly into consideration as modifications. As the northern hemisphere, according to medieval theory, contained far more land than the southern hemisphere and this landmass, according to Toscanelli (who cited Marinus of Tyre), stretched over 225 degrees longitude, Columbus may have reached the conclusion that the Atlantic was of a navigable size.

The southern hemisphere on the other hand was generally considered to be predominantly covered by water although since the days of Crates and Ptolemy, who had claimed that Africa extended far to the south, it was assumed that there was a fourth continent lying somewhere to the south of Asia or Africa. Early medieval authors still expressed themselves carefully about it,[41] but even Isidore mentioned a fourth continent[42] and by the 12th century on the more detailed maps of the world there is a sector to the south of Asia (partly also to the south of Africa), separated from the rest of the land mass by a symbolic equatorial ocean and called *Terra australis incognita*.[43]

Interestingly enough, one of the strongest opponents of the idea of a fourth continent was Pierre d'Ailly (1352–1420). Considering that as an encyclopedist he was usually extremely tolerant and far-sighted in geographic matters it is all the more surprising that he denied the existence of the southern continent and thereby the existence of the Antipodes.[44] It is most likely, however, that his ecclesiastical position played a role here since he was a Church cardinal, and whereas the question about the existence of a southern continent (which would only be discovered 300 years after Columbus) did not create any ideological controversy, the question of the inhabitants of the same, namely the Antipodes, was an extremely delicate one (see later).

The most important reason for the Church's resistance to the idea of the Antipodes has already been mentioned. The argument was the limitation of Noah's descendants to the three continents mentioned in the Old Testament. It was St Augustine who first used this argument. As a result of his immense authority in theological questions in the Middle Ages it was regarded as authoritative until early modern times. Augustine considered the list of peoples and countries recorded after the Flood, as given in Genesis,[45] to be definitive; it was a complete register which allowed for no extension. Thus, the descendants of Noah, and hence also Adam's offspring, only lived on the three continents

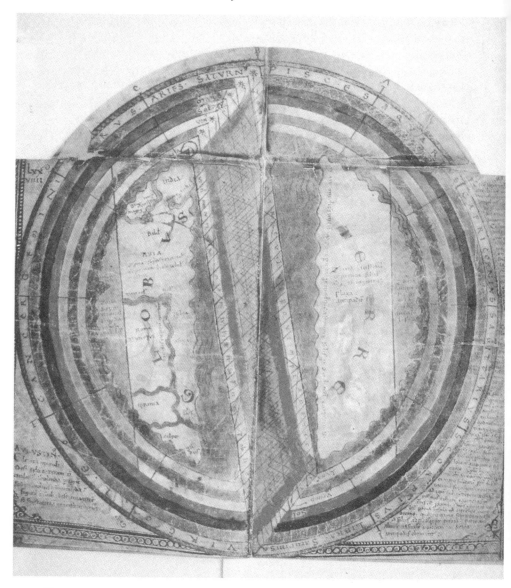

Figure 19. Large mappa mundi from Lambert of St Omer: Liber floridus (c. 1120). St Omer, Bibliothéque municipiale, MS 776, f. 92v–93r.

named in the Bible, and therefore the idea of there being people on a fourth continent, even if it really did exist, was simply inconceivable.[46] In addition to this, Ptolemy had stated that the southern hemisphere of the earth was inaccessible because of the burning heat on the equator. Therefore Noah's descendants could never have reached the southern continent anyway. Evidence to the contrary was not provided until the Portugese expeditions of 1472.[47] This geographical theory that the hot equatorial zone could not be crossed carried a theological consequence. Even if, for some reason, people did live in the hypothetical southern continent, this continent could not be reached because it was impossible to cross the equator. Therefore, Christ's missionary task: 'Go to *all* peoples and teach them' could not be fulfilled. If this was true then the whole question of the act of salvation was put into question. But the idea that Christ might have issued nonsensical instructions was wholly implausible. As the impossibility of crossing the equator was considered a simple matter of fact, the only possible way open for the Church was quite simply to reject the existence of the Antipodes.

Despite these weighty arguments the 'legend' of the Antipodes persisted. It continued to be refuted which meant that the possibility of its existence remained a matter of scholarly interest and subsequent discussion. At the time of the Church Fathers there were two determined opponents of the sphericity of the earth: Cosmas Indikopleustes and before him, around AD 300, Lactantius (whose Classical style of writing led him to be called the Christian Cicero). The latter emphatically denied the existence of the Antipodes. Cosmas had no influence on the development of the discussion in the west since he wrote in Greek. His works were never translated into Latin, remained unedited until the 17th and 18th centuries and therefore were totally unknown in the west until much later than the time we are concerned with.

On the other hand Lactantius was far more influential. He was frequently quoted by opponents of the Antipodes theory, supposedly even by Columbus's adversaries at the Council of Salamanca.[48] Even Copernicus saw occasion to refute Lactantius' views. Like Cosmas, Lactantius rejected the sphericity of the earth and considered the supposition of Antipodes to be foolish. He also opposed the teaching of gravity without which the idea of the Antipodes would be nonsensical.[49]

We know of an interesting controversy in the 8th century concerning the topic of the Antipodes. When he was Bishop of Mainz, Boniface (672/5–754; the Anglo-Saxon missionary whose life was brought to an abrupt end by some heathen Frisians) wrote a letter to the pope, Zacharias (741–752), asking or complaining about the Irish monk Virgil (d. 784). In his answer to this query, dated 748, Zacharias rejected Virgil's opinion about the sphericity of the earth and the existence of people at the other side of the earth completely, saying that it was a 'twisted and unreasonable teaching'.[50] It is not known whether Zacharias later reconsidered his opinion or whether his rejection of the Antipodes was even contrary to contemporary scholarly views. The controversy certainly had no ill effect on Virgil's ecclesiastical career, far less leading to his condemnation, since he was consecrated bishop of Salzburg in 767.[51] Obviously, at this point of time a belief in the Antipodes was certainly not considered to be heretical as it would become in the 14th century.

Another scholarly theological controversy on the topic of the Antipodes is known from the end of the 11th century. It centred on whether pagan knowledge could be assimilated by Christian scholars. The itinerant friar and later Augustinian canon Manegold of Lautenbach attacked a certain Wolfhelm of Cologne because of his defence of the heathen author Macrobius and his *Weltbild*. Although Manegold rejects Macrobius' views, he is able to cite him competently and obviously knew the cosmographical work of this 'heathen' author only too well.[52] Thus it appears that it was not simply a lack of knowledge of the theories about the Antipodes from Classical times which led some medieval authors to their negative views, but rather it had more to do with the fact that these advocates were pagan. Yet, such considerations would have applied to the majority of cosmographical knowledge. Consequently it seems that the theological arguments in favour of Noah's descendants being the exclusive settlers of the three continents (to which the world was thereby limited) were convincing enough to lead scholarly zealots, such as Manegold, Zacharias and Boniface, to attack their opponents. The complaint that those believing in the Antipodes were heathen and thus lacking credibility is secondary and only supplied additional fuel to their argumentative fires. Apart from the occasion discussed above, the Roman author Macrobius was considered to be a cosmographic authority even with good Christian authors of the Middle Ages, among them scholarly clerics from Honorius of Autun to Albertus Magnus and Thomas Aquinas.[53]

It seems almost incredible that even as late as the 14th century people were burnt at the stake for supporting the theory of the existence of Antipodes. This happened to the professor of medicine in Padua, Petrus of Abano, in 1316 and to the astronomer from Bologna, Cecco da Ascoli, eleven years later, both of whom were attacked by the inquisition apparently for their belief in the Antipodes.[54] However, a contemporary countryman of theirs, Dante Alighieri (1265–1321), was a strong advocate of the theory (even if it is extremely uncertain if the treatise *De aqua et terra* was really written by him or not). He spoke out in both the *Divina comedia* and in the *Convicto* repeatedly in favour of an inhabited southern continent[55] without ever having to suffer any consequences for having done so. However, the fact that others did apparently suffer for adhering to such beliefs suggests that the consequences for the biblical teaching of the creation and salvation, as interpreted by Augustine, meant that it gave opponents of the existence of the Antipodes plenty of ammunition. They could always quote Augustine's views in their favour. If their difficult adversaries believed in the Antipodes then they had an ideal excuse to denounce them, even if this had not been the real reason for the accusations.

The increasing tenacity of Church doctrine in the 14th century is surprising because during the 12th and 13th centuries almost all the better known encyclopedists and astronomers had spoken in favour of the existence of the Antipodes. The scholar Alexander Neckham (1157–1217, made abbot of Cirencester in 1213), who hardly deals with cosmography in the narrow sense of the word in his most important work, the encyclopedic *De naturis rerum*, refers to the Antipodes. Although he was able to describe them correctly as living underneath our feet, he did not explicitly say whether he actually believed in their existence or not.[56]

Albertus Magnus was much more lucid in expressing his belief in the existence of the Antipodes. He systematically dealt with the problem of where people could actually live on earth and how the stars rise and fall in the sky from their geographical situation.[57] William of Conches was equally clear in his detailed discussion of the differences between the daytime and the seasons for the peoples of the inhabited part of the world, the Antipodes and the inhabitants of the same longitude on the southern hemisphere.[58] He no more doubted the existence of the Antipodes than his contemporary, the encyclopedist from Flanders, Lambert of St Omer. Lambert showed, on the climatic zone maps given in his *Liber floridus*, the Antipodes as inhabiting the southern temperate zone and names this area unmistakably the 'region of the Antipodes'[59] (Figure 18). He copied his zone maps and the Antipodes from Macrobius, which suggests that, despite being a canon in St Omer, he had no qualms whatsoever about quoting a pagan authority. In western Europe the scholarly climate of the 12th and 13th centuries was considerably more liberal than in the Italy of the 14th century; we have no indication that anyone in England or France suffered because of questions concerning the existence of the Antipodes.

What is striking about the discussion of the existence of the Antipodes in the Middle Ages is the way in which the sphericity of the earth and gravity were taken for granted. The question as to whether a people living 'down under' would have difficulty 'holding on' because of being on the other side of the earth is never posed because it never occurred to medieval man. Ideas such as this are modern inventions as a result of erroneous judgements about the knowledge of the Middle Ages.

CHAPTER FIVE

To the Ends of the Earth

The Far-Off East

Columbus's plan and, even more, the journey west itself must have filled his contemporaries, let alone his fellow travellers, with fascination and fear. One reason for this was that sailing westwards from Spain and Portugal meant a sea voyage of unknown length. However, the land that lay at the end of the voyage was certainly no less fascinating for all that. Everybody involved knew that they were heading for 'India' which at the time was synonymous with the greater part of the continent of Asia. Columbus had used this vague term but clarified their actual destination by talking of Cathay (China) or Cipangu (Japan). So the expedition knew which countries and islands they were hoping to reach. However, despite reports from occasional travellers and tales of incredible sights, these places were still so unknown that the authority of established authors was needed to lend sufficient credible basis to actually setting sail and looking for them.

Columbus used the works of eminent and trustworthy authorities, and no doubt took them with him on his voyage. We know that he owned the encyclopedic Latin cosmography written by Pierre d'Ailly. He carefully annotated his copy[1] and he was greatly influenced by its author's views. The two other works which Columbus held in high esteem were the journal written by Marco Polo and Sir John Mandeville's *Travels.*

Marco Polo (1254–1323) did not write the record of his visit to China himself. On his return home from his travels in China, which lasted from 1271–95, he was imprisoned in Genoa, a town at that time in conflict with his hometown of Venice. In 1298 he dictated his experiences to his fellow prisoner Rustichello who wrote them down in a mixture of Italian and French.[2] Within a few years the account had been translated into many different languages and was known throughout Europe. There are still about 140 manuscripts of his work extant today.[3] The book was called *Le Devisement du Monde* in French, but was better known under the title *Il milione,* a title which, interestingly enough, reflects the opinion of his contemporaries about the immeasurably exaggerated figures given. Nowadays this work is usually simply known as Marco Polo's *Travels.* He described Chinese customs from the standpoint of a virtually unprejudiced observer who, as a plenipotentiary, became as well

56

acquainted with the Kublai Khan as no other foreigner had. Most of the stories told by Marco Polo were indeed true (as we now know), but because of the inconceivably high population figures he gave for Chinese towns (see later in this chapter) he was known as *Messer Milione*, on the basis that he must have been bragging for effect. He was reputedly implored to repent and give up his boasting even on his death bed.[4] Taken all together the stories just seemed too incredible for the Europeans of the 13th and 14th centuries to put too much trust in them. The popular title by which the book was known in the Middle Ages shows all too clearly the ironic scepticism with which it was regarded.

In the late Middle Ages, the destabilisation of the Mongol Empire had made travelling to the far East much more difficult if not too dangerous. In consequence far more faith was put in Sir John Mandeville's *Travels* or else *Travails*, possibly the most fictitious travelogue of the period. The exact identity of this popular author has never been totally ascertained. We know very little more than that the book was first written probably either in French or else in Anglo-Norman around 1360 and that its author was either an English knight who sought refuge for some reason or other in Flanders or else a Flemish barber surgeon.[5] His name was probably assumed and despite being one of the most accredited travel authors of the Middle Ages it is very unlikely that he had travelled further than Egypt, if even that far. He probably died in Liège where his gravestone could be seen until the time of the French Revolution. Other than this we know virtually nothing about him. This medieval Karl May[6] described all the countries of the world in great detail with such remarkable finesse that he became a pseudo-authority on geographical matters despite his own limited experience. His technique was essentially identical to that of all other armchair travel writers through the ages: he copied everything from any travel journals and encyclopedias[7] which he could lay his hands on and passed the information on as his own experience. His accounts were considered to be far more trustworthy than those of Marco Polo. This was simply because most of the things he wrote about, however strange they sounded, could be checked upon in books written by 'authorities' of the ancient and contemporary world, and thus confirmed. Apart from this, John Mandeville was a skilful travel writer who was perfectly capable of linking the matter of fact with more exotic details. Like Marco Polo's, his work was translated into numerous languages and was the bestseller of medieval travel literature. It is represented by over 200 manuscripts[8] and countless very early printed versions still extant today.[9]

In early modern scholarship Mandeville was considered a liar and a distorter of facts. Nowadays one attempts to see his work in the light of its astounding influence. His book was read by his contemporaries and travellers in later centuries as a geographical encyclopedia which was used as the basis for geographical exploration, and not as a novel. It was of fundamental importance to Columbus, and was also used by Martin Frobisher, in search of the North-West Passage in 1576, and Sir Walter Raleigh on his journey to America in 1595.[10]

John Mandeville used the medieval encyclopedias as his primary sources. He consulted Isidore of Seville's *Etymologia* written in the 7th century and the *Speculum majus* (the greatest compendium of the Middle Ages) compiled by the French Dominican, Vincent of Beauvais, who wrote his work a century before Mandeville. Besides these he consulted all the older travel records which he could find. For example he made use of newer or older journals written by pilgrims to Jerusalem (William of Boldensele, 1334, or John of Würzburg, 1165) as well as travellers to Asia. It did not concern him whether they were records of actual experience, such as Marco Polo's record or that of the Franciscan Odoric of Pordenone, or else fabulous tales such as the romance about Alexander the Great's journey to India or even the letter of Prester John.[11] This information was embellished with tales from collections of legends[12] and also included thoroughly scholarly quotations from astronomical literature.[13] John Mandeville was able to invent such convincing stories about Asia because at his time much was already known about even the most distant regions of this continent. Europeans had learned a great deal about Africa and Asia from the Crusades which had begun in the 11th century and the conquest of Jerusalem. The foundation of the Crusader State in 1099 marked the beginning of a time of intensive cultural exchange between Europe and the Near East. However, in 1187, after less than a century, Saladin reconquered the Holy City in the name of Islam. From this date the political influence of Europeans in the Near East was drastically reduced. Politically and militarily the Christians were on the retreat. The number of pilgrims permitted to travel to the Holy Land depended on the tolerance of the current Islamic rulers. Not only were pilgrims faced with high taxes but often enough with directly hostility, such as being stoned[14] which made the pilgrimages a relatively dangerous adventure.

It is therefore not surprising that European rulers, especially the popes of the 13th and 14th centuries, looked out for allies in the fight against Islam. They believed that they had found one in the Tartars and their mighty Khan who had terrified both Christians and Moslems equally by a series of raids into Eastern and Central Europe in the first half of the 13th century, reaching as far as Poland, Silesia, Hungary and even Eastern Austria in 1241. In the process he wiped out two major western armies at Liegnitz and Mohi.[15] Pope Innocent IV was expecially interested in these diplomatic contacts and repeatedly sent clerics as ambassadors to the Mongols from 1243 onwards. The most important of these was a certain Italian Franciscan, John of Plano Carpini, who, despite his advanced years (he was over 60), set off in 1245 for what was to be a two-year journey via Kiev to the newly elected Great Khan Güyük, a grandson of Genghis Khan. Carpini's mission brought a letter from the Khan back which caused a sensation in Europe because of its apparent arrogance. Despite the adverse wintry conditions on his return journey which was full of privations Carpini managed to write a scholarly but personal record of his experience while still en route, the *Historia Mongalorum*.[16]

Another Franciscan (from the Flemish province), William of Rubruck, set out in 1253 from Constantinople for Asia. Despite being sent by the French king Louis IX (the Saint), he travelled eastwards not as an ambassador but more as a missionary. He reached the Great Khan Mönke (who he called Mangu) in 1254 and was astounded (as were all the other Europeans) at his religious tolerance. In May 1254 the Khan even organised a theological discussion between the Franciscan, Nestorians, Buddhists and Moslems.[17] After his return William reported to the king in Paris, but also told the English scholar Roger Bacon about his experiences.[18] The record of his travels which he then composed is one of the most vivid medieval travel journals in which the marvels seen do not eclipse his own experiences with onerous natives, foreign cuisine, bad horses, and other personal discomfort suffered during his time abroad.[19]

The third East Asian traveller whose description was widely read was the Friulian Franciscan Odoric of Pordenone[20] who travelled to Asia at some point around 1314. He later spent four years in China (1324–1328) and travelled among the archipelago of the Nicobar islands where he even made the acquaintance of a tribe of cannibals.[21]

Marco Polo also mentioned cannibals living on an Indian island far to the south,[22] and even if the Franciscan began a discussion about their distasteful custom with the inhabitants, it is clear that European travellers were by no means surprised to come across such phenomena. They knew about the existence of such *anthropophagi* (the Greek word for cannibals) who had been an integral feature of the European encyclopedias whenever mention was made of fabulous races[23] ever since the natural histories written by Pliny and Solinus. It is no doubt conceivable that Odoric might actually have spoken with the natives on the subject, on the lines that it would be scandalous to allow friends and relations to be eaten by worms after their death instead of being eaten by their friends. This sounds remarkably similar to the explanation given in medieval European literature about the Patrophagi (parent-eaters) who fatten up their parents before their death in order to share them with friends at a feast held in their honour.[24] When Columbus came across cannibals on Cuba, this fact must have strengthened his belief that he had arrived in southern Asia, as both Marco Polo and John Mandeville, the latter of whom had copied his information about the island of Dondin from Odoric's report,[25] claimed that this is where the cannibals were to be found.

Cannibals and other 'fabulous' peoples who the travellers met, or said they had met, on their journeys to far-off regions, and who absolutely fascinated the Europeans, are the subject of the next chapter. The fabulous races were by no means the only phenomenon for the travellers 'to write home about', since from all medieval travel records to East Asia it is clear that, despite some limits to their own horizons, travellers realised increasingly clearly just how boundless the inhabited world in the east was. There was no edge to a disc-shaped earth (which no-one believed in anyway), no fence at the end of the world,[26] not even the wall with or without flames around the earthly Paradise which might have been expected from the world maps and old handbooks and even the Alexander

Romances of the high Middle Ages.[27] The only travel record in which Paradise occurs at all is the one invented by Sir John Mandeville. Ironically enough, by talking of the possibility of returning from East Asia to Europe by a direct route, he confirmed that the inhabited world had no limits. He related in an anecdote that the only reason why he returned overland was that he had actually reached his homeland by going straight on, but, because he had obviously come from the wrong side, he had not recognised it whereupon he had turned round and gone back the other way again all round the earth.[28]

The gradually increasing awareness of the sheer size of Asia was particularly impressive for travellers to Mongolia as they passed through northern Asia. It was augmented by the fact that however far east they went, they still found people, often living in areas where on the basis of the *mappae mundi* and information from antiquity they had assumed they would only find fabulous races and wilderness.

The most lasting impression not only for travellers to Mongolia, but especially for those to China was the high population density of eastern Asia, the size of the towns, the huge armies, and the numerous provinces. If Marco Polo was mocked for being a *Messer Milione*, then this was predominantly because the size of Chinese cities were simply inconceivable for Europeans of the late Middle Ages. Although the town of Babylon was said to have been so big that three days' journey was needed in all directions before its limits were reached, this belonged to the biblical past, along with other exaggerated claims such as Noah's and Methuselah's respective ages (950 and 969 years). Europeans of the 13th and 14th centuries could do little else but laugh with incredulity at the apparently ridiculous claims being made when they compared what they were being told with what they already knew from their own experience. In 1377 London had a mere 35,000 inhabitants, Rome a decade before had even less, only 17,000, whereas Paris, the largest city in Europe, with its court and university had only 280,000 inhabitants in 1383. Venice, Marco Polo's hometown, was the third largest town in Europe (after Paris and Naples) at the end of the 13th century, but even so only had about 100,000 inhabitants.[29] Such figures were negligible compared to cities described by Marco Polo on his travels, such as the town of Kinsai (today Hangchow) comprising 1.6 million houses, with a circumference of 100 miles and 12,000 mostly stone bridges. Even Sugiu (Su-chau in Kiang-su or Suzhou in Jiang-su) is said to have had 6,000 bridges[30] and Cambaluc (Beijing) apparently had 1.2 million inhabitants by 1270.[31] Apart from these facts Marco Polo always knew how to fascinate his audience with what would interest every European, especially merchants. His tale is full of pearls, gold and jewels, spices and herbs,[32] and of strange customs, such as paper money which was used in China from the 10th century onwards. The wealth attributed to a country increased the further it was from Europe. Marco Polo never set foot in Cipangu (or Cimpangu = Japan) since the Mongolian attempts to subjugate the country in 1274 and 1281 had failed miserably.[33] Using information from other travellers he described this archipelago as lying 5000 miles from China, and was so 'boundlessly' rich in gold that the royal palace had roofs which were tiled two fingers deep with gold. Even the floors were said to be gilded, quite apart from the presence of other riches including jewels and red and white pearls. Consequently it is little wonder that with such a description in front of him Columbus should have been at least as interested in landing in Cimpangu than arriving in India, if not more so.

The medieval concept of 'India' was far broader than ours today. On some small world maps India stood for Asia, in the same way as Libya could be used as a *pars pro toto* term for Africa. From the discrepancy of information about where India actually lay, whether it lay to the far east, or else in southern Asia or else between Africa and Asia, the notion arose that there were either two or even three Indias.[34] The encyclopedias written by scholars, such as Gervase of Tilbury and Vincent of Bauvais,[35] refer to two Indias: Upper India (*India superior*), which was said to have been Christianised by one of the apostles, Bartholomew; and, Lower India (*India inferior*), which had fallen under the missionary zeal of another apostle, Thomas. The division of India into three parts, an Ethiopian, a Median and a Far Eastern, was suggested in the Pseudo-Abdias from the 6th century and occurs relatively frequently on the *mappae mundi*. The same description appears in the letter by Prester John (of whom more later), as well as in all the hagiographic sources dealing with St Bartholomew.[36] Wherever it might lie, there had been a realistic picture of India with regards to its size and physical geography since Alexander the Great's campaign there.[37] It was an empire with distinctly fabulous characteristics and was described like no other country with a mixture of facts and fiction. It was considered to be extraordinarily large and densely populated, very fertile and extremely rich in gold and jewels.[38] This attractive description was admittedly somewhat spoilt in many sources by tales of the great dangers en route (such as the poisonous snakes in Mesopotamia) and not least by the fabulous races there. Nevertheless India was considered to be the ideal destination for Europeans as is evident from the three directions of European expansion. Whether the route led directly overland to the east, or round Africa, or even, as Columbus tried, by the western route, the destination of all these journeys was India.

Sir John Mandeville was at least one source that confirmed the existence of the earthly Paradise to the east of India. According to older cosmographies and the *mappae mundi* it lay in the furthest east of Asia, that is, somewhere near China and Japan. Yet even Mandeville admitted[39] that he only knew it from hearsay and could be no more specific as he had not been there himself. In any case Paradise was enclosed by a wall and had deserts full of wild animals surrounding it, preventing any mortal from entering. Ever practically minded, Mandeville further commented that the rivers of Paradise were not navigable because they were raging torrents, as many a high-spirited prince had discovered to his cost. Nevertheless he also knew that Paradise lay higher than the surrounding countryside and that its four rivers, the Nile, Ganges, Euphrates and Tigris, which all flowed with gold and jewels, had their source in the fountain at the centre of Paradise.

Mandeville even talked about China, and although his source for the power and riches of the Tartar khan was Marco Polo, he added more information not in genuine eye-witness accounts. Among these additions are tales of fabulous animals such as the griffin, a bird which was so big that it could carry away a horse and rider as well as a whole ox cart in its claws.[40] He also described amazing flora, such as a tree whose fruit turned into living birds.[41] Mandeville's information was the result of combing through old encyclopedias and romances in search of fabulous pseudo-facts in order to be able to embellish his fictitious record. Consequently, his work contrasts markedly with the records of Marco Polo, Odoric and Carpini. They had all voluntarily undertaken journeys to Mongolia or China, had fulfilled a mission there and therefore concentrated their reports on the politics, religion, court customs and the economy of the countries they stayed in.

These records differ yet again from the one left by Johannes Schiltberger,[42] a Bavarian soldier, who spent more than three decades involuntarily in the east. He was part of King Sigismund's army which found itself annihilated by the Turks in 1394 at Nicopolis, below the Iron Gate on the lower Danube. Schiltberger was probably no more than fourteen years old at the time and it was only his youth that saved him from being executed. Instead he was sent into slavery, at first in service with the Turks, then he fell into Mongolian hands after the Turks had been conquered by the Tartars. In this way he came from Asia Minor, Egypt and Mesopotamia to south-western Mongolia. His unsophisticated tales include information about India and Paradise, although he never went there himself and freely admits it. Only after thirty-three years of forced journeying as a slave of war did he manage to escape and in 1427 finally returned to his homeland. Although his tale sounds fresh and simple he had augmented his experiences with other sources in order to tell his story. Consequently his adventures are a strange mixture of traditional western knowledge, mixed with extensive use of legends and stories heard on his travels. In the same straightforward firsthand way he described both the eating habits of his Mongolian rulers, who ate salted meat and drank mare's milk, his precarious attempts to flee, at the same time as he told of princesses in inaccessible castles or of a Crusader tale about the red town walls of Antioch being painted with the blood of Christians.

All of the travellers to Asia, even those pilgrims who only went as far as the Holy Land or perhaps to Egypt or the Sinai peninsula,[43] provided Europe with information about Asia and its inhabitants. In this respect, both Schiltberger's descriptions of Islamic customs[44] and Marco Polo's notes on the religions of eastern Asia with their bovine and other zoomorphic deities[45] are thoroughly objective and informative. At the same time they almost all perpetuate western prejudices about the exotic regions of the world since the authors of the travel books usually used older travel records as well as the encyclopedias available when writing down their experiences.

There were various reasons for making use of older travel books. Firstly, the popular handbooks provided the less educated traveller with a frame of reference. The knowledge thus acquired was confirmed during the journey to a certain degree even if experiences made ought really to have contradicted it. Man in the Middle Ages travelled with a certain *Weltbild* in his head which was pre-shaped by knowledge from books. This preconception influenced, to a certain degree, what was seen on the journey and how it was mentally classified. Therefore it is hardly surprising that nearly all travellers to Asia claim, for example, to have seen a unicorn. Illustrations in late medieval and early modern travel books depict the fabulous unicorn as a mythological creature just as it was imagined in the Middle Ages. Only one traveller, Marco Polo, who even in this instance showed himself to be open to his own perceptions and less prejudiced or pre-conditioned than others, commented somewhat disappointedly that the unicorn did not resemble its popular image. It turned out to be an ugly, plump and fat-legged animal with a short horn. He thereby provided us with a thumbnail sketch of a rhinoceros:[46] 'there are also many unicorns, which are hardly smaller than the elephants, with a head like a pig lowered to the ground; they live in water and mudholes and have a horn on the forehead which is rough and black'.* But even an eye-witness account did not serve primarily to 'demythologise' the unicorn, as a critical description like this confirmed for the European reader once more that there were indeed unicorns.[47]

The case is not so different for today's travellers. Their attitude, as a result of modern individualism and a different kind of education, is directed more towards the extraordinary rather than the common. They also tend to see the 'sights' recommended by, for example, the Michelin guides rather than other at least as obvious attractions and therefore, back home, only repeat what they have already read about in the book beforehand.

Secondly the travel writer could use written sources to aid his own memory whilst writing his account. Although the pilgrims to Rome or Jerusalem could refer to quite detailed and accurate pilgrim guides,[48] the traveller who had been further afield had to rely more on the fabulous information of the medieval encyclopedias. These combined Classical, Arabic, and European knowledge in a frequently quite unbalanced way with fictitious fabrications. These accounts could naturally enough be confirmed by additional information which added more weight to the rest even if the traveller perhaps could not check the information from his own experience, but still wanted to include it for the sake of completeness.

Thirdly, the agreement between the actual experience and the traditional

---

* *do sint ouch vil eynhorn, dy luczil cleyner sint wen die elephant, das houbt sam eyn swyn krum czu der erdin; sy wonen gerne in dem wazzir und in den pfülin und han eyn horn mittin an der stirnen unde das ist grob unde swarcz*

knowledge known from books gave additional credibility both to what was said and to who said it. This is where the medieval concept of knowledge differed quite drastically from the modern one, insofar as experience was measured on the authority of the books and not vice versa.[49] Mandeville's fictitious travels, based on older books, was therefore without doubt the most trustworthy of its genre for the medieval audience since it offered virtually nothing new and therefore did not deviate from the tradition of older more authoritive works.

The Hot South

Mappae mundi and geographical texts agreed that, apart from a narrow strip on the Mediterranean, Africa was desolate and in the equatorial zone it became completely uninhabitable. It was thought that because of the extreme heat caused by an overhead sun human life was impossible.[50] Accordingly, there were no known travel records about Africa. That does not mean that none existed. In fact a wealth of information about Africa existed in the fascinating travel book by the Moroccan Islamic writer, Ibn Battuta, but this only reached Europe in the 19th century. Like many of his countrymen Ibn Battuta had not only fulfilled his religious duty by going to Mecca, but he subsequently also spent many years (1325–1354) travelling. His journeys took him via India, the Maldives, Ceylon, and Java as far as China. Later he travelled in Spain and Central Africa as far as Timbuctoo.[51] His lively record is full of details and confirms the high standard of Arabian culture which the Europeans had little knowledge of. Another work about Africa was one by the Spanish Jew Benjamin of Tudela. He travelled from Spain via Asia Minor to Baghdad and India and on the return journey via Ethiopia and Egypt visiting the Jewish communities en route.[52] However, like the Arabic work of Ibn Battuta, this record was not even known in scholarly circles in medieval Europe.

Central and western Europeans did not know much more about Egypt, Tunisia, and north-west Africa than what could be gleaned from late Classical sources and the Old Testament. Admittedly, many wealthier pilgrims to the Holy Land went via Egypt[53] in order to see the Nile and Alexandria, some probably being taken there by captains who had trading calls to make in the Nile Delta. Egypt was indeed the best known of all African countries. Few travellers penetrated any further into Africa. Even Classical authors were silent about interior Africa for want of information, and the entries on maps and the descriptions in cosmographies are correspondingly meagre.

It was known that West Africa, beyond the pillars of Hercules (Gibraltar-Ceuta), bordered on the Atlantic Ocean. It was supposed that the south extended to the southern ocean at some great distance. It is unclear whether Africa was believed to stretch out to and beyond the equator or whether a hot ocean divided possible landmasses on the southern hemisphere.[54] Both possibilities are found on *mappae mundi.*

The Roman provinces of Egypt, Libya, Tripolis, Pentapolis, Byzacena, Numidia and the (occasionally mentioned two) Mauretanias were listed and augmented geographically by the addition of legendary Ethiopia, which (like Libya) could be synonymous for Africa. In the cases of the North African provinces there were at least towns like Babylon[55], Alexandria, Carthage, or Hippo (where St Augustine had lived) which could be pointed out, but in the case of Ethiopia any description was a matter of pure fantasy. Just as with India in the furthest east and Scythia in the far north of the inhabited world, Ethiopia in the south was presumed to be the home of monstrous races and fabulous animals. It was known from the history of the Punic wars and the wars against Jugurtha that there were elephants in Africa.[56] What other animals there were did not come from Roman historiographers but from Pliny's natural history, the compendium of curiosities by Solinus and Isidore's encyclopedic works[57] which enthusiastically reported fabulous phenomena such as herds of wild onagers, the ostrich, the rhinoceros, snakes with two heads, the chameleon, and also basilisks and dragons.

Medieval man was fascinated by the concept of fabulous peoples (see Chapter 6) and any other amazing phenomena. Information about miraculous minerals and waters, and in particular the descriptions of fantastic animals, were an integral part of any medieval description of the world. Even the eye-witness records of travellers far afield were no exception to this. There is a natural tendency to view this predeliction for anything fabulous and exotic as typically medieval, but a glance at television documentaries of the late 20th century shows the fascination still caused by the animal world, and in particular anything considered to be exotic (that is, whatever the observer is not permanently confronted with).

Apart from the natural history written by Pliny in the 1st century AD and the extracts from it made by Solinus revealing his relish for the unusual,[58] this taste for the fabulous was satisfied by the so-called *Physiologus,*[59] written at some point between the 2nd and 4th century. The *Physiologus,* which dealt exclusively with animals, was originally written in Greek, then in Latin and in numerous vernacular languages. It was extremely popular. The title actually referred originally not to the book itself but to its author, a 'natural philosopher'. In its medieval versions it was a specifically Christian work and gives a theological interpretation after every description of an animal, which accounts for some of its popularity. In a later development, the *Physiologus,* the animal chapters in Isidore of Seville's *Etymologiae* and other encyclopedias were compiled to create so-called bestiaries which began to emerge from the 10th century onwards. Their contents were wider in scope than the *Physiologus,* but they rarely dispensed with the spiritual interpretation.[60] They were also more voluminous and sub-divided into mammals, birds, reptiles and fish, as well as occasionally including chapters on plants and minerals. In most of them the originally brief theological interpretation extended to moralising fables about animals and nature in general.

The bestiaries mention well-known animals about whom elevating stories were told. Yet the main emphasis lay quite clearly on the more exotic creatures amongst whom monsters and fabulous animals had their place. The favourite of all the real animals was undoubtedly the elephant. It had homes in two peripheral areas of the inhabited world: India and Africa. Larger *mappae mundi* repeatedly include a picture of the elephant to indicate India. It seems most likely that the elephant illustrated on the Ebstorf world map was too much temptation for someone. Of the thirty original sheets of parchment making up this large map the one showing India was cut out and removed.[61] Notwithstanding this vandalism the map retained another elephant, a small one in West Africa,[62] until it perished in flames during the Second World War. The second large medieval *mappa mundi*, displayed in Hereford Cathedral, shows an elephant in India complete with a fighting turret on its back,[63] a feature which, together with the sheer size of the elephant, apparently impressed the medieval authors most.[64] The longevity of elephants (reputed to be 300 years) was impressive and only exceeded by dragons. The elephant's long gestation period of two years was also worth mentioning, as was the fact that the animals turned away from each other during mating, which was a sign of their chastity, according to the *Physiologus*. The well-known characteristic that, despite their size, elephants are afraid of mice is a tale that is nearly 2000 years old.[65]

Of all the real animals, the European encyclopedists were also fascinated by the afore mentioned unicorn (identified, by Marco Polo at least, as the rhinoceros), camaelopards (giraffes), the African onagers (wild asses), antelopes, panthers, tigers and even crocodiles. All these animals gave the descriptions in the bestiaries an exotic charm as well as a reason for spiritual edification. The exemplary modesty of the elephants, the humility of the unicorn and the zeal of the panther contrasted greatly with the foulness and baseness of the crocodile which served as a negative example.[66]

Many of the animals, listed to embellish the description of exotic regions, were even further afield from our modern concept of reality than the spiritual interpretations given. Griffins and basilisks, dragons and giant ants, the manticore and the phoenix were just as much a part of medieval reality as far-off countries were, and so were the stories of the self-castration of the fleeing beaver and the pelican ripping at its own breast to feed its young. Nonetheless the spatial distribution showed that the fabulous beasts were located on the peripheries of the known *orbis terrarum*. The griffins which attacked people in Scythia in the north, the basilisks who killed with their looks, the terrifying dragons in the south of Africa, the manticore with the human head and the three rows of teeth vouched for India, and Arabian phoenix which destroyed itself by fire and rose from the ashes.[67]

The description of the fabled animals was almost completely characterised by a dichotomy which is less noticeable on the world maps and travel descriptions than in the miniatures in books of hours and the stone statues of medieval cathedrals, where their metaphorical role is all too frequently obscure to us. All of the animals, even the monstrous, were seen to be part of God's creation and therefore had their place in the divine plan of creation. This is certainly true for their natural habitat where each plays its part in a complex hierarchy with other animals. Whether the part was as a dominant or subordinate, the thought seems very Darwinian. This hierarchy also extended to the part that animals played in man's world, which the bestiaries gave just as much space to in the spiritual exegesis as they gave to descriptions of the natural world. On the other hand, the fabled animals symbolise an aspect of the medieval world which man experienced as something alien, different, and terrifying. By classifying them as 'fabulous' he could make them notionally submissive and at the same time invoke an association with the boundaries of the inhabited earth and thus of man's existence.[68]

The Bleak North

Not only were the furthest east and south of the inhabited world normally considered to be inaccessible, but so was the far north. It remained so well into the 19th century when circumnavigations of the world and expeditions into the darkest interior of Africa were no longer a novelty.

The idea of reaching the North Pole did not even enter the medieval imagination, although the question about what countries lay in the north of Europe and Asia had bothered both Classical and medieval authors. The historical exploration of the north began with Herodotus in the 5th century BC, who only got as far north as the Black Sea, though. Pytheas, a Greek traveller born in Marseilles, wrote down eye-witness accounts of western and northern Europe in the 4th century BC, when he travelled along the Atlantic coast to the British Isles and then further, probably thereby visiting the islands of the North Atlantic, the Orkneys, Shetlands, Faroes, and perhaps even Iceland. One of these places, though it is not certain which, he calls the island of Thule.[69] There are no copies of his work 'About the Ocean' preserved today, but the information given was used by Hipparchus (2nd century BC). Since the days of Pytheas the search for the island of Thule was a continuing fascination for Classical and later geographers, yet the lack of actual knowledge in the north of Europe is quite striking. The Classical authors from Aristotle and Plato to Tacitus[70] had little to report and even on the medieval *mappae mundi* the information contained on northern Europe is scant. In the extreme north the river Tanais (Don) has its source in the Riphaean mountains; this then flows to the Black Sea, forming the border between Europe and Asia. It flows through Scythia which the Scandinavians, after the eastern expansion of the Viking era, called Greater Sweden.[71] To the east of this lies the densely forested area of Hyrcania.

Further west lie Germania and the island of Britannia which are described in some detail.[72] For the northern part of Europe, there is only some vague information about the 'islands' Dacia (Denmark), Suecia (Sweden) and Norvegia (Norway) whilst the afore-mentioned Atlantic islands rarely appear on maps.[73] Thule was usually identified with Iceland, but this second, native name led to a misunderstanding that there were two islands, namely Thule and Iceland, or even three islands, Thule, Iceland, and the Indian island of Thile which was often confused with the former simply because of the similarity of the names.[74] For most Europeans the inhabited earth was finally at an end with these islands for the North Atlantic had not lost its terror since antiquity.

One of the oldest vernacular cosmographical texts from the 11th century, the Old High German poem, *Merigarto*, tells of a trader who went to Iceland.[75] It also tells of a 'Liver-sea', 'a fabulous, dangerous coagulated sea in which the ships could not move'.[76] This was obviously thought of as being in the north-west and probably referred to the frozen polar sea.[77] Attempts to understand the *mare coagulatum* as being an early allusion to the Sargasso sea[78] is unwarranted, even if the *Image du Monde* by Walter of Metz located this coagulated sea to the west of Africa. Similarly, links to the legendary magnetic mountain, as found both in the Middle High German *Herzog Ernst* and in the *Legend of St Brendan* are old but are not original. Similar comments about the northern sea can be found earlier in the writings of the Irish cleric Dicuil[79] as well as in Isidore of Seville's work[80] and they were subsequently incorporated into standard encyclopedic knowledge. Even so it seems that, particularly in western Europe, vernacular tradition played a role of some importance since even in the Latin text of the ecclesiastical historian Adam of Bremen (between 1073 and 1080) the word *Libersee* ('Liver-sea') is found written in German, no doubt as a result of there being no adequate equivalent Latin expression.[81] Otherwise people living in central and western Europe knew nothing about Scandinavia, if one excludes various comments about fabulous races.[82] Only the Scandinavians themselves extended the horizon northwards and to the north-west, as discussed above.[83]

One reason for the scanty knowledge about northern Europe in the Middle Ages was the view of Classical authors that the north was uninhabited, and uninhabitable. This is evident in ancient teaching on the climatic zones which attributed strips of the known earth to astronomical climates. This meant that the earth, and in particular Europe, was divided into strips of latitudes. In these strips the inhabitants of a climatic zone observed more or less the same stellar constellations from their homes, had the same length of day and to a certain degree similar metereological conditions. The latter was only of secondary significance and is only tangible in the modern meaning of 'climate'. As it is less a case of an exact theoretical-astronomical division of the inhabited world than a list of places and countries for practical comparative purposes, it hardly matters that only a narrowly limited area of the inhabited world is covered by it, as the following list of the seven climates may demonstrate:

Diameroes	India – Red Sea – West Africa
Diasyenes	India – Persia – Arabia – West Africa
Dialexandrios	India – Thaurus – Alexandria – Carthage
Diarhodos	Filipones – Greece – Sicilly – Gibraltar
Diaromes	Caspian Sea – Macedonia – Rome – Spain
Diahellespontum	Hellespont – south of Germania
Diaboristenes	Miotian marshes – Germania – Britannia

The weaknesses in this system were already recognised by Martianus Capella[84] (5th century AD) and an eighth climate was introduced to cover the Ripheaen mountains (*Diaripheos*), but whereas the Scandinavian authors did not deal much with these weaknesses or the climatic theory, the English astronomer Robertus Anglicus felt his country was clearly at a disadvantage, a feeling he voiced in his commentary on John of Sacrobosco's *Liber de sphaera* made in 1271: 'To what is said contrary to the authority of Alfraganus and Ptolemy, who assume that the first climate begins this side of the equator, I say that this proof is not conclusive, for the last, seventh climate only contains a little of England – not even as much as two days' journey – but from which it does not follow that England is uninhabitable, because the philosophers of that time only divided well-known inhabited areas whereas at this time it was not yet inhabited and no rumour had reached us of it. In short, they divided not only inhabitable but generally known inhabited land to which access and departure was easily possible.'[85]

Despite such corrections made by English clerics and the far superior geographical knowledge of the Scandinavians northern Europe remained for most Europeans an unknown zone on the periphery of the inhabited world.

Excursus: Hope in the East: the Indian Kingdom of Prester John

In the year 1165 a letter appeared in Europe which was passed on by the Byzantine emperor, Manuel Comnenus (1143–1180), to the Emperor of the Holy Roman Empire, Frederick I Barbarossa (1152–1190), and which began as follows:

Prester John, by the Might and Virtue of God and our Lord Jesus Christ King of Kings, greets Manuel, leader of the Romans and wishes him the lasting grace of God.[86]

The letter did indeed go to Frederick Barbarossa, but where it came from, as it was supposedly originally written in Greek and then translated into Latin (as the letter itself states), was and still is uncertain.

After an introductory formula of greeting and allusion to a supposed exchange of gifts between the two rulers the letter talks about the power and the riches of Prester (a contraction of *presbyter*, a priest) John. It claims that he ruled over seventy kings and owned incredible amounts of jewels. Then the letter turns to the description of the three Indias which John ruled over. This longest section of the letter is a list of everything that was known in western literature about fabulous things in India. The text names jewels and herbs with miraculous properties, exotic and fabulous animals (phoenix, unicorn, and salamander), the pepper wood, fabulous races such as the Amazons, Pygmies, Centaurs and Dog-heads,[87] the enormous Indian rivers and a sandy sea.[88] The last part of the letter ties up with the beginning and describes the ideal theocratic regime which Prester John practised according to the teachings of St Thomas in which there were to be no poor, no sycophants, no thieves, no adulterers, and no heretics. Finally the palace and the courtiers of Prester John were described. Despite this insolent description of his kingdom he still went on to boast of his humility by saying that he spurned the title of king because he knew no higher rank than that of being a priest of God.[89]

This arrogant letter was of course a forgery and the reason why it was thought to be real in the Middle Ages is predominantly because the description of India confirmed everything that was known about India from travel literature and even more so from the encyclopedias. Like in Sir John Mandeville's book of travels this accord between the new text with the Latin authorities was not the result of identical experiences but of the respective authors' compilation of extracts from older works to make a new text. Although the letter claimed to have a Greek source, such an earlier form is highly unlikely.[90] The author of the letter was probably a western European cleric who primarily wanted to expose the conditions in Europe where the conflict between Emperor and Pope (Alexander III) had reached a new low. During the schism antipopes were elected (Victor IV 1159–1164, Paschal III 1164–1168) and in addition there was the external threat from Islam (Edessa fell in 1144, and the Second Crusade, 1147–1149, failed) which Europeans were becoming increasingly aware of. In this situation it was the aim of the author of the letter to present the emperor of the Holy Roman Empire as well as the Pope and the Church at large with the ideal of a theocratic rule, a Christian Utopia in comparison to the Europe of his time.[91] His second aim was probably to strengthen European resolve in the struggle against Islam – thus perhaps strengthening the morale for another Crusade – by inventing a mighty Christian ally to the rear of the Islamic enemy.[92]

As far as politics are concerned, the author undoubtedly failed on both counts. The papacy and the empire had enough on their hands with their struggle against each other, and if the hope of finding an ally in the east was sufficient to raise speculations, hard-core information was missing and the next (third) Crusade did not come off until 1189.

On the other hand, as a literary work, the fictitious letter of the priest-king John was a complete success. It was translated from Latin into English, German, Russian, Serbian, French, Occitan, Italian, and even Hebrew,[93] with twenty manuscripts alone of the Old French translation preserved[94] and almost a hundred manuscripts of various Latin versions known to Zarncke[95] in 1879.

The text was still extremely popular at the time of the incunabula.[96] The reason for the quick and wide distribution of the short and, because of the concentration of the descriptions, relatively monotonous text lay surely not in the above-mentioned authorial intentions, as far as we can reconstruct them,[97] but rather primarily in the fact that most of the information about India found in the scholarly sources in Europe was collected here and presented in concise and clear but also very popular form. The dependence of the text on Latin tradition meant that the knowledge of the scholars was confirmed; for others, the vague fragments of information about India were augmented with additional material. Thus, this compilation itself became a source for later works, such as the travel description (1389) of Johannes de Hese,[98] a pilgrim to Jerusalem, the *Dreikönigslegende* ('Legend of the three Magi') by Johannes of Hildesheim[99] (written c. 1351–1370) and not least the previously mentioned fictitious *Travels* by Sir John Mandeville.[100]

Considering the substantial 'literary' success of Prester John's letter the question as to the identity of its author arises, or to put it in a different way: what were the historical sources which led the anonymous author of the actual text to invent Prester John? In recent scholarship on the subject of Prester John there has been a tendency to merge and harmonise the various older attempts at interpretation to a complex construction.[101] The literary basis of the anonymous author would appear to be derived primarily from two letters about the historically proven visit of a patriarch called Johannes to Pope Calixtus II in Rome in the year 1122 or 1123. This patriarch is said to have been an Indian cleric and the two letters about his visit report in detail about the Thomas-Christians in India. It is not completely certain where these Thomas-Christians came from if they can indeed be traced to an eastern evangelising by the apostle Thomas, or, as is more likely, that they are descendants of Nestorian Christians who were dispersed throughout Asia after the condemnation of Nestorius as a heretic at the Council of Ephesus on 22 June 431.[102] The Indian priestdom of Prester John can probably be explained by this visit of the patriarch Johannes. The story about his visit was subsequently exaggerated and he was transformed into a mighty ruler and enemy of the Muslims. This hostility is no doubt the result of a different historical event, namely the battle of Katvan near Samarkand in the year 1141 in which the Mongolian army leader Ye-lüh Ta-schih wiped out the army of the Seljuk sultan Sanjar. The news of this major defeat of the Turks soon reached Europe where it was greeted with joy and the Mongolian army leader was thought of as a potential ally.[103] The first written reference to this army leader is in the chronicle of Bishop Otto of Freising from the year 1145. He had heard of the battle from a Syrian bishop from Gabula during his visit to Rome in 1144. Otto gave this army leader the name of Prester John[104] and this is the name under which the Mongolian general went down in medieval history. The reason for Otto giving him this name might have originated in another far-off Christian king, the Christian (Nestorian) Ethiopian king. These kings, ever since the Christianisation of Ethiopia in the 4th century,

encyclopedic literature does not explicitly refer to this central position of Jerusalem,[6] it plays a significant role in the writings of crusaders and pilgrims.[7] Numerous detailed descriptions of the city[8] reflect the interest in the city at the centre of the world awakened in pilgrims and crusaders. So also do a series of illustrative plans of the city of Jerusalem,[9] which gave a stylised and ideal picture of the city rather than being a town plan in today's sense (Figure 20). Besides these there were pilgrims' guides to Jerusalem which served the same purpose as modern guidebooks by offering a form of checklist so that none of the important pilgrimage sites would be missed. These works included the so-called Jerusalem breviary, dating from around 550,[10] the *Libellus de locis sanctis*, written in 1173 by a certain Theoderic,[11] and the 13th century *Descriptio terrae sanctae* by Burchard de Monte Sion.[12] These guides then in turn served as the model for personal records made by the pilgrims.[13] Even if nowadays the earlier suppositions about large numbers of manuscripts and early printed pilgrim guides have been somewhat modified, one can hardly presume that every pilgrim actually owned such a guide or even needed one.[14] Just how important the bought 'Michelin guides' were for the individual traveller is uncertain. Similarly the role of oral information passed on by travel guides should not be forgotten altogether. Whatever the role of the written and oral advice was for the travel journals, one thing is certain: the number of holy sites to be visited in Jerusalem was impressive. Among the 'musts' of the most important sites were the two largest buildings in the city: the Basilica of Constantine and the Holy Sepulchre. The former was known as the *Templum Domini* despite having been dedicated to the Virgin Mary in 1141.[15] It had been built in 661 as Omar's mosque and was the successor to the temple of Solomon destroyed in AD 70 by the Romans. The crusaders had redesigned it and slight structural alterations had made it the second most important ecclesiastical building in Jerusalem. The latter, the *sepulcrum Domini*, was the church destroyed in 1009 and re-built in 1042–1048, marking the grave in which Christ was laid prior to the resurrection. This was joined together with the crusaders' church (*Templum sancte crucis*) to form a building complex covering the sites of the grave and Golgotha which in turn was completed on 15th July 1149.[16] Apart from these monumental buildings there were numerous other sites to be visited which were well-known from the Old but more especially from the New Testament: the graves of Adam, the Virgin Mary and St Stephen, the room of the Last Supper, the Pentecost room, Peter's prison, David's tower, Pilate's palace and naturally the *via dolorosa*.

Beyond the city of Jerusalem itself there were more authentic, or at least reputed, holy sites to be visited. These included the garden of Gethsemane, the pool of Siloam with a spring which never flowed on the Sabbath,[17] the valley of Josaphat, but also the palm from which leaves were ripped for Jesus's triumphant entry into Jerusalem, the mountain of the transfiguration and Lazarus' grave in Bethany.[18] The Palestinian countryside round about was visited by pilgrims less often and less keenly than the holy sites themselves. Nonetheless most pilgrims included Jericho, the Jordan including the site of the Baptism of

Figure 20. Plan of Jerusalem (12th century). Stuttgart, Württembergische Landesbibliothek, MS bibl. 2–56, f. 135r.

the Lord, the Dead Sea and Mount Hebron on their agenda even if they did not visit Nazareth and Bethlehem. However, some of the pilgrim's journals mention so many Old Testament sites in Palestine that the descriptions begin to appear like a geographic register to Bible history (such as *De situ terrae sanctae*, written by an archdeacon called Theodosius in the 6th century).[19]

In the early Middle Ages most pilgrims from European countries, especially those from Britain, Germany, Ireland, and Scandinavia, travelled overland. The two main routes (along the Danube and from Belgrade onwards across the Balkans or else via Italy, Albania and Macedonia) took them to Constantinople, after which they were forced to take the difficult, risky, and dangerous stretch over the Turkish highlands of Anatolia from Nicea via Caesarea to Antioch, the route also taken by the crusader armies.[20] However, later it became more usual to take a ship from Venice to Tyre or Acre, from where it was a mere 'five long days' journey' to Jerusalem. From the 13th century onwards the sheer numbers of pilgrims led to the advent of a regular pilgrim industry which began with buying provisions and booking places onboard ships in Venice and led onto the organised immigration and accommodation in Acre which often left much to be desired.

Pilgrim accommodation was also organised in Jerusalem itself. From the 5th and 6th centuries every episcopal church had its own hostel and numerous religious orders ran hostels for visitors.[21] The crusades brought a distinct increase in the importance of the various crusading orders for pilgrim care. The part of the Al-Aksa mosque granted by Baldwin II in 1119 to the first Templars under the leadership of Hugo de Payns, subsequently to become the seat of the Templars, was able to house up to nearly three hundred Templars in the 1270s by converting the old Herodian temple vaults below into stables.[22] The Templars and the Hospitallers kept hostels for pilgrims not only in Jerusalem but also in the harbours and by the main approach roads. Apart from these, accommodation was set up and maintained by private grants and foundations. The hostels run by the orders participated likewise in the generosity of the pilgrims who were only too happy to have reached the Holy City at long last.

Pilgrimages to the Holy Land began in the third century with Christian communities travelling together with their bishops in order to see the holy sites in Jerusalem with their own eyes.[23] In 313 the Roman emperor Constantine ruled that Christians should finally receive the freedom to practise their own religion, and even Helena, Constantine's mother, travelled to the Holy Land in 327. Her journey was probably the most important pilgrimage of early times due to the effect it had. Helena brought numerous relics back to Rome with her, not only the 'True Cross' on which Christ was crucified, together with the nails and the seamless garment, but also the table on which the Last Supper was eaten and numerous other relics.[24] Apart from this she was active in the Holy Land itself as a keen restorer of holy sites. In doing this she had anticipated the example, possibilities and purpose of later pilgrimages and had also given the relics market a significant impetus. From Helena's time on Jerusalem has become the most important goal for all Christian pilgrims who want to see the sites of Christian belief with their own eyes and physically touch them.

In the Middle Ages there were a number of other motives for going on a pilgrimage apart from the purely religious ones. These motives are difficult to separate from pure faith, because today's separation of a secular and religious activities does not apply to the holistic medieval way of looking at the world. As a result it is not easy to distinguish between the individual components leading to the desire to make the pilgrimage. There was curiosity and the urge for adventure, the desire to visit the holy sites or the longing to die near to them (and therefore to be one of the first to be resurrected on the Day of the Last Judgement), the wish to regain Jerusalem for Christianity by warlike methods, the acquisition of relics for material or religious reasons, and finally the pilgrimage as a penance or even as a paid replacement for somebody well-to-do.[25]

There have been itineraries of pilgrimages for nearly as long as there have been pilgrims to Jerusalem themselves. The journal made by one pilgrim from Bordeaux who visited Constantinople and Jerusalem in the year 333 is probably the oldest extant report,[26] but in the following centuries time and again descriptions of journeys made by pilgrims to Jerusalem appeared. The early records, invariably written in Latin, show the differing interests of the pilgrims as well as the frequently adventurous circumstances in which they came to the Holy Land and then went back home again.

One very early and detailed journal, whose popularity is reflected in the existence of more than twenty manuscripts, is that written by Bishop Arkulf. Before 687 the Gallic bishop travelled to Palestine and spent nine months in Jerusalem. On his journey home he was shipwrecked on the Hebrides and told the story of his travels to Adamnan, an Irish monk, who had been abbot of the monastery of Iona (founded in 563 by St Columba) since 679. He also made four plans of churches in the Holy City, among them the Church of the Holy Sepulchre, drawing them onto a wax tablet which Adamnan then copied into the manuscripts. The resulting book, the 'Three Books about the Holy Sites' written by Adamnan was dedicated to King Aldfrith of Northumbria and had a far-reaching influence since manuscripts of the work spread throughout the whole European continent as a result of the missionary zeal of the Irish-Scottish monks. The Diagrams included in the work meant that the foundation plan of the Church of the Holy Sepulchre (from the time prior to the end of the 7th century) was known, especially in the monasteries of what is now South Germany and Austria, at a time when journeys to Jerusalem were extremely rare.[27] Another early pilgrim to Jerusalem, Willibald, was later to become bishop of Salzburg. His journey to the Holy Land between 721–727 along with seven companions was documented by a nun in Hildesheim[28] and later repeatedly reworked.

After a marked increase in the number of pilgrimages during the reign of Charlemagne resulting from more stable political circumstances, the pendulum soon swung the other way so that there was a drastic deterioration. By the turn of the millennium there were virtually no pilgrimages being made. The uncertainty and dangers facing the pilgrims not only in the Near East but also in central Europe can be seen on the example of St Koloman, an Irish pilgrim, who made his way in 1002 overland to Palestine. His obviously foreign clothes meant that the indigenous population near Vienna took him for a Bohemian spy and lynched him. Only posthumous miracles saved his reputation and he was finally laid to rest at the Benedictine monastery at Melk and subsequently venerated there.[29] The deteriorating political situation in the Near East – from the point of view of Christian pilgrims – was also the reason why calls for the liberation of Jerusalem became louder. This in turn led to the First Crusade in 1096. In the year 1099 Jerusalem fell to the Templars and for the next two centuries there was much toing and froing between Europe and Palestine during which time hardly any distinction was made between pilgrimage and armed crusade.[30] The Anglo-Saxon pilgrim Saewulf in 1102 tells of attacks by Islamic bandits on pilgrims travelling from Jaffa to Jerusalem.[31] Other travellers in the 12th century, on the other hand, had travelled to the Holy Land in the hope of more violent and heroic adventure. One of these was the Norwegian king, Sigurd Magnusson, known as Jórsalafari ('the one who went to Jerusalem'), who made the journey between 1107–1111. He sailed from Norway through the Straits of Gibraltar and on to Palestine before making the return journey overland via Germany. Despite his lack of involvement in any great battles apart from the siege of Sidon and Tyre the moral support given by a Norwegian king was certainly not without significance for Baldwin, King of Jerusalem.[32] Later on, Scandinavians frequently took part in crusades, the Fifth Crusade (1217) in particular being supported by the Norwegian crown.[33]

Another Scandinavian traveller had quite different interests. The Icelandic Benedictine abbot Nikulás went to the Holy Land between 1149–1154, describing this journey in a detailed itinerary written in Old Norse which he dictated on his return to Iceland. He does not only comment that the middle of the earth lay in the church of the Holy Sepulchre but also added the inaccurate observation that the sun shone down from directly overhead there. His astronomical observations were, however, correct when he used his own eyes, such as his information on the height of the polar star as seen from the Jordan. He explained that a man lying on his back who pulled up his knee and then set his fist with the thumb stretched out on top of this, would see the polar star at this height.[34]

Only a few years after Nikulás another cleric made a pilgrimage through the eastern Mediterranean, the Holy Land, and Asia going as far afield as China. He, too, left an itinerary behind him. This pilgrim was a Jewish rabbi from Spain, Benjamin of Tudela, who not only pursued religious and social interests, but also examined the situation of his brothers in religion in the diaspora of Europe and Asia. His records offer us a picture of the Jewish communities in the 12th century from Europe to Central Asia.[35]

In the 13th century the Christian kingdom of Jerusalem became increasingly threatened. With the fall of Acre in 1291 the last toehold of the Templars in Palestine had fallen. Consequently pilgrimages became notably more difficult so that the Holy See even forbade all pilgrimages east of Cyprus for a short time.[36] In spite of this this there was a resurgence in the number of pilgrimages made in the 14th century, reflected in the increasing number of pilgrimage journals, many of which were written in the vernacular.[37] This may in part have been due to a search for religious solace following the horrors of the plague in the mid-14th century,[38] but it was probably also the result of an increasingly mobile and urbanised population of western Europe. Their more developed self-confidence manifested itself in the journeys themselves just as in the many records written about them.

It should not be forgotten that Jerusalem was not the only great goal for pilgrimages among western Europeans. Travelling to Rome involved a journey of many months for Germans, English, and Scandinavians which exhausted the physical and financial resources of many a pilgrim. One Icelandic pilgrim guide reckoned on a period of three weeks' travel from Denmark to the Brenner pass over the Alps and then a further six weeks from there to Rome (with another fortnight's foot march from there to Bari and then yet another fortnight's sea voyage to Acre).[39] Since the discovery in Rome of the bones of St Peter and St Paul in 319 by Pope Silvester I, the eternal city had become a worthwhile destination for a pilgrimage. The growing importance of the papacy with its right to grant a plenary indulgence had attracted pilgrims ever since the foundation of the Papal States in the 8th century.[40] In addition to this, of course, came the ecclesiastical significance of Rome as the seat of papal power which made the city a frequent destination for many secular and religious clerics. For the latter, papal acceptance of diverse orders was indispensable, whereas for the secular clergy it was a matter of the personal acceptance of the pallium after the episcopal election.

Rome had found itself in a cultural and political nadir in the Middle Ages. From the Norman destructions of 1084 to the end of the schism in 1417 Rome had been time and again shaken by internal and external struggles. However, the number of the apostles and martyrs buried there was so great and the other relics to be admired or even acquired so evident and plentiful that many pilgrims regarded a visit to Rome as the fulfilment of their greatest wishes despite the outward decay of the city. Understandably, a journey to Rome was not considered to be as meritorious as a sea voyage to the Holy Land so that there are only a few pilgrim records of journeys to Rome. To compensate for this there is a mass of secondary literature for pilgrims to Rome. Itinerary maps and descriptions of the way to be taken listing the stations of their route for the German and Scandinavian pilgrims[41] and city guides of Rome, which gave detailed information about the (Classical and Christian) sights of the city, the obligatory churches to visit and, not least, the indulgences which could be gained in doing so. A walk around the seven main churches, among which were San Paolo fuori le mura and Sta. Agnese fuori Porta Pia, could strain the most ardent Rome pilgrim.

However, a pilgrim was not only able to visit the buildings,[42] perhaps familiar to him from Classical historical writing, but also a remarkable number of relics, including the bodies of the apostles Peter and Paul and St Lawrence as well as innumerable martyrs from the early Christian persecutions.[43] As in Jerusalem, pilgrims could rely on information both about the churches as well as about Classical buildings from manuscript pilgrims' guides. The oldest of those known was written in the 9th century and conveniently divided the city sights, much like its modern counterparts, into twelve separate walks.[44]

The third most important pilgrimage centre of the west, albeit only since the 9th century, was Santiago de Compostela in Spanish Galicia. It was here that the apostle James, who had miraculously appeared here, was buried. According to legend he had aided the Christians in their fight against the Saracens in the battle of Clavijo in 844.[45] Germans, English, and French were particularly numerous in their pilgrimages to the grave of St James. They made use of a well-kept pilgrim's trail which reveals an early form of organised tourism since it was amply provided with hostels, especially over the Pyrenees and through northern Spain. There are no extant medieval records of journeys to Compostela written in German, but the Latin *Liber Sti. Jacobi*,[46] which was both a travel guide and legendary in one, gives us an impression of what the pilgrimage to Santiago must have been like.

We know of pilgrims in the 13th and 14th centuries who visited Jerusalem as well as both Rome and Santiago,[47] and whoever travelled to the Holy Land overland, usually also visited Constantinople. Despite the separation between the western church and the orthodox church, the capital of the Byzantine Empire had an incredible number of relics, as well as the impressive buildings. This made the city a worthwhile destination for the pilgrims. In Constantinople there were not only the graves of the saints Philip, James (the Younger), Luke, and Timothy. There were also parts of St Stephen, and also the skulls of Abraham, Isaac and Jacob, the apostles Thomas and Matthew, the evangelist Luke as well as John the Baptist (supposedly in two examples). Other impressive relics included the manger from Bethlehem, the crown of thorns, the trumpets from Jericho, the cross that the emperor Constantine had seen in heaven, and, last but by no means least, the axe which Noah had used to build the ark.

Nevertheless the real pilgrimage centre was Jerusalem and the Holy Land because it was only here that Christ had actually lived. The situation of Jerusalem at the intersection of the three continents was additionally responsible for its position as the centre of the earth's surface,[48] and in Adamnan the city is explicitly called the *umbilicus* of the world (*umbilicus mundi*).[49] Jerusalem also lay *on top* of the globe,[50] that is, on the 'visible' side; only thus can we understand why the road from Europe to Jerusalem is said to be *uphill* and the road from Jerusalem to East Asia leads *downhill* again. Even after the discovery of the New World, Jerusalem remained the centre of Christianity, but the Copernican revolution in astronomy and the newly discovered continent removed the city from being the physical centre of the world. The unbroken spiritual significance of the city is made clear by Columbus's fanciful plans to reconquer Jerusalem, but this, coming at the end of the 15th century, decades after the fall of Constantinople (1453) and two centuries after the final fall of Acre and of the Latin Palestine kingdom (1291) was, of course, only a lost dream, and Columbus's suggestion for the financing of a new Crusade nothing more than an anachronism.

CHAPTER SEVEN

The Fruits of Original Sin: Monstrous Races on the Edges of the World Known to Man

The Discoverers and the Cannibals

Among the stories which Columbus and other travellers brought back from America and which fascinated their European contemporaries most were the tales about wild natives in the newly discovered islands and countries. They were so far removed from human (European) and divine law that not only did they run around naked but they also even ate each other. This morbid interest is occasionally found reflected in the titles of the works, such as Hans Staden's ethnographical report on Brazil *Warhafftige Historia und beschreibung einer Landtschafft der Wilden/ Nacketen/ Grimmigen Menschfresser Leuthen/in der Newen Welt America gelegen*[1] (1557) ('True History and Description of a countryside of wild, naked, fearsome cannibals in the New World of America'). In the texts themselves and the illustrations, which as a rule copied other woodcuts quite freely,[2] cannibalism constituted a major topic in any discussion of America. Apart from the more detailed travel descriptions[3] this was particularly true for the broadsheets – publications deriving from letters and mostly dealing with a single topic, in this case the discoveries in the New World – and which were the precursors of today's newspapers.[4]

The actual reason for this strong impression which the cannibals suddenly made on the Europeans was not only their mere existence but rather that there were now shiploads of sailors who had seen them with their own eyes or else travellers like Staden who had lived among them (and survived). It had been known for a long time that peoples far away had the strange habit of devouring their enemies, and even their own relatives, but what Columbus and his successors were able to report about actual human farms exceeded anything that the encyclodedias had ever had to tell (even if one leaves the human sacrifice as practised by the Aztecs aside).[5] What it said about the 'anthropophagi' (as cannibals were called in scholarly literature from Classical times, using the Greek term for the phenomenon to mitigate some of its horrific associations) was comparatively harmless: the peoples in question were those naked tribes living in easternmost India who ate human flesh and drank blood.[6] Even the peoples Gog and Magog were said to be cannibals, but Alexander the Great had shut them up behind a wall on the Caspian Sea and the rest of humanity were

Figure 21. Cannibals in Hans Staden, Warhafftige Historia (1557).

safe from them until the Day of Judgement.[7] East Asian cannibals such as these did indeed present a threat for the unsuspecting but their atrocities were, in the eyes of European scholars, exceeded by far by the anthropophagi who ate their own relatives.

Of all the tribes practising endocannibalism[8] these so-called patrophages were especially frequently mentioned in the encyclopedias.[9] They were the people who ate their own parents when they had become old and frail. First they were fattened up, slaughtered and devoured by these people in the company of their friends and relatives, thus supposedly honouring their parents: 'and they believed that they would treat them very badly if they let them get old without killing them and let them die thin'.[10] Sir John Mandeville also wrote about the parent-eaters on the island of Sandin, telling in great detail of how this fabulous race asked the medicine man if a sick person had a chance of recovery or not. If not, then the sick person was suffocated, boiled, and roasted after which he was eaten by all his friends and relations during a festive meal.[11] This form of cannibalism is also mentioned by Marco Polo in his journal in connection with the islands of Java and Sumatra and especially for a kingdom called Dagroian (in northern Sumatra).[12] Furthermore, despite not ever having been there, he assumed that there were aggressive cannibals in Cimpangu (Japan), who even attacked strangers and then cooked them if an adequate ransom was not forthcoming.[13]

From his knowledge of Mandeville's and Marco Polo's works Columbus must have expected to be confronted with cannibals on the islands he landed on. Nonetheless he appears to have been shocked by the extent of the cannibalism he encountered. The word 'cannibal' itself dates to Columbus's first voyage: he notes in the log that the inhabitants of Cuba called the people of Puerto Rico *caniba*, and that they ate human flesh. He began to use the term *canibales* himself to denote other similarly inclined man-eaters on the Caribbean islands. This word was quickly adopted by those writing travel journals so that although anthropophagi were mentioned in the German version of a letter written by Columbus in 1494,[14] *Canibali* were spoken of in German by 1508[15] and *cannibals* in English by 1553. By the mid-16th century 'cannibal' had replaced 'anthropophagi' as the term most commonly used throughout Europe. From a cultural historical point of view this aspect, too, is symptomatic of Columbus's first journey: he sailed away expecting to find *anthropophagi* and returned having met *cannibals*.

Alexander and the Wonders of the East

Cannibals were not the only strange peoples that a traveller could encounter abroad in medieval times. There was a whole catalogue of such 'fabulous' races. Travellers in Classical times had for example already recorded the strange and wonderful people who were to be found in India. In his memoirs written in around 400 BC, Ctesias of Cnidos, the Greek physician to the Persian king, wrote of his experiences in the east, which he called *Indika*,[16] describing the Pygmies, Cynocephali and Macrobii in India. The first were only three spans high, the other race had heads like dogs, and the last were born with white hair which gradually darkened with age. His contemporary, Megasthenes, who was an emissary to India and who recorded much about the actual customs of the Indians,[17] confirmed the existence of the Pygmies and added the Astomi to the list of races living in deepest India, a people who lived only on the smell of apples.[18] Homer's *Odyssey* was more important than these works for propagating the knowledge of fabulous races. It is also the oldest known text in which fabulous races are recorded. Homer described the Cyclopes, whom he assigned to Sicily,[19] and hairy women in India. He also included the tale of the battle between the Pygmies and the cranes. This was possibly based on historical facts, such as the catching of cranes during their migration over central Africa.[20] Even in the *Iliad* Homer refers to a fabulous race, the Hippomolgi, or mare-milkers.[21]

Another traveller, better known than either Ctesias or Megasthenes and whose fame far exceeded even that of Odysseus, was Alexander the Great. Alexander's life and especially his campaign through Asia, during which he reached India in 326 BC, made him the most popular Classical hero during the Middle Ages. The legends about Alexander, prolific from soon after his death, only became available around 200 BC in a romance, probably written in Alexandria. It was later attributed to Callisthenes, a nephew of Aristotle and one of Alexander's companions. This romance by 'Pseudo-Callisthenes' in which many fabulous and legendary details of Alexander's campaigns were included, formed the basis for numerous medieval texts about Alexander. The material became known in the west in two Latin translations and many versions of them.[22] Of about eighty versions in thirty-five languages the most important was the Latin *Alexandreis* by Walter of Châtillon.[23] It was the source for many of the west European vernacular versions.[24]

In the different versions of the Alexander Romances there were numerous descriptions of fabulous races. The mere fact that these races were associated (albeit only by occurring in the same text) with the name of Alexander meant that the races achieved a degree of popularity that they would not otherwise have enjoyed. The wide distribution of the Romances spread knowledge about the fabulous races included in them, just as it increased Alexander's fame. In the Alexander romances there were peoples with (to Greek eyes) strange eating habits, such as the fish eaters (Ichthyophages) whom Alexander forbade to eat fish. However the Alexander Romances concentrated more on the social behaviour and appearance of fabulous races. They included the people who had six hands, the headless (Blemmyae or Acephales) and the dog-headed (Cynocephales), all of whom were extremely popular with medieval audiences. These exotic-looking races served primarily as exotic embellishments to Alexander's campaigns. More important, though, were the peoples whose social behaviour gave the authors the opportunity to use Alexander's imperialistic judgements to pass comment on alien customs, condemning them for being uncivilised or praising them for being exemplary. When Alexander came upon the terrible cannibalistic peoples Gog and Magog, who (already as a result of the prophecy in the Old Testament)[25] were considered to be a severe threat to the rest of humanity, he immured them north of the Caspian Sea, thus liberating the world from this threat at least until the Day of Judgement. The case was quite different with the Oxydraces (naked Indian wise men, also called Gymnosophists) who were possibly modelled on Indian yogis or Buddhist monks. Faced with the threat of war these extraordinarily peaceful people sent Alexander a letter in which they explained to him the pointlessness of his campaign since he was only mortal and his achievement would die with him. Alexander, in his discussion with them, did not fail to stress his role in the plan of creation, but one cannot help noticing the criticism (from a spiritual point of view) of his imperialist attitude voiced here by Christian authors. The Amazons, too, whom Alexander also encountered in northern Asia, sent Alexander a letter in which they explained their way of life. Even Alexander was unable to avoid admiring the wisdom and prudence of their social structure. It may seem surprising for an era such as the Middle Ages, which is hardly known for having a liberated attitude towards females, that this land of women was founded on reason. The influence of Classical tradition was probably predominant in this case.

The Europeans and the Monsters

The main sources for the fabulous races in the Middle Ages, besides the literature on Alexander the Great, were the works of Pliny and Solinus. In his huge work, *Naturalis Historia*, Pliny the Elder, who was killed during the eruption of Vesuvius in AD 79,[26] claimed to have consulted two thousand older works and in so doing compiled all there was to know in Classical times about natural science, including fabulous beings. He is also partly responsible for the misunderstanding about the identity of India and Ethiopia, which in turn led in the Middle Ages to the idea that there were three Indies[27] and which also resulted in both these regions being considered to be the homes of fabulous races in medieval texts. Solinus used Pliny's *Naturalis Historia* two centuries later as a source for his *Collectanea rerum memorabilium*,[28] in which, as the title suggests, he concentrated exclusively on strange matters so that his work is solely composed of strange and wonderful things that he found in Pliny, including all the fabulous races. Both the topic and relative brevity of Solinus' work meant that it achieved much greater popularity in the Middle Ages than Pliny's *Naturalis Historia* and as a result the fabulous races, originally listed in the latter, often came into medieval handbooks either directly or indirectly from the *Collectanea*.

It is by no means clear to us today why lists of 'fabulous' races were a feature of most of the popular collections of geographical and cosmographical texts. However, the fact that medieval collections which dealt vaguely with natural history or ethnology always contained such lists indicates quite clearly that the fabulous races were considered to be just as factual as was the settlement of the three continents by Noah's three sons. The fabulous races were not considered primarily to be miraculous (that is to say, belonging to myths and legends), but rather as a standard feature of geography. Consequently, short lists of fabulous races are found both in Latin as well as vernacular handbooks which otherwise deal exclusively with geography and cosmography.[29] Only scholars of the 14th century, such as Konrad of Megenberg, began to be sceptical enough of the their existence to leave them out of their collections or at least add them only as an appendix to the main work.

The literature about Alexander the Great referred to the fabulous races purported to live in India or along his route there. However, medieval encyclopedic literature, following the example of Pliny and Solinus, attributed the fabulous races to the three remotest areas of the earth: the Arctic wastes of

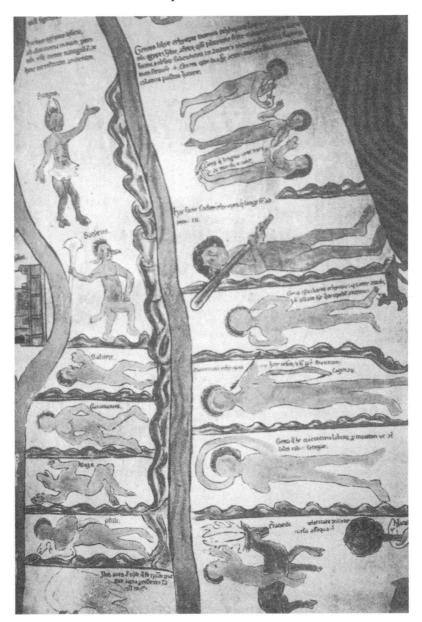

Figure 22. Fabulous races from the Ebstorf mappa mundi (13th century).

Figure 23. Skiopode on the Beatus map by Burgo de Osma. Copy in Miller: Mappae mundi, vol. 1, 35.

Scythia in the north of Europe and Asia, furthest India, and Ethiopia in equatorial Africa. Scythia played only an insignificant role, although the Amazons (or some other land of women), the Cynocephales and the Pygmies are said to have lived there. Only in the Scandinavian tradition is there a notable tendency to include more fabulous peoples in these relatively close – but still clearly frightening – regions of northern Asia.[30] The confrontation between Lapps and Eskimos might have played a role here, but the sighting of a Skiopode (a man with one foot) on Labrador, which can be read in the old Icelandic sagas about the discovery of America by the Icelanders in the 10th century, is nevertheless somewhat peculiar.[31]

European scholars in the Middle Ages followed their Classical predecessors and ever since Isidore of Seville in c. 600 tended to think that fabulous races lived in India and Ethiopia.[32] However, apart from the information given in encyclopedias compiled by Honorius[33] and Hrabanus,[34] both of whom used Isidore intensively, the large-scale world maps in particular depicted the fabulous races predominantly in Ethiopia. Both the Hereford map[35] and the Ebstorf map[36] – as well as the fragment of a third large *mappa mundi* from Cornwall[37] – show over a dozen fabulous races drawn on a symbolically suggested southern continent to the south of Ethiopia. But as many smaller maps in manuscripts confirm, for example the London psalter map,[38] this was the result of an iconographic tradition in cartography which was already very old. Fabulous races were already depicted as living on the southern continent in one of the oldest groups of European world maps: the *mappae mundi* in the manuscripts of the commentary on the apocalypse by Beatus of Liebana from the 8th century. These show a solitary Sciopode sitting on the southern continent protecting himself from the sun's rays by his large foot and serving as a symbol for all the fabulous races which were assumed there.[39]

It seemed harmless enough to think of the fabulous races as being far away to the south, but the assumption of fabulous beings on the southern continent had theological consequences. If, as mentioned in the discussion about the Antipodes,[40] the southern continent was uninhabitable for mankind, then it must be equally impossible for fabulous races to live there, otherwise the humanity of the fabulous races had to be queried.

The inclusion of the reports about fabulous races by Christian historians and encyclopedists in the early Middle Ages led to speculation about the role of these fabulous races (who in many cases could hardly be described as human) in the divine plan of creation. The question of whether they could be regarded as human was the one that attracted most attention in the Middle Ages. On the one hand the issue was raised as to whether these peoples were descended from Adam and Noah like everyone else, subsequently creating the need to ascertain where they actually lived. On the other hand thought was given to the characteristics which made an often only physically deformed fabulous being human and conversely what made him a different sort of creature.

This question of human identity, even if certain human parts of the body and organs were missing, has only recently aroused interest again. The problems are obvious when we consider the diversity of physical diversity of medieval fabulous beings, such as in the lengthy early medieval lists of fabulous beings included by Isidore and Martianus Capella, compiled from Pliny and Solinus.[41] Isidore describes the Troglodytes (swift-footed and dumb cave-dwellers), Antipodes (with backward-turning feet, correctly 'Antipedes') and gigantic Titanes as inhabiting Ethiopia.[42] Martianus adds the headless Blemmyae, the goat-footed Satyri and Aegipanes and the thin-limbed Himantopodes.[43] In the teratological chapter (teratology = the doctrine of wonders and miraculous occurrences) actually dealing with fabulous beings, Isidore[44] lists Hermaphrodites, terrifying giants (Gigantes), dog-headed Cynocephali, one-eyed Cyclopes, yet again the headless Blemmyae, Panotios with enormous flappy ears, Artabatitae who crawl along on all fours, horned and goat-footed satyrs and fauns, the Scipodes with their one huge foot, the hoofed Hippopodes, the tiny Pygmies and an Indian tribe of women with an extremely short life-span.

These various deformations provoked the question of the humanity of these people on genealogical and theological grounds. The most important medieval German book about natural history, *Buch von den naturleichen Dingen* ('Book

*Figure 24. Panoti from a Latin-Old English list of fabulous races.
London, The British Library, MS Cotton Tiberius B V, 83v.*

of natural things'), written by Konrad of Megenberg shortly before 1350, reveals just how important the question of whether the fabulous races were descended from Adam was for scholars in the fourteenth century. He copied his material entirely from the *Liber de Natura Rerum* by Thomas of Cantimpré, but went beyond him in his reflections about the reasons for the origin of the fabulous races and their role in creation: *Ain vrâg ist, von wannen die wundermenschen kömen, die ze latein monstruosi haizent, ob sie von Adam sein komen*[45] ('A question is the origin of the monstrous races, whether they descend from Adam').

A popular biblical-historical answer to this issue among the Church Fathers was that the fabulous races were descended from Cain, whose descendants were cursed by God in the form of visible anomalies.[46] However, it was not until St Augustine that a viable explanation was found which became the valid doctrine for centuries to come.

Augustine's astute view was that if the fabulous races were human at all then they must be descended from Adam. Furthermore their collective monstrosities could be compared with deformities of individual people. The role of these races of deformed peoples, just like the single deformities occurring among ordinary people, was hidden from human understanding, but had significance in God's plan of creation.[47] This explanation was simplified by Isidore and subsequently became the common explanation for the Middle Ages. Monsters and fabulous races appear to be unnatural but nothing in creation is against nature because God simply wanted it like that.[48]

Attempts at less simplistic explanations, such as Aristotle's, were only made again in the 13th and 14th centuries in the work of Albertus Magnus and especially that of Nicole Oresme. Around the mid-14th century Oresme, a French university teacher (made bishop of Lisieux in 1377), formulated a detailed theory of teratology in his book *De causis mirabilium* which discussed in great detail monsters, deformities and other such phenomena. In his opinion, deformities and fabulous beings were well within the divine plan of creation. They should not be interpreted as portentous in any way (as had been the case in Isidore[49]), but rather should be seen as the result of a deficiency during conception or in subsequent development, caused perhaps by the physical environment, which was either too dry, too wet or too arid.[50] The idea that adverse climatic conditions could be responsible for the deformation or deficiencies of the fabulous races had long been suggested by the encyclopedias as the cause for peculiar appearance and social behaviour, for example of the Ethiopian Troglodytes or Sciopodes.

Nicole Oresme, because of this assessment that deficiency or malformation of the male sperm was the cause of deformities and the idiosyncracies of the fabulous races, regarded these beings as a kind of pre-stage in human development. Thus the Pygmies, whom scholars used as their main example for fabulous races, were considered to be on a developmental stage somewhere between the apes and man,[51] a surprisingly modern and Darwinistic kind of solution.

The supposition that fabulous races were a stage between man and anthropoid apes was found in a somewhat different form in the writings of the great German scholar, Albertus Magnus. He regarded the deficiencies of monsters and apes to be less physical than of mental control over the body (*disciplinabilitas*). He set up a three-step hierarchy to demonstrate the degrees of control. Man was at the top, the Pygmies (representing all fabulous races) were in the middle and at the bottom were the apes.[52] In Albertus Magnus' opinion, however, other fabulous races, in particular the Cynocephales, could be regarded as simians

Figure 25. Cynocephales from a Latin-Old English list of fabulous races. London, The British Library, MS Cotton Tiberius B V, 80r.

anyway,[53] thus following an explanation made by Solinus.[54] The rationalistic classification, at least of the dog-headed race, was an apparently popular solution to the whole controversy about the classification of the fabulous races since the Ebstorf map includes both the Cynocephales as well as the satyrs and fauns among the six different types of simians.[55]

These interpretations of the fabulous races give one explanation of the physical origins for human deformities, but not of their typological background. The medieval opinion about this appears to be that the fabulous races were Cain's children, according to which certain children bore the sign of their ancestors' sins. One even more detailed theological explanation is only to be found in the so-called *Wiener Genesis* (Viennese Genesis), an early Middle High German biblical poem from the second half of the 11th century from the region of what is today Bavaria or Austria. It says that God explained to Adam the danger that certain herbs have for pregnant women, but that Adam's descendants had ignored this advice and had therefore deformed their own children by eating the forbidden herbs.[56] According to these explanations, man's disobedience towards the will of God was the reason for the origin of deformed people.[57]

The scholars of the whole Middle Ages reflected in a thoroughly reasonable way, but they accepted on the whole that fabulous races actually existed. Not even critical scholars such as Albertus Magnus[58] and Nicole Oresme, or even Roger Bacon (in his *Opus Majus*) doubted their existence. This principal acceptance reaches far into the late Middle Ages where the fabulous races found in India are recorded in the *Ymago mundi* written by Pierre d'Ailly, and used by Columbus. He does not include as many fabulous races as Isidore, whom he refers to, but in his chapter 'The wonders of India',[59] he nevertheless describes the Pygmies, the Macrobii, the Bragmani, the Ichthyophagi, the Antipedes, the Arimaspi, the Blemmyae and the Astomi without, however, naming their Greek names in most cases.[60] Thus, Columbus was undoubtedly not only prepared by the journals of Sir John Mandeville and Marco Polo to encounter fabulous races, but also by scholarly cosmographies.

However, Columbus did not only expect to see – in European eyes – deformed people. He was probably aware that his voyage would bring him into contact with peoples and races with strange customs and eating habits. Many of the medieval fabulous races were distinguished from 'normal' people by European standards, not by physical deformation but rather by differences in social behaviour or in their eating habits. The latter plays a great role in the mutual assessment of peoples even today. Many national prejudices are expressed with insulting references to eating customs. Thus the French are known as 'frogs', the Germans as 'krauts' whereas the British used to be and might still find themselves referred to as 'limeys'. The rejection of foreign culinary habits led (and still tends to lead) to a wholesale rejection of the foreign culture itself. Explicitly denouncing foreign cuisine as inferior was all part of a positive reinforcement and legitimisation of one's own values.

Both in social and dietary habits the question of the humanity of fabulous peoples played only an insignificant role. In this group of monstrous races the Greek tradition was probably more strongly felt in which a clear interest in the social behaviour of foreign peoples was manifest. Of the fabulous races which can be ultimately traced back to Pliny, quite a number are distinguished by their dietary habits. These do not only include the afore-mentioned cannibals (*Anthropophagi, Patrophagi,* Gog and Magog), the *Panphagi* (eaters of everything) or the race that exclusively survived on fish (*Ichthyophagi*), but also such unrealistic races as the Astomi who survived solely on the smell of the apples growing just outside Paradise,[61] the straw-drinkers who only had a tiny mouth, the snake-eating Troglodytes,[62] the dog-milking *Cynomolgi,* and mare-milking Hippomolgi. Both of the latter races show how the actual habits of a race (the

Figure 26. Ichthyophagi from a Latin-Old English list of fabulous races. London, The British Library, MS Cotton Tiberius B V, 80r.

Tartars indeed used to milk mares) could be exaggerated to become the fictitious custom of another. In the case of this group of fabulous races the historical 'core' of the fiction is more tangible than in the cases of others. Cannibals and fish-eaters originated from occasions when Classical travellers encountered the dominant eating habits of a particular people. Even the idea of the apple smellers might have some foundation in the Tibetan habit of using camphor as a prophylactic against certain illnesses.[63] The question of the historical credibility or the element of ethnological truth is in the case of peoples with a different diet almost as unimportant as in the case of those with unusual social habits. Here, too, the form in which a fabulous race is characterised says more about the *Weltbild* of the observer who is describing the phenomena than about the real or fictitious races themselves.

Naturally, the habit of eating one's own relatives, cannibalism and dietary habits generally count as part of social behaviour in the wider sense. However, in this respect there are several other races which should be mentioned who differed from the European norm by the form or the absence of social structure. Three races in particular from this group had – in contrast to most of the other fabulous races – rather exemplary characteristics for the Europeans, which is emphasised by a correspondingly moralising stance in the texts. The Amazons with their warlike and well-organised state were most widely known,[64] whilst the Gymnosophists and Brahmans only found their way into encyclopedic tradition through the Alexander Romances. The Bragmanni (an oral distortion of the Indian brahmans) were described as being naked white cave dwellers, whilst the Gymnosophists, according to Pliny, stood with their feet in glowing sand all day and stared into the sun,[65] which is obviously a description of shamanistic practices of the predecessors of the Indian yogis, as they had already been described by Megasthenes.[66]

The Maritimi and the Troglodytes are only socially strange by their peculiar choice of places to live. Admittedly, the former are described by Pliny as having four eyes, but he actually only wants to stress their particular sharpsightedness with this,[67] a detail that Solinus[68] and the medieval interpretors (*Elucidarius*, Gervase of Tilbury, Bartholomew Anglicus) no longer understood as such.[69] In point of fact the Ethiopian Maritimi received their name from their homes on the sea, as well as eating fish, as did the Ichthyophages. The Troglodytes, similarly settled in Ethiopia, are mentioned far more often in medieval encyclopedias; they were dumb cave dwellers who could hunt animals with a club because of their fleetness of foot.[70]

The third group of races, which are characterised by social behaviour and were therefore considered to be fabulous, were those whose sexual behaviour was considered by the Europeans to be unusual. The most obvious of all was the physiological sexual exoticism of the Hermaphrodites who provoked in medieval authors the comment time and again that everyone there could have children with everyone else.[71] Less widespread was the race of the Wife-Givers, but they were still mentioned by such a reliable witness as Marco Polo. They offered any passing travellers their wives or their daughters and considered it an honour if the travellers then slept with them. The unmarried girls thus got rid of their unwanted virginity and could then acquire gifts which in turn improved their marriage chances.[72]

The popularity of fabulous races in the Middle Ages cannot only be explained by attempts to create exotic texts, but should also be understood representing the desire of the Europeans to emphasise their 'normality' which itself made it necessary to define the boundaries of what was 'normal'. It is in these terms that we should understand the continuity of a fascination in fabulous races still being with us. Now we call them 'aliens' and have pushed them further and further to distant corners of the ever expanding universe of our experience and research. Thus, fabulous (or at least strange) humanoid races belong to the

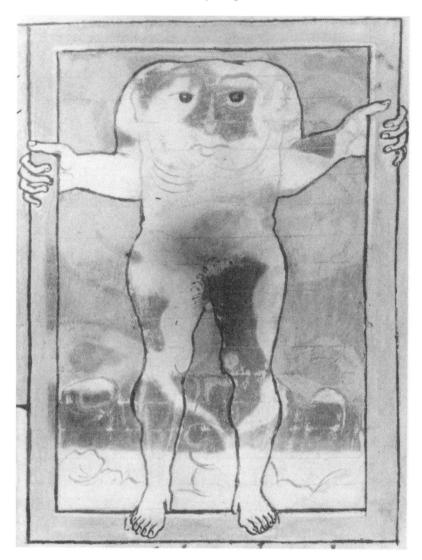

Figure 27. Blemmyiae from a Latin-Old English list of fabulous races. London, The British Library, MS Cotton Tiberius B V, 82r.

standard inventory of most of the works of the huge genre of the science fiction novel and film.[73] Furthermore, when making judgements concerning the credibility of such fabulous races,[74] we should not forget the often ignored question about the reasons and factual origins for such beliefs in the Middle Ages and the Classical world. Admittedly, this second point is not essential for the intellectual position and the literary verbalisation, but it does help to avoid prejudices or making sweeping judgements too lightly about medieval knowledge. For example, the frequently mentioned possibly matriarchal societies could perhaps be the factual basis of the legend of the Amazons, whereas distorted customs of Indian yogis could be the root of the tales of the Brahmans, whilst overexaggerated reports about the physical – or cosmetic – characteristics of certain races might be the basis of some physical deformities, as well as the afore mentioned bird catching being the origin of the battle between the Pygmies and the cranes.[75]

Under these circumstances we should not be surprised that fabulous races are an integral part of medieval encyclopedias[76] just as of chronicle historiography[77] and travel literature. Fabulous races, aliens, or people from Mars, call them what you will, still fulfil today a release function for man's uncertainty. The virtually exclusively literary life which they led (and lead) means they can be seen less as a threat to man and rather as a complement for the diversity of creation.

CHAPTER EIGHT

God's Mysterious Ways or the Hidden Powers of Nature:
Astro-Meteorology in the Middle Ages

Meteorological and astro-meteorological phenomena such as thunderstorms, comets, northern lights, and compass deviation cause little surprise today, as they have long been the subject of scientific research, but in Columbus's time they could cause consternation and even fear. From time immemorial until well into modern times these natural phenomena were not only explained 'naturally' but also allegorically, as bad omens, or concrete signs of forthcoming specific, usually terrible, events. There were popular explanations for most natural phenomena which in many cases had survived the Christianisation of Europe unscathed and were of a natural-mythological nature. For example, thunder and lightening were interpreted as the rumbling of a god of thunder (or a giant). In southern Germany there was a folk-belief in earthquakes being caused by tremors of the world serpent, the Germanic Midgard serpent.

In addition to this came other natural processes which, despite no longer being inexplicable, still cause us some amazement. When, for example, Columbus sailed into the Sargasso sea in light winds (16th September 1492), progress through the water was slowed down. His sailors feared that the 'grass-sea' and the calm would mean that they would be stuck on the open infinite sea for ever as the sluggish winds made any return seem impossible.[1] Although Columbus knew about the phenomenon from older sailors, the terror did not disappear until it was discovered that it was caused merely by a kind of drifting seaweed that hindered the ships' progress. Similarly the observed deviation of the compass from due north was eventually discovered to be caused by magnetic north being located some distance from true north, and also because the pole star itself was not located precisely on the celestial pole.[2] Until then sailors became confused and panicked when they appeared to be off-course, simply because the phenomena had not been noticed.

Apart from such newly discovered phenomena, even the most important causal links in nature and meteorology were still unknown. Nevertheless, all these natural occurances as part of the physical environment were observed with great interest and not only academic interest. Many of them, such as thunderstorms or earthquakes, presented potential existential threats. For farmers, hail could mean a winter of hunger and so its threat was very tangible. By far the majority of the population had not the slightest idea about the explanations for natural phenomena as propounded by the scholars. The meteorological inter-pretations (as far as things could be interpreted in the Middle Ages) would have interested them, but they were simply not accessible.

Several problems had already been solved in Classical times, for example the role of volcanism and erosion in the formation of mountains[3] and these results remained known in the Middle Ages, even if little progress was made in detailed knowledge. The actual achievement of the Middle Ages lay in the conveying and popularisation of knowledge, not in deepening it. One example of this is the explanation of the rainbow (*arcus coeli*, see below). Although the physical reason for the rainbow was known since Classical times, the interpretation of it in the Middle Ages was on the whole allegorical and theological.[4]

Contrary to modern popular opinion, the physical environment was un-questionably a topic of interest for medieval scholars. This was particularly true from the scholarly Renaissance of the 12th century when scholars began to be acquainted with the corresponding works of Aristotle, such as *De meteorologica*, *De physica*, *De mundo*, but only through the indirect medium of Arabic authors. These works then formed the basis for the scholars to develop their own theories.[5] The medieval preliminary stage to modern physics developed out of this mostly very theoretical-philosophical research, and was only possible when the existence of natural laws was recognised. The discovery of natural laws, however, made slow progress in the Middle Ages. The term 'natural law' itself is only found at the end of the 13th century in Roger Bacon's works,[6] who incidentally also coined the phrase *scientiae experimentalis* (experimental sci-ences) for the subjects known today as natural science subjects.[7] Nature was usually thought to be permeated by God's will and totally subject to his free volition. Therefore there were no natural laws beyond the divine. In the Middle Ages it was not necessary for an explanation of the physical environment to presuppose a concept of nature with a force of its own until the time of the late scholastics.

From the 12th century onwards there was an increase in speculative research into nature and natural phenomena, but even so it was relatively seldom for a medieval work to deal systematically with all aspects of inanimate nature. This may have terminological reasons, for, ever since Pliny the Elder's time in the first century AD, 'natural history' had been primarily equated with zoology and botany and not with inanimate matters. Such treatises were correspondingly based in particular on extracts from encyclopedic literature, especially from Isidore's *Etymologiae* (more seldom from Martianus Capella and Macrobius's commentary on Cicero's *Somnium Scipionis* from the beginning of the 5th century). One of the most important sources for scholars of the high Middle Ages in addition to these were the various works by the first western European 'scientist', the English monk Bede (672/3–735). He was called 'venerabilis' (venerable) because of his numerous works in which he linked Classical know-ledge with medieval Christian thought. He drew much of his information from

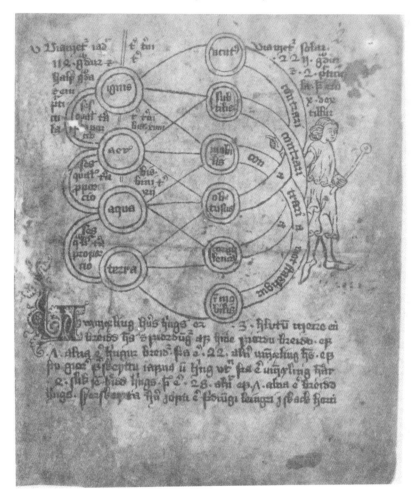

Figure 28. Table of the four elements according to Bede from an Old Icelandic manuscript (c. 1400). Copenhagen, Arnamagnaeanisches Institut, AM 736 III, 4to, f. 2r.

Isidore and Pliny, but was more critical than either of them and in cosmographical matters far more concrete than Isidore. His concise, but very informative works, *De natura rerum*, *De temporibus*, and *De ratione temporum* were of paramount importance for natural history and historiography in the subsequent centuries. This is reflected in the fact that more than 125 manuscripts of *De natura rerum* are preserved today.[8]

Surprisingly few of the compendia that were interested in natural history within this encyclopedic tradition deal (next to astronomy) with geology,[9] meteorology, optics,[10] and such topics in a more general form (besides them there is a limited number of monographs on various sections of natural history).[11] Short chapters about hydrological and meteorological, only very seldom geological phenomena were included in encyclopedias orientated towards natural history from the 12th century onwards, for example *De imagine mundi* by Honorius of Autun or *De philosophia mundi* by William of Conches. However, although Aristotle's works (translated in Spain from the Arabic)[12] were beginning to find circulation, these texts by Honorius or William were mostly based directly on Venerable Bede. Detailed discussion of geological questions in the Middle Ages are even more unusual. Besides Albertus Magnus (in his *De mineralibis et rebus metallicis*) and Alexander Neckham (*De natura rerum*), the only others who concerned themselves (apart from alchemists) in any detail with geological, mostly metallurgical questions, were scholars from Britain. Amongst these were Adelard of Bath (early 12th century) in his *Quaestiones Naturales*, Radulphus Higden (c. 1299–1365) in the *Polychronicon* and Michael Scotus (c. 1235) in his *Mensa Philosophicus*.

The rare sections about natural phenomena were usually classified with contemporary logic according to the four elements earth, water, air and fire, out of which the so-called sublunar area was made, that is, the whole space beneath the lunar orbit. This innermost sphere of the universe had at its centre the globe of the earth, since the earth as the heaviest element always tried to descend lowest and the lowest point of the spherical universe is its centre.[13] Arranged around it there was water, somewhat unevenly but nevertheless covering the majority of the earth, above that was the air, and finally fire. The specific weights (or perhaps more appropriately, lack of weight) in medieval opinion were: earth (one), water (twelve), air (eighteen), and fire (twenty-seven). Or to put in another way air was 18 times lighter than earth.[14] These ratios are problematic to reconstruct and to interpret today because if earth was twelve times heavier than water, then it must refer to certain minerals or metals, but quite certainly not the mineral-organic mixture which we usually call earth today.

The four basic elements were not only related to each other in the mathematical relationship of the weight-ratio, but in a far more complex connection which was called syzygy. Every element not only had a place in the scale of weights, but also particular characteristics which corresponded to the following ranking:

earth *(terra)*	cold	dry	immobile	viscous	blunt
water *(aqua)*	cold	wet	mobile	viscous	blunt
air *(aer)*	warm	wet	mobile	fine	blunt
fire *(ether)*	warm	dry	mobile	fine	sharp

This had the effect that every material object could be defined in its characteristics according to its elemental components; for example onion is warm and wet, garlic on the other hand warm and dry and therefore sharper than the former. Diagrams of the elements and their qualities are found in most of the medieval handbooks,[15] but also in numerous special explanations of syzygy (Figure 28). The doctrine of macrocosmos-microcosmos was such that not only

101

did the world up to the lunar sphere consist of the four elements, but it also included man, in whom concentrations of certain elements led to particular temperaments.[16] As a result of this, human temperaments are also often included in these illustrations.

Earth

The first element, earth, is the heaviest and therefore the most important element. Whenever the authors of medieval cosmographical natural histories wrote about earth, apart from describing the shape of the world, the zones, and the climates,[17] earthquakes in particular were considered to be important. The causes for the latter had been the subject of discussions from Classical times, arriving admittedly at very diverse explanations.

The classification according to elements occurs in a natural historical treatise attributed to Bede but which in fact was only written in the 11th to 12th century in southern Germany.[18] The chapter dealing with earth is divided into *Forma Terre, Zone, Climata, Terremotus*. In this treatise there was a whole range of attempts at interpreting earthquakes *(terrue motus)*. They were explained by the water which flowed through underground caverns like human arteries. The movement of the water was so strengthened by winds entering the cave system that the earth quaked as a result (Isidore, *Etymologiae* XIV, I, 2f and Honorius, *De imagine mundi* I, 5). This explanation which was known from the 5th century BC was the most prevalent interpretation of earthquakes in Classical times and in the Middle Ages.[19] Another explanation was the subterranean collapse of mountains in the interior of the earth, which was thought to be hollow. A third interpretation which is obviously based on Germanic mythology is that the movement is caused by the snake Leviathan (the Midgard serpent), which is wrapped around the earth and which causes the waters and even the earth to quake.[20]

The popular attempts at interpretation given here were completely non-scholarly, whereas in the 14th century Jean Buridan (Johannes Buridanus) offered a scholarly cosmological solution which found great support then and afterwards. Because of the different distribution of earth and water on the earth's surface the centre of gravity of the earth and the geometric centre were not identical. Consequently there was a natural tendency to balance this discrepancy. As soon as mountains eroded somewhere and were swept away, the whole globe of the earth would make a movement in an attempt to rebalance.[21] This theory corresponds best to today's interpretation of earthquakes being caused by the shifting of the earth's tectonic plates.

However, even popular and vernacular works did not contain exclusively inaccurate information. Konrad of Megenberg, the canon from Regensburg, who devoted a whole long chapter[22] to earthquakes in his *Buch von den naturleichen Dingen*, translated from the French in the mid-14th century,[23] spoke out decisively against the 'great fairy tale' that a fish-like being (like the Leviathan or the Midgard's serpent, which he calls Celebrant) could cause earthquakes. He explained them correctly as being a consequence of volcanism. He also mentioned the poisonous volcanic gases and added a list of major earthquakes which occurred during his lifetime.[24] He refers to Avicenna, whose geological work was available from the 12th century in Latin,[25] as well as to Albertus Magnus[26] who also saw the connection between volcanism as the origin of earthquakes and the formation of mountains. One popular view about the origin of volcanoes and volcanic activity originated in Aristotle and his ideas about the eruptions of Etna on Sicily. Aristotle had assumed that just as the waves disturb the otherwise calm sea, they also moved the subterranean base of the mountains which was completely riddled with caves and tunnels. In this way the sulphur which was inside was ignited, leading in turn to fiery eruptions.[27] Nearly all the encyclopedists of the Middle Ages accepted this theory just as Classical scholars had done, such as Lucretius (1st century BC).

In his treatise, Konrad of Megenberg enumerated the particular signs of an impending earthquake, including the various colours of the sun, some kinds of cloud formations, and certain planetary constellations. In contrast to Konrad, many authors of the 15th century suggested that comets and animal behaviour were amongst signs indicating severe earthquakes were likely.[28]

Astrology played a role in the 'scholarly' forecasting of earthquakes; however, it played a far greater role in scholarly meteorology, going beyond explaining only natural phenomena, so that for the Middle Ages we can speak with good reason of astro-metereology.[29] The art of prognostication, that is to say, forecasting the weather, was exclusively based on astrological principles. In addition to this we should not forget the everyday folk knowledge relating to metereology. This would have included farmers' rules, rhymes, and the signs suggesting a change in the weather, surely used then just as they still are today. These must have been used even more intensively than nowadays because of the greater dependence of a primarily agricultural society. However, there is no noteworthy systematic description in scholarly literature. The reason for this was probably that an audience for the writings about predicting weather and phenomena was to be found among academics and at court where the corresponding manuscripts could be afforded.[30] Farmers, few of whom would have been able to read, would have had little access to manuscripts and probably would hardly have had the education and the leisure to devote to complex astrological computations. The fact that the monasteries, despite their agricultural activities, seldom owned works concerned with prediction of phenomena was probably the consequence of astrology not being theologically accepted. Indeed there were repeated voices raised against investing any belief in the stars. Thus, in astro-meteorological texts there were seldom allusions to weather conditions which might also have been significant for agriculture, such as hail, thunderstorms, floods, and frost. Instead they are almost exclusively concerned with forecasting rain.

Only in the late Middle Ages were the simplified astro-meteorological laws united with farmers' weather rules in calendar-like collections. These farmer's almanacs, which used chronological points such as the so-called critical days and saints' days, were supposed to make short-term or long-term weather forecasts possible. Even in this relatively practical structure of prediction the Latin tradition still dominated and astrology never completely lost its influence on metereology until far into modern times.[31]

Water

Everyone, not just farmers, was interested in how the more unusual weather conditions, such as hail, snow, fog or dew, were caused. Treatises dealing with explanations for these were a curious mixture of truths and half-truths from our point of view. Clouds *(nubes)* and fog *(nebula)* were always understood to be the evaporation of water by the sun's radiation, even where natural science had little influence (see Isidore, *Etymologiae*, XIII, 7, 1–2). Important details such as the drop in the temperature of saturated air through the cold surface of the earth or winds were not yet mentioned. Konrad of Megenberg described how fog became so heavy by being mixed together with smoke that it could not lift above the ground despite solar radiation,[32] which partly reflected reality, although the degree of saturation is not mentioned either by him nor by anyone else.[33] The origin of rain *(pluvia)* was explained in different ways. Whilst the treatise from the early 12th century still believed that the clouds were squeezed out, so to speak, by the wind,[34] Konrad explained condensation by comparing the cold layers of air with the cold iron lid of a cooking pot on which steam has condensed:[35]

The rain comes from watery vapours which the sun's heat has sucked up into the middle layers of the air, but because of the cold there, the vapours become water again, as we can see from the steam rising from a boiling pot on the fire: when the steam touches the cold iron lid of the pot, it turns into drops of water.*

These observations led Konrad to conclude that the size of the rain drops depended on the temperature of the air in its middle layers. Despite his generally critical attitude, Konrad still repeated elements of folklore, such as the fall of red rain (which he identified as having red dust mixed in with it, rather than blood as folklore claimed) or the raining of small fish or frogs. This latter he rationalised by accepting the phenomenon as fact. He commented that the

---

* *Der regen kümpt von wäzzrigem dunst, den der sunnen hitz auf hât gezogen in das mitel reich des luftes, wann von der kelten, diu dâ ist, entsleuzt sich der dunst wider in wazzer, als wir sehen an dem dunst, der von dem wallenden hafen gêt ob dem feur: wenn der dunst die kalten eisnenne hafendecken rüert, sô entsleuzt er sich in wazzers tropfen.*

dampness in the clouds already contained traces of fishspawn or frogspawn which during certain planetary constellations then came to life.[36] Such additions from folklore are not found in Konrad's model, the Latin *Liber de natura rerum* by Thomas of Cantimpré.[37] The digressions, however, show how seriously Konrad examined all natural phenomena that he knew, even if he could not totally free himself from medieval folklore.

With regard to rain Konrad commented also that some mountains were so high that the rain could never reach them, as the layers of air in which the processes of weather took place lay lower than the highest mountain peaks.[38] This consideration shows just how true an Aristotelian he was, since Aristotle had (*Meteorologica* I, 4) likewise assumed this considerable height of mountains. In the Middle Ages the relative height of mountains was a topic of academic speculation. Scholars were usually of the opinion that the mountains were of no consequence in relation to the size of the globe of the earth.[39] One vivid comparison described the size of the mountains on the earth 'like grains of sand on a skittle ball'. The idea behind this derives from Pliny who gives an account of attempts to measure the height of mountains (which gave results which were almost correct). He sceptically quotes the consequences resulting from this, namely that the mountains in comparison with the globe represent insignificant elevations.[40]

All relevant treatises on natural history, when treating the elements water and air, also dealt with hail, snow and dew. The reasons for the formation of hail (*grando*) and snow (*nix*) are given reasonably correctly as being related to the temperature either of lower, or else higher, layers of air through which the precipitation was falling.[41] No thought was given to the reasons for the rising of moist air. Albertus Magnus first described snow crystals in the 13th century. Dew (*ros*) and hoar frost (*pruina*) were interpreted correspondingly as condensation of moisture through the nightly drop in temperature, or else as frozen dew.[42] In connection with these meteorological phenomena gossamer (*estas*) and shooting stars (*stellae cadentes* or similar) with the ensuing jelly-like 'stellar phlegm' were also considered in the treatises. These were thought to be atmospheric phenomena of the sublunar area (phenomena to do with weather). In actual fact, both can be traced back to organic origins. Gossamer was thought to be the dried-up residue of the air following dew. It was believed that spiders made their webs from it, whereas gossamer is actually spider's webs, i.e. not the means but the end. 'Stellar phlegm', on the other hand, which was mentioned both in the treatise entitled *De mundi celestis terrestrisque constitutione*[43] as well as in Konrad of Megenberg's *Buch von der Natur*,[44] was explained as the result of the fall of shooting stars, whereas in fact it is the result of blue algae developing after rain.[45]

Water was thought to be sphere-shaped like the earth, both because of the shape of the single water drop and also because of the form of the waters surrounding the earth (hydrosphere).[46] Whenever the element water was mentioned, one problem for medieval observers of nature became obvious. Water,

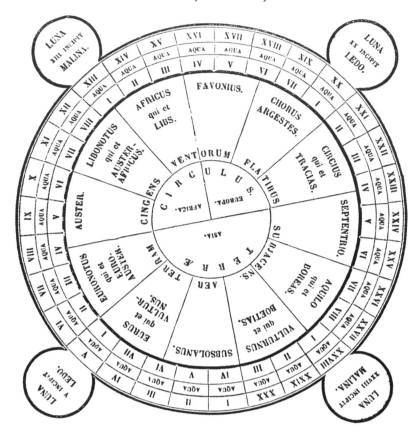

Figure 29. Circular diagram of the influence of the moon on the tides according to Bede. Copy in J.-P. Migne, Patrologia Latina 90, cols. 259–260.

as the second element, was supposed to surround the earth, but did so only very incompletely (as was obvious from the continental landmasses) and had a constant tendency always to finds its own lowest level. The irregular distribution of water and land could be interpreted in two ways. Edrisi, the Arabian cosmographer, claimed, on the basis of computation, that the sea actually lay higher than the land. This view was repeated in the work of the English Augustinian abbot of Cirencester, Alexander Neckham (1157–1217). He also thought that the sea formed something like a mountain (which according to his statement could be confirmed by looking at it) and would only be held by God's will in its coasts despite the higher position.[47] The other more complex interpretation, which was put forward by Jean Buridan in the 14th century, was the aforementioned theory that the hydrosphere and the sphere of earth have different centres, thereby explaining why part of the globe of earth rises up above the water whereas the majority of it is covered.[48] The logical consequence, but only

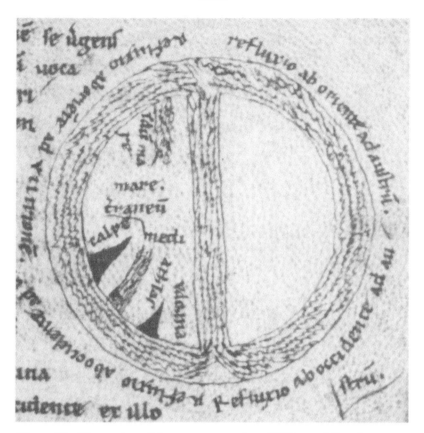

Figure 30. Illustration of the sea currents from William of Conches: Philosophia mundi. Vienna, Österreichische Nationalbibliothek, MS 1736, f. 55r.

rarely noted, of this argument was to refute the existence of a southern continent because the sea must be at its deepest there.[49] A third theory offered a way out of the problem, by assuming an irregular hydrosphcre which then could divide the surface of the earth into several dry sections.[50]

It was almost a matter of course that in treatises dealing with water the cause of the tides (*aestus*) would be considered. The change between ebb and flow, the spring tides (*malines*), and neap tides (*ledones*) were particularly striking and at first glance inexplicable natural phenomena. The reasons were included by Nicole Oresme (died 1382), theologian, natural philopher and mathematician, in his teratological work *De causis mirabilium*. He correctly attributed them to the moon's pull on the sea, as well as to an independent perpendicular motion of the sea.[51] This explanation had been known at least since the time of Bede[52] but it was not included by Isidore; maritime natural phenomena were not covered at all by Konrad of Megenberg. In this context the Bavarian treatise *De mundi celestis terrestrisque constitutione*[53] mentions the ocean serpent once more, this time responsible for the tides (as before it had been described as the cause of earthquakes). This shows how powerful and durable the myth of the world serpent was up to the High Middle Ages. From the time of Bede there were attempts to illustrate the influence of the lunar phases on the tides diagrammatically, mostly in the shape of circular diagrams (Figure 29) which were a common technique in the Middle Ages for all sorts of illustrations of topics of natural history.

The sea currents (*refluxiones*) were considered to be closely linked with the tides.[54] William of Conches, in particular, dealt in great detail with their origin, significance and direction.[55] In William's opinion divine wisdom was the reason for sea currents existing. They carried the warmth stored up in the water in the equatorial zone around the landmasses of the three continents lying on the northern hemisphere and lapped round them with warm water. The point of departure for the sea currents was the (assumed) ocean at the equator, from which currents went to the north and the south, assuming a system of two such currents in the east and one in the west (of the three continents). William included also the possible deviation of the sea currents through submarine mountain ranges and explained in detail which seas were fed by which currents. The manuscripts of his work contain many illustrations of this system of currents. In other medieval works the currents are not illustrated, as far as I know (Figure 30). As the earth was considered to be immobile, the deviation of the currents through the revolving of the earth was of course totally unknown.

The rarely mentioned whirlpool was also considered to be a consequence of sea currents. Right up to the 17th century it was believed that they existed at the poles of the earth and sucked the water into the interior of the earth.[56] This belief in a whirlpool or maelstrom appears to be at the bottom of the description made by the church historian Adam of Bremen in the 11th century. He reported how daring Frisian sailors had been caught in the mighty suction of a whirlpool near to the North Pole and had only been able to save themselves with great difficulty.[57] The maelstrom caused by strong tidal currents in the Norwegian Lofoten islands could be the historical foundation of this tale.

The natural philosophers of the 12th and 13th centuries no longer merely discussed miraculous fountains when dealing with water, but they are dealt with in great detail in encyclopedic literature. Wells and springs from all parts of the world were mentioned, many of them in pairs, for example the two Greek wells, one of which strenthened the memory whilst the other made one forgetful (Isidore, *Etymologiae* XIII, 12, 3–4). There were the two Sicilian springs, one of which made women pregnant, the other made them infertile (*Etymologiae* XIII, 13, 5). One spring in Italy was said to heal eye disorders, whilst one in Africa produced a clear voice (*Etymologiae* XIII, 13, 2), and one in Greece increased the libido (*Etymologiae* XIII, 12, 3–4). Where the Troglodytes live in Ethiopia there was reputed to be a well whose fresh water turned salty and unpalatable three times a day (*Etymologiae* XIII, 13, 9), and where the Garamantes lived water froze during the heat of the day, but was warm at night (*Etymologiae* XIV, 5, 13). Legends like these were found in the large compendia next to pages giving a variety of information: the red colour of the Red Sea which was explained quite rationally as being the result of the red earth surrounding it (*Etymologiae* XIII, 17, 2–4). There were accounts of the Dead Sea on which there were no storms due to its viscosity, on which a burning lamp would float but an extinguished one would sink because the Sea pulls everything which is dead down into itself (*Etymologiae* XIII, 19, 3–4). There are also the descriptions from Classical times about a coagulated frozen sea in the North Atlantic, which the Old High German *Merigarto*, a fragment dealing with noteworthy bodies of water, mentions in the 11th century.[58] The mixture of logically reconstructable and factually correct information with legendary accounts from Classical times and quite simply fabulous elements characterise chapters covering water in the encyclopedias from Isidore onwards. The same had been the case with the descriptions of animals in the *Physiologus* and the bestiaries.

Air

As was the case with water, when it came to dealing with the third element, air, medieval encyclopedists were again able to observe natural phenomena, primarily the winds. The Classical system of four main wind directions and eight subsidiary wind directions for each of the four made thirty-two sections. These were reflected in the division of the Portulan maps just as modern compass plates are divided into thirty-two sectors. This concept was completely integrated into medieval scholarship and illustrated in numerous circular diagrams of the winds. The usual attribution of the main winds to the directions and these then to the appropriate seasons, ages of man, and elements led to complex diagrams. In these diagrams the topical connections of totally different areas of life were made apparent. Medieval man enjoyed taking recourse in such matters (Figure 31).

The origin of the winds was explained by Bede. He attributed them not only to differences in temperature, but also to the pressure of air against high mountains. The main wind directions were thought to cover a far greater area than today: the warm east wind was supposed to emanate from the warm sea current to the east of Asia.[59] Apart from this, the movement of the planets was also thought to influence the winds. It was assumed that just as the movement of the firmament transferred itself to the planetary spheres, the planets also set the atmosphere around the earth in motion.[60]

In the atmosphere of the earth more natural phenomena could be observed which remained partly inexplicable, such as thunder and lightening or the northern lights (*aurora borealis*). For lightening (*fulmen*) and thunder (*tonitrus*) the southern German treatise, *De mundi celestis terrestrisque constitutione*,[61] gave a whole list of explanations. One of them was the collision of clouds driven

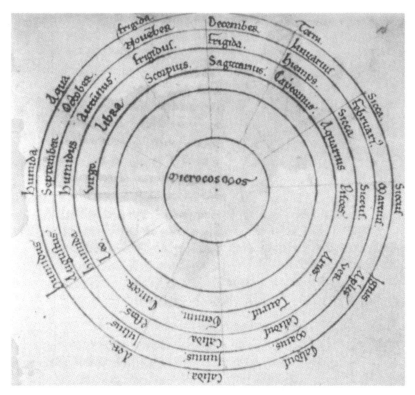

Figure 31. Large circular picture of the directions of the wind, ages of man, elements etc. from William of Conches, Philosophia mundi. London, The British Library, MS. Add. 11.676, f. 16 (13th century).

together by the four main winds, creating either pressure or heat or cold, which expressed itself in a loud noise and light. Another interpretation, which had already appeared in Isidore[62] and Bede[63] was that thunder was a wind 'locked up' within clouds (a sort of excess pressure). Their reasoning was that a blown-up bladder creates a loud noise when it bursts despite its relatively small size. A third attempt at interpretation compared the process with the sound made by glowing iron when it is thrust into cold water which could be traced back to the fact that the cold condensed water in the clouds meets together with tiny bits of fire falling out of the empyreum. Both Thomas of Cantimpré and his translator Konrad of Megenberg subscribed to the latter.[64] The older texts also agreed that when lightening struck, it left a kind of stone behind, or that the thunderclap was a stone anyway.[65] Konrad of Megenberg contradicted this notion vehemently, pointing out that people who had been struck by lightening never suffered wounds, but only ever burns.[66] In connection with this, Konrad commented on the differing speeds of light and noise as the lightening was seen

before the thunder was heard. He confirmed this opinion with another historically interesting example taken from contemporary every-day life. This was the
beating of the washing with bats: if one stands on a hill and looks at someone
beating washing in a stream from some distance, then although the bat hitting
the clothes can be seen it takes a little while before the sound can be heard.[67]
However, he had no idea about the electrically conductive properties of metal.
He explained the observation that a flash of lightening could strike a sword and
destroy it whilst the leather sheath remained unharmed by saying that the hard
steel gave more resistance to the 'hot vapours' of the lightening than did the soft
leather. His explanation relies rather on the lacking flexibility and the greater
density of materials than on the conducting qualities.

Rainbows were considered to have more to do with the properties of air than
water. High and late medieval texts were often very detailed in their discussion
about them. They described how droplets of water contained in the haze and
clouds refracted the sunlight at a certain angle of incidence, thus causing a
rainbow. However, they only knew red, green, and yellow as the colours of its
spectrum.[68] This physical explanation hardly played little more than an allegorical role. The colours were supposed to remind man of the colours of fire,
water, and sulphur. Their significance was the conflagration of the world on the
Last Day, the waters of the Flood and the sulphur rain which fell on Sodom and
Gomorrah.[69] This kind of interpretation corresponds to the treatment of the
animals in the *Physiologus* and the bestiaries[70] where the physical aspect was
dealt with only briefly (mostly limited to the appearance and eating habits). It
also reflects the authors' primary interest which was in the symbolism. Bede was
aware of four colours, green, purple, yellow, and red, which he equated with the
four basic elements.[71] Despite the dominance of the allegory, the rainbow
example shows that in this case both meteorological knowledge about the
storage of water in the clouds in the form of smallest drops, as well as optical
awareness (the refraction of light through water drops)[72] were available, even
if little usage was made of this knowledge.

Fire

Although there were explanations for climatic phenomena of the atmosphere
which were partly characterised by everyday experience and therefore in touch
with reality, there were certainly no empirical data availiable for occurrences in
the fourth element of the sublunar area, the fire, or rather ether. It should be
noted that there was an uncertainty about the limits of ether. Did it end at the
lunar sphere as the fourth sub-lunar element? Or did it extend to fill the whole
space between the earth's atmosphere and the firmament? Authors who placed
the ether in the sublunar sphere still described different planetary processes and
events as happening in the ether, despite the contradiction. These included solar

and lunar eclipses and also comets, shooting stars and other phenomena of the heavens, such as the *aurora borealis*, or 'northern lights'.

Shooting stars were generally seen as a form of fiery precipitation unlike watery precipitation which fell as rain or hail. The idea that shooting stars might be smouldering stars which were falling to earth had already been dismissed by late Classical times. They were understood to be the remains of smouldering fragments which were carried into the atmosphere from the fiery empyreum.[73] The belief in viscous residue from shooting stars has already been mentioned and even an astronomer such as Michael Scotus (c. 1175–c. 1234) who wrote a commentary on John of Sacrobosco's textbook, *De sphaera*, considered shooting stars to be primarily a topic for astrologers, as comets were (see below).[74]

Occurrences such as the northern lights (also known as polar light and only from the 17th century as *aurora borealis*) were virtually never discussed in medieval scholarly works, although sightings of these electro-magnetic phenomena were by no means seldom. It is difficult to differentiate between meteor showers, shooting stars, and the northern lights in medieval sources.[75] However, thanks to the forms described, we can assume that Konrad of Megenberg (in his chapter *Von den fewern in den Lüften*) meant the northern lights when he talked about a fiery vapour in the form of a bright crown, and a shower of meteors when he described a process like the quick ignition of many candles. He calls the meteor shower *springende gaiz*[76] ('jumping goat') and this is probably the only medieval evidence for the usage of the term *capra* ('goat'), used in Aristotle and Seneca, for this phenomenon.[77]

On the other hand the comets had been considered to be ethereal phenomena ever since the revival of Aristotle in the 12th century. Until the 15th century comets were still thought to be a product of earthly vapours. In the Middle Ages the older (and as we know today, correct) theory, which can be traced back to Seneca and was included by Bede and Hrabanus Maurus, that they are stars with very long orbits, was usually dismissed.[78] Honorius of Autun devoted a short chapter to this very topic called 'Why comets are not stars'.[79] He explained his disapproval: comets could not be counted among the fixed stars because they wander, nor do they keep to the path (known as the 'ecliptic') of the planets and sun through the signs of the zodiac; it was apparently inconceivable that they might be a different form of star. William of Conches presented a similar argument. The treatise *Questio de Cometa* by the theologian Heinrich of Langenstein explained comets similarly as a smouldering conglomeration of earthly vapours.[80] This treatise was interestingly enough commissioned by King Charles V who wanted to speak out against the astrological interpretations of comets on the occasion of the one sighted at Easter in 1368. As is only too well known, comets were widely thought to forecast anything disastrous, from an earthquake to the demise of a ruler. A treatise on comets by the Ulm teacher Jacob Engelhardt (or Jacobus Angelus, physician to the archduke Leopold of Austria) on the occasion of the comet of 1402 agreed with this Aristotelian opinion of the nature of the planets. However, he also recounted several other theories, probably under the influence of the commentary on Aristotle made by Albertus Magnus, written 150 years earlier, which is similarly structured and includes the same authorities.[81] Amongst these is the opinion of one of the oldest Christian authors who dealt with comets, John of Damascus, one of the Church Fathers (c. 650/75–c. 750) who considered comets to be short-lived and extraordinary divine creations. Another late medieval theory saw them as reflections of planetary light.[82] Comets were considered less as natural phenomena and far more as forewarnings of natural catastrophes such as earthquakes and floods but also of the death of kings and noblemen.[83] This is why Isidore of Seville's idea of the comets as *portenta* held true well into modern times.

One question not yet discussed is that of the extent of the distribution and the comprehensibility of relatively popular treatises such as *De mundi celestis terrestrisque constitiutione*. If I have repeatedly mentioned popular scholarly representations, then only in relation to specialized scholastic research, as the named treatise was more or less certainly on the most recent level of scholarship of its time. It told facts in a way which did not demand any background knowledge of astronomy. Nevertheless such a treatise stood far above the pure accumulation of knowledge used as a basis for homilies and catechisms, so often found in the cosmographical sections of popular encyclopedias and compendia like the nearly contemporary *Elucidarius* by Honorius of Autun, the *Lucidarius* or the *Book Sidrach*. The level of knowledge of natural history in these works was probably equivalent to the current level of teaching at universities and within religious orders. These views were thus typical only of well-educated clerics and some laymen with a university education. They were only rarely transmitted to a wider audience, although this could have happened orally via sermons, the most important medium of popularising theories and views. This only changed slowly even in the late Middle Ages, for example through vernacular works like Konrad of Megenberg's *Buch von der Natur*. Only in the 15th century did wider circles of the urban population gain access to such documents and the information contained within.

CHAPTER NINE

A New Continent, a New Earth, a New World:
from Columbus to Galileo

On 12th October 1492 Columbus set foot for the first time on San Salvador, one of the islands belonging to the American continent. He must have been aware that he had just completed a historic voyage, but not aware of the full extent of his discovery. He had not only discovered a completely new continent, but a *fifth* continent. Although Australia would not be discovered by Europeans for another three centuries,[1] the existence of a southern continent was as good as a foregone conclusion. On his deathbed in Valladolid fourteen years later Columbus may have had a glimmering that he had not only discovered new islands or even a new continent, but that he had discovered a 'new world' in the literal meaning of the term. Even so, to the end of his life the contours of this world were still unclear to him, the nature of the discovery confused and the consequences totally unforeseeable. In 1506 he was probably only interested in settling his claims with the Spanish crown; cosmographical implications and the significance of his discovery on world history were no longer of any consequence to him whatsoever.

It is significant that the first reports about the discovery of America often have *De mundo novo* ('On the new world') somewhere in the title. There was a reason for this. The term *mundus* sounds somewhat strange here since in medieval Latin the word meant 'world' in the meaning of 'cosmos', or 'universe'. *Terra nova* might have been the more expected term for the newly-discovered islands and countries. This strange choice of word went so far that even the Latin word *orbis* was used for the New World, as in a Spanish work which appeared in 1511 entitled *De orbe novo*,[2] just as if what was being described was a totally new planet Earth. Columbus himself never spoke about the newly discovered islands as being anything other than Asia or India. The name, America, came from Martin Waldseemüller who used it on a map which accompanied a 1504 edition of Amerigo Vespucci's account (see below). The name 'America' was popularised through his own *Cosmographia introductio* (published 1507).[3]

The gradual change in the *Weltbild* from the beginning of the 16th century was even reflected in the words for 'world'. This raises the question of innovations which took place and how they altered the medieval *Weltbild*, as described in the preceding chapters, to the modern *Weltbild* of the 17th century. The 16th century was a period of transition, especially with regard to the physical *Weltbild*. Reports of voyages of discovery and Copernicus' theories about a sun-centred solar system only became known during this century. As further progress made in understanding the universe was relatively slow, reception of the new knowledge even in scholarly circles was no more than gradual. This chapter deals briefly with the most significant changes and developments from the 15th to 17th centuries in geography and astronomy.

Geography

As the terms used for the New World show, Columbus's discovery was more than a mere extension of the three known (and the fourth assumed) continents. If the Portuguese had discovered a new continent south of Africa or Asia, or if Brazil (at first called Terra de Vera Cruz),[4] which they first sighted and landed on in 1500, had proved to be a continent of manageable dimensions in the southern hemisphere, this would have been a significant extention of the medieval *Weltbild*. However, it would not have shattered the image to the same extent as Columbus's discovery did because it would only have confirmed what some Classical and medieval authorities had already assumed about the existence of a southern continent.

The amazing aspect for the early 16th century was that Columbus's discovery was of a completely unknown and unsuspected continent which seemed to stretch immeasurably far to the north and south. Moreover, there was only a gradual realisation that the landfall made by the Genoese sailor John Cabot (Giovanni Caboto) who discovered Labrador in 1497–1498 for the English crown,[5] Columbus's discoveries in Central America, and the new land found by the Portuguese in Brazil all belonged to one and the same landmass. The geographical *Weltbild* had been quite literally shattered, and it could never be restored. The earth with its familiar three continents on the northern hemisphere suddenly burst at the seams to the west. Where previously there had been an immense, but theoretically navigable, ocean between western Europe and Asia, a gigantic new land mass suddenly appeared. The shock for the Europeans could hardly have been greater than if Atlantis had suddenly re-emerged from under the waves in the western Atlantic.

The first definitive record we have which confirms the realisation of the enormity of the discovery is a letter from Amerigo Vespucci to Lorenzo di Medici, dated 10th March 1503. He states that as a result of his voyages of discovery along the east coast of the South American continent he had come to the conclusion that the new discoveries were not only new islands on the way to Asia, but rather a whole new continent of immense dimensions. This became widespread knowledge through the printing of Vespucci's report in 1504. It was graphically illustrated by Martin Waldseemüller's map which accompanied the book and it was on this map that the continent was called America after Amerigo Vespucci for the first time.[6]

The discovery of America and its extent was not the only innovation in the geographic *Weltbild* of early modern times. The Portuguese navigator Bartholomew Diaz had reached the Cape of Good Hope, at the southernmost tip of Africa, on 1st May 1488, thus determining the full southerly extent of Africa. In May 1498, after rounding the Cape and then crossing the Indian ocean his compatriot Vasco da Gama arrived in Calicut (now Kozhikode) on the Indian coast and was therefore the first European to reach India by sea, albeit after an eleven month sea-voyage.[7] This and the other voyages of the Portuguese to India (in 1500, 1503, and from 1505 at ever shorter intervals)[8] had at first at least as much influence on the extension of the European *Weltbild*. In addition to this the Portuguese brought 'loads of pepper, ginger, nutmeg, cloves, but also other products such as camphor, nard, borax, wormwood and aloes'.[9] As an economic basis for further voyages these were more promising than the small amounts of gold and pearls and 'Indians' which Columbus brought back to Spain. In this way India entered European consciousness in the early 16th century twice over. Not only had the Portuguese gained entry to the long sought far-eastern fairyland of spices and jewels, but it was also assumed to be the ever increasing new land in the west.

Admittedly, as the Spaniards forced their murderous way through Central America, the land did prove to contain enough gold. However, the further they went the more different America turned out to be from the India of late medieval expectations. Ultimately America became more important as the land of hope for European colonisation than as a source of gold. Nevertheless, the gold coming from Central America to the Spanish crown, apart from the quite considerable amounts (which should not be underestimated) which arrived in Europe via unoffical channels, was to have quite significant economic consequences for western Europe.

From an economic point of view all four of Columbus's voyages were unsuccessful. Spices and larger amounts of gold were not forthcoming during Columbus's lifetime. Only the ruthless policy of exploitation conducted by the Spaniards in Central America in the 16th century finally began to show financial success. The real profits gained by the Spanish crown came less from the gold taken from the Mayas, the Incas, and the Aztecs, and far more from the mining of Central American silver deposits. The shares from the import of American precious metals usually ammounted to only 10% of the entire budget of the Spanish kings in the 16th century, and even in the record year of 1598 stayed below 20%.[10] Nevertheless this extra income was sufficient to make Spain one of the richest European countries in the 1500s. There was also the extra financial strength of the Spanish traders to America who had grown rich on the proceeds, investing their profits primarily in land and property. As a result of this the Spanish financial dealings (as well as private profits) fell increasingly to foreign trade concerns, in particular French, but also English and Dutch. Thus, the constant flow of precious metals from America to Europe was distributed relatively quickly throughout western Europe.[11] Despite protectionistic customs policies and high tax yields Spain was not the only beneficiary of the exploitation of the New World, quite apart from the increasing significance of smuggling and piracy towards the end of the 16th century.

The division of the earth, which had been sought by the Spanish crown at the papal curia was sealed by the papal bull of Alexander VI dated 4th May 1493. It was modified in the contract (the Treaty of Tordesillas) agreed between Spain and Portugal on 7th June 1494. The arrangement appeared at first sight to be quite clearly in Spain's favour. The line, which ran 370 Spanish miles to the west of the Cape Verde Islands (off the west coast of Africa), divided the Atlantic and therefore also the unexplored areas into a western Spanish and an eastern Portuguese half. This not only put Portugal, as intended, into possession of the eastern route to India via Africa, but unintentionally also into possession of the immense landmass of Vera Cruz (later Brazil) which was discovered accidentally by Pedro Alvarez Cabral in 1500. This historical division of the new discoveries between Spain and Portugal is still obvious in South America today by the distribution of languages.[12] During the course of the 16th century Portugal was at hardly an economic disadvantage. Apart from a consequence of reaching India via the eastern route, this was particularly the result of Brazilian resources even if those were far less unscrupulously exploited than those of the Spanish colonies. The protection of the Indians by the crown led to a conflict between the Portuguese colonial government and plantation owners.[13] Only Castillian foreign rule over Portugal from 1580–1640 ended Portugal's independent economic power.

The 16th century was in many ways characterised by the attempts made by all the monarchs of western European states to gain some share in the riches of the New World. These extended from direct exploitation or colonisation, or by disruption of the Spanish-Portuguese monopoly through privateering expeditions or by expeditions to areas of North America which had not yet been claimed. One positive consequence of all this for scholarship at least was that cosmography made immense progress through the sheer numbers of expeditions now being financed. Hartmann Schedel's world chronicle (published in 1493) still shows the three continents known in the Middle Ages on a map of the world which, except for the Ptolemaic orientation to the north, hardly reveals any post-medieval influence.[14] Only fourteen years later the 1507 world map by Martin Waldseemüller included a very detailed drawing of Africa, which appears to be correct in its proportions, even if it seems a little overdimensional in comparison to Europe. Apart from this, Waldseemüller's map also includes the West Indian islands known by then and a longish section of the Brazilian coast as well as a small part of North America, particularly around the Gulf of Mexico.[15] The entry for this area reads, significantly, *Asiae pars* which shows that it was still believed to be part of the East Indies. As little as forty years later the *Cosmographia Universalis* by Sebastian Münster (published in Basle in 1544) included a map, which despite inaccuracies and distortion, shows both American continents entitled *Novus orbis*. The new double continent is shown with all its coasts in its correct position between Europe and Africa, and Japan and China.[16] Within half a century the transition from the medieval to the modern view of the world had been accomplished to a considerable extent in cartography (which here may be considered to be representative for cosmography). Except for topographical details and the polar regions, the only thing that was absent from 1601 to c. 1800 was the discovery of Australia, before the basic contours of the landmasses of our earth were established.

Astronomy

A change in the medieval *Weltbild* with regards to astronomy came later and took far longer than the change in geographic perception. The process of transition from the Ptolemaic planetary system to the Copernican took from the 13th century to the end of the 17th before all the different stages of knowledge could be merged into one system which found general acceptance.

Nevertheless, the beginnings of the actual Copernican revolution in astronomy began much earlier, at a time when Columbus was spending his first few months in the New World. After studying in Germany and Italy, Nicolaus Copernicus spent the winter of 1492–1493 studying the planetary theories of the Austrian early humanist, Georg von Peurbach (1423–1461), in Krakow. He grew dissatisfied with what he read to the extent that he began making his own observations of the planets. These observations eventually led to the publication in 1543 of his main work *De revolutionibus orbium coelestium* ('On the revolutions of the celestial bodies') where he expounded his planetary theory.

Copernicus's work contained several revolutionary conclusions. Firstly he said that not all celestial movement has a common centre. Secondly, all circular orbital movement has the sun as the centre. Thirdly, the distance of the earth from the sun is insignificant in comparison with the distance of them both from the stars. Finally, the daily movement of the sun and the stars across the sky is only an illusion. In reality the earth turns around its own axis.[17]

In more recent research into the history of astronomy there has been a tendency to reject the idea of a genuine Copernican revolution[18] because none of these concepts was completely new. The realisation that not all the planets orbited around one common centre was at least 300 years old, since the observation that Venus and Mercury revolved around the sun and not around the earth (see Chapter 2 and Figure 5) had already been made in Classical times by Herakleides of Pontos and then rediscovered again in the Middle Ages. The possibility of a whole heliocentric planetary system had already been postulated by the astronomer Aristarchus of Samos in the 3rd century BC, and his theories were not only known to Copernicus but to all other late medieval astronomers.[19] The humanist Copernicus had merely drawn his hypothesis from a different Classical source than his predecessors. Even the explanation of the

Figure 32. Woodcut showing the collapse of the medieval astronomic Weltbild, supposedly from the works of Nicolaus of Kues, in reality in Camilo Flammarion, Meteorologie populaire, Paris 1888.

planetary motion and the apparent rotation of the firmament via the rotation of the earth on its own axis had already been suggested in the 14th century by Jean Buridan and Nicole Oresme on the basis of the principle of simplicity. However, both were too steeped in Ptolemy's teachings and accepted his authority to too great an extent to be able to trust their own hypothesis.[20]

Copernicus's theories were only one step in the process of the so-called Copernican revolution. Much of the preliminary work had already been done by the early humanists. Georg von Peurbach with his *Theoricae novae planetarum* (printed by Regiomontanus in Nuremberg in 1473) was still a firm adherent to the theory of the geocentric system, but nonetheless gave detailed studies of the planetary movements. Johannes Regiomontanus (1436–1476) himself excelled through his humanistic search for Classical natural historical works and his commentary on Ptolemy's work (*Epitoma in Almagestu Ptolemei,* Venice 1496).[21]

With the generous financial support of the Danish king Frederick II, Tycho Brahe (1546–1601) was able to improve the accuracy of astronomical observations with the naked eye quite considerably. He produced the most accurate star catalogue yet created. However he never deviated from the geocentric system.[22]

Copernicus had had the opportunity to consult older teachings of a heliocentric system, but only Johannes Kepler (1571–1630) completed the break with the Ptolemaic *Weltbild* of the Middle Ages. He had been Brahe's assistant and used the new star catalogue to make observations and calculations in an effort to explain the eccentricities in the movements of the planets, which had been traditionally interpreted as the result of innumerable spheres. Eventually his calculations came up with the unprecedented discovery that the planets move round the sun in elliptical, not circular, orbits. As a result Kepler was able to compute three laws of planetary motion which provided the basis for future astronomical research and destroyed for ever the concept of multiple spheres. The first and most important of these was, that the planets move round the sun in elliptical orbits with the sun occupying one focus of the ellipse.[23]

The completion of the transition from the medieval astronomic view of the world came after Galileo Galilei (1564–1642) who wanted (after initially opposing Copernicus's views)[24] to prove Copernicus's hypotheses. Pope Paul V reprimanded Galileo in 1616 for teaching the Copernican system. In 1633 he was tried by Pope Urban VIII and obliged publicly to refute Copernicus's teachings. This should not only be understood as the struggle of the papacy against the emancipation of secular sciences, but also as an element of 17th-century European politics. It had grown out of tension between the papacy and the Habsburg Empire, and between conservative Roman circles and more open, but similarly politically entangled members of the Roman curia on the other.[25] The trial of Galileo was, despite its notoriety, only an insignificant chapter in the development of modern astronomy and thus of the acceptance of the modern heliocentric *Weltbild*. Too many of Galileo's theories were already generally accepted by the 17th century, because they had been introduced by Copernicus and even Kepler. Although certain church circles repeatedly demanded that the heliocentric system could be taught only as a hypothesis and not as truth, this had only a formal legal significance at this time. In 1758 the general prohibition on books by Copernicus was lifted and they were no longer on the index of the Catholic Church. From 1821 onwards works which taught the Copernican system could finally be published with the Catholic imprimatur.[26]

This acceptance of the Copernican system sounded the death knell of the Ptolemaic *Weldbild* of astronomy which had survived for nearly one and a half millennia and which had thus characterised the entire Middle Ages. Ptolemy's sphere-shaped universe was exploded. The earth no longer rested at its centre but was merely one of many planets, and even these since Kepler's theories no longer rotated round the centre of the universe in circular perfection. If Konrad of Megenberg in the 14th century had been overawed at the sight of the night-time starry sky in an apparently limitless universe,[27] in the 17th century the lack of a protective cover of the firmament had become reality. The unity and the harmony of the old *Weltbild* had been destroyed and the heavens stood open. Post-medieval man was no longer protected by the all-encompassing sphere of the cosmos; he was forced to live with the openness of an inconceivably large and almost empty universe which was marked by the contradiction of chaos and natural laws.

Interpretation of a Medieval World Map
Based on the *Mappa Mundi* in Hereford Cathedral

At first glance the *mappae mundi*, as discussed in Chapter 4 (a), may appear difficult to understand. The reason for this is not only because medieval world maps were designed to serve a different purpose from modern maps, but also because modern maps have different contents and use different modes of representation. It is these two aspects which make the medieval maps seem 'wrong' to a modern viewer, or at least distorted. A modern observer uses modern cartographic criteria and expects distance and topographical features to be drawn in their correct spatial relationship and at the same scale. In contrast the medieval user was mostly interested in places from biblical stories, historical sites known to him from fables and legends, and illustrations showing fabulous races and animals. All these had to be easily recognisable.

The following interpretation analyses the most important elements of a medieval map from a modern point of view and tries to give an explanation of the medieval interest in each entry. The purpose is only to enhance our modern understanding but is totally unhistorical because a medieval map was built up from layers of information drawn from various written sources, such as biblical texts, Classical authors and historiographers, medieval chorographies, legends of the saints, and natural history works etc.

The world map from Hereford Cathedral has been chosen to serve as an example as it is the only complete large-size medieval world map which has survived (diameter: 132 cm). The larger Ebstorf map from northern Germany was destroyed during Allied bombing of Hannover in 1943 (original diameter: 356 cm). Of the Cornish map (original diameter: about 156 cm) there is only a fragment (61 x 53 cm) remaining. Large maps such as these were rare in the Middle Ages.

As was the case with the Ebstorf map, it is by no means certain that the Hereford map originally served as an altar picture, a theory which has been repeatedly suggested[1] because both maps have been kept in churches. The history of the map between the time it was drawn in around 1290, and 1682, when it is first mentioned in Hereford, is unknown although on the basis of details concerning English and Welsh history and geography on the map it may be assumed that the map was drawn not far from where it hangs today.[2] Since

Map 1. *Mappa mundi from Hereford Cathedral, England (end of 13th century). Complete reproduction.*

then it has been one of the treasures in the cathedral, generally unnoticed until 1988 when plans were hatched to sell the map through Sotheby's to raise funds for the renovation of Hereford Cathedral. However, fears that the map might be purchased by industrial concerns overseas (in particular Japanese) led to a fund-raising organisation being formed to keep the map in Hereford. This was eventually successfull thanks to various fund-raising enterprises, including the sale of symbolic shares. In the end the cathedral chapter saw its way to financing the renovation of the cathedral without having to sell the map.

The Hereford *mappa mundi* is a circular map with a diameter of 132 cm framed by the remainder of the vellum. The frame shows Christ as the Judge of the world at the top in an illustration of the Last Day, seated between angels with trumpets who indicate to the souls either their salvation (to the left) or damnation (to the right: Rev. 20,12). The bottom left-hand corner includes an (inaccurate) quotation from the Gospel according to St Luke (Luke 2,1) with the command from Caesar Augustus for the whole world to go and be counted. Beneath this the author has named himself, a certain Richard of Haldingham and Lafford, whose identity has not yet been fully ascertained. The bottom right-hand corner shows a rider and a hunter with a dog as well as the words *passe avant* 'forwards!', no doubt an instruction for the person looking at the map. These entries outside the actual map are predominantly in Anglo-Norman, whereas the entries on the map itself are made in Latin.

The double circular frame of the map itself is divided on the outside into the four points of the compass, and on the inside into the four main wind directions. The outer edge of the whole vellum bears both an ornamental and an inscribed border.

The world map is easted, that is, east is at the top, and corresponds roughly to the most widespread structure of medieval world maps, the T written within an O (thus, also known as T–O maps). The cross-bar of this T divides Asia (the eastern half of the inhabited earth at the top) from Africa (bottom right) and Europe (bottom left). The vertical bar of the T represents the Mediterranean, interspersed with several islands, whilst the left-hand half of the cross-bar symbolises the Don (in the Middle Ages called Tanais), the divider between Asia and Europe, and the right-hand half of the cross-bar the Nile, which separates Asia from Africa.

As on numerous other T–O maps the cartography of the Hereford map was to some extent influenced by the so-called hemisphere maps. These did not only aim to show the three continents of the northern hemisphere but rather the whole earth with its continents. Therefore it also depicts the equatorial ocean whose existence was assumed as well as the likewise supposed southern continent. On the Hereford map all that is left of the ocean and the southern ('Australian') continent is a narrow strip of water in the south of Africa and a strip of land further south still (along the right-hand edge of the map). This vaguely indicated southern continent is full of fabulous people and animals.

When the Hereford map is reduced in size, it appears to be grossly overladen

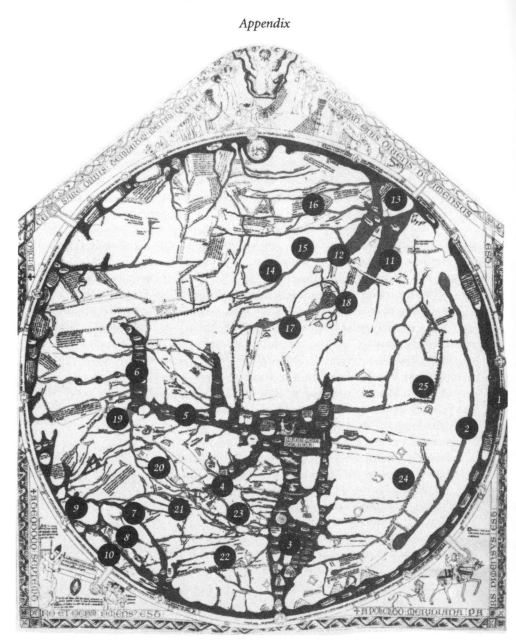

Map 2. Mappa mundi from Hereford Cathedral: islands, mountains and rivers.

with entries. Indeed there are about a thousand entries, at times extremely detailed, sometimes carefully illustrated. What follows is an attempt to help the reader to gain a better insight into the structure of the map through the layering of topographical, architectural, and ethno-zoological entries. It should be noted that only a small number of entries have been included by means of example. For a complete illustration of the map see Figure 16.

The ring of water (1) around the outside of the circular inhabited earth is the visible part of the hydrosphere on which the inhabited continents only take up a relatively small part (see above Figure 13).

To the right of the picture and extending parallel to the southern coast of Africa is a strip of water (2) which symbolises the assumed equatorial ocean which divides the northern from the southern hemisphere, and which makes the latter inaccessible for mankind. This form of illustration comes from the hemisphere maps.

From the centre of the map to the bottom (to the west) is the Mediterranean (3) with its numerous islands. It has bays to the north-west (bottom left), the Adriatic (4), to the north (left), the Aegean Sea (5), and as a continuation of the same, the Black Sea (6).

On the bottom left (north-west Europe) the English Channel (7) divides England (8), Scotland (as an island in its own right) (9) and Ireland (10) from the mainland. On the other hand Scandinavia is only marked by a number of completely arbitrary peninsulars and islands which defy any attempt to classify them realistically.

On the top right the finger-shaped bays (in the south-east), originally marked red, are the Red Sea (11) and the Persian Gulf (12) with the large legendary island of Taphana just off-shore. This is probably an inaccurate positioning of the island of Taprobana (Ceylon or Sumatra) (13). The Euphrates (14) flows into the end of the Persian Gulf, and further to the east so does the Tigris (15), not far after that the Indus (!) (16). North of the Red Sea towards the centre of the map the River Jordan (17) is shown together with the Sea of Galilee (18) with the two towns of Sodom and Gomorrah pictured within its waters. The lake is disproportionately large because of its great significance as an important site in the Holy Land.

Apart from the rivers already named, there are only a few which are particularly prominent on the map: the Danube (19) which flows into the Black Sea on the left of the map and numerous tributaries (among them the Salzach (20) with Salzburg) and the Rhine (21) which flows into the Channel on the bottom left.

The map includes numerous mountain ranges, recognisable from the rows of symbolic mountains, but few of them are easily recognisable on the reduced form of the map. Noteworthy, in particular, are the Pyrenees (22) (bottom of the map) which divide the Iberian peninsular from the rest of Europe. Somewhat above the Pyrenees and just about recognisable is the long semi-circular curve of the Alps (23). The two mountain ranges in Africa are more striking

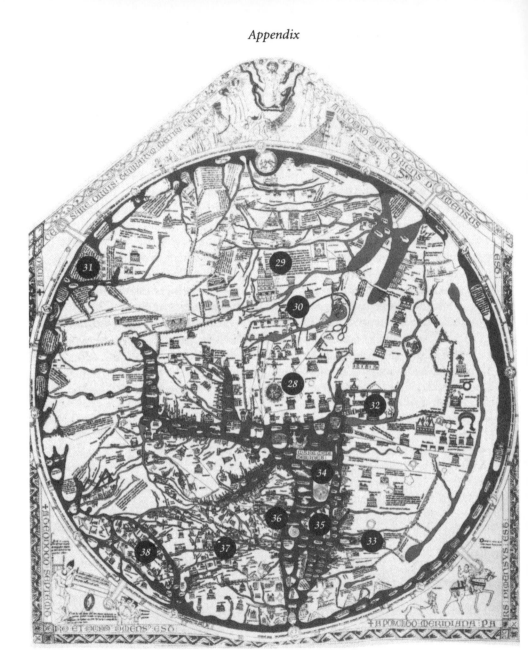

Map 3. *Mappa mundi from Hereford Cathedral: buildings and towns.*

with both running in an east-west direction, the lower (more western) the Atlas (24) whilst the mighty range above it, to the south of the Nile, is marked as 'very high Ethiopian mountains' (25).

In Asia the only distinct mountains are the Taurus (26) to the east of the Black Sea and the Armenian mountains (recognisable by the inclusion of Noah's Ark) whilst the numerous Near Eastern mountains known from the Old and the New Testaments are only depicted as relatively small.

As on almost all medieval world maps, Jerusalem lies at the centre of the map. It is depicted as being surrounded by a circular city wall (28, cf. also the city plan shown in Figure 20).

Not far above Jerusalem is the tower of Babel, shown as a magnificent structure (29), with the town of Damascus shown immediately below it (30). All of the more important sites in the Holy Land (over sixty are given) are at the centre of the map. Otherwise there are few towns to be found in Asia, which corresponds to the lack of knowledge about the continent, even though there are more than four hundred town names on the map, two hundred and twenty in Europe alone. Particularly striking is the wall (31) in the north-east of the earth (left) with which, according to legend, Alexander the Great immured the terrible races of Gog and Magog.[3] In the southern half of the world we can see Alexandria (32) with the lighthouse in the estuary of the Nile (Solinus 32, 43) and Hippo (33) on the African Mediterranean coast where St Augustine is shown in full episcopal regalia. It is, furthermore, interesting that on the African coast nearly all of the towns known from Classical times are included.

In the Mediterranean Crete (34) and Sicily (35) lie close to each other, whereby the former shows the labyrinth of the Minotaur (Virgil, *Aeneid* V, 588 and VI, 27; Isidore, *Etymologiae* XV, 2, 36) drawn in detail following the northern European tradition.[4] Immediately to the left Rome is illustrated as a large castle (36) and thus, after Paris (37) the largest town in Europe. This was by no means accurate (see above Chapter 5), but corresponds to its religious significance. On the British Isles and Ireland which, despite the distortion caused by the round edge of the map, are drawn more realistically than on other *mappae mundi*, there are over thirty town names, Hereford (38) being one of them.

A significant factor on the map are the many entries which deal with people and animals, including numerous fabulous ones (see Chapter 7). In Europe there are only a few such pictorial entries, including a skiing Norwegian in the far north, but also a bear (39) and a monkey (40) (who probably appears there by some misunderstanding).[5] To the east of the Pyrenees there is a buffalo (41) which the illustrator probably thought was typical for southern Europe. In the south-west there are the leopard (42), the legendary basilisk (43) and in Ethiopia the unicorn (44). In the south of Africa there are several fabulous peoples, such as the Troglodites who live in caves (45), but the majority of these fabulous races are found on the strip of land, suggesting the southern continent. In the west (bottom) the naked Gangines (46) can be seen, the four-eyed Maritimi, the

Map 4. Mappa mundi from Hereford Cathedral: animals and peoples.

headless Blemmyae, the Psilli (who test the legitimacy of their children by letting them play with snakes), Hermaphrodites, the mouthless, the one-legged and the ear-less races in the east, to the left of that, already in Asia, the horned Satyrs and the Amycterae (48) with their big lower lip. Besides fabulous peoples Asia contains numerous illustrations of animals, next to the Satyrs on an island in the Nile a crocodile ridden by a man (49), to the east of that on the island of Taphana two cute dragons (50), in eastern India an elephant with a fighting turrret on its back (51). Right in the north of Asia near to the peoples of Gog and Magog (52) there is a Crane-Head (53) who is leaning on a stick, next to him a pelican (54) ripping at its breast to feed its young with its blood, and next to that a two-humped camel (55). Further to the north there is first a (here somewhat displaced) Minotaur (56), then the griffons (57) against which the Pygmies (here seen with swords) are fighting. Immediately underneath these there are two Anthropophagi (cannibals), ripping human limbs apart and devouring them (58). In the extreme north of the earth two Cynocephales (dog-headed people) are sitting quite alone on a peninsula (59). The cartographer repeatedly states that he has gleaned the information about the animals from Solinus. He appears to have used the same source for the majority of his fabulous peoples.

NOTES

Notes to Preface

1   The word *world* can be used to denote both the earth as well as the entire universe in the wider sense of the word. In order to avoid any misunderstandings in this book it is usually used in its meaning of 'universe'.

2   A. J. Gurjewitsch, *Das Weltbild des mittelalterlichen Menschen*. 4th ed., Munich 1989; J. Huizinga, *Herbst des Mittelalters*. 11th ed., Stuttgart 1924; A. Borst, *Lebensformen im Mittelalter*, Frankfurt, Berlin and Vienna 1979.

3   Gurjewitsch, 72f.

4   C. Burnett (ed.), *Pseudo-Bede: De mundi celestis terrestrisque constitutione. A Treatise on the Universe and the Soul*. London 1985 (= Warburg Institute Surveys and Texts. 10), 18.

5   Even though the 'fabulous' or 'monstrous' peoples are dealt with in Chapter 7, this is not because they should be considered to be part of the everyday life of the medieval European, but because they are a standard element of the description of far-off countries.

6   A. Koperska, *Die Stellung der religiösen Orden zu den Profanwissenschaften im 12. und 13. Jahrhundert*. Freiburg (Switzerland) 1914.

Notes to Chapter One

1   G. Prause, *Niemand hat Kolumbus ausgelacht. Fälschungen und Legenden der Geschichte richtiggestellt*. Munich 1988, 49ff. Prause is even able to take his examples for this myth from current school textbooks.

2   S. de Madariaga, *Kolumbus*. Berne 1989, 189.

3   Only one other member of the commission is known by name, and that is the lawyer, Rodrigo Malonado (cf. G. Granzotto, *Christoph Kolumbus. Eine Biographie*. Reinbek 1988, 105).

4   If the commission had really spent any length of time at the court, it would have had to move with the court, as Ferdinand and Isabella were constantly travelling: Granzotto, *Christoph Kolumbus*, 105f and 109f.

5   One of the inventors of this myth is Columbus's famous 19th century biographer, Washington Irving: W. Irving, *The Life and Voyages of Christopher Columbus*. Author's revised edition. London 1876, 34–49.

6   See Irving.

7   Lactantius, *Divinae institutiones* III, 24 (S. Brandt (ed.), *L. Caeli Firmiani Lactanti opera omnia* I. Prague, Vienna and Leipzig 1840, 254ff).

8   C. Kretschmer, *Die physische Erdkunde im christlichen Mittelalter*. Vienna 1889, 55.

9   B. de Montfaucon, 'Cosmae Indicopleustae Topographia Christiana'. In *Collection Nova Patrum et Scriptorum Graecorum*. Vol. 2. Paris 1706; only Book 1 and extracts from Book 3 were printed before, namely in Paris in 1663; see W. Wolska-Conus,

Cosmas Indikopleustès. Topographie Chrétienne. Vol. 1–3, Paris 1968–1973: vol. 1, 44–123.

10   See below chapter 3; for the sphericity of the earth, see Ch. W. Jones, 'The Flat Earth'. *Thought* 9 (1934), 296–307; A.-D. v. d. Brincken, 'Die Kugelgestalt der Erde in der Kartographie des Mittelalters'. *Archiv für Kulturgeschichte* 58 (1976), 77–95; R. Simek, 'Die Kugelform der Erde im mittelhochdeutschen Schrifttum'. *Archiv für Kulturgeschichte* 70 (1988), 361–373; J. Tattersall, 'Sphere or Disc? Allusions to the shape of the earth in some 12th-century and 13th-century vernacular French works'. *Modern Language Review* 76 (1981), 31–46.

11   Granzotto, 106f; E. G. Jacob, *Christoph Columbus. Bordbuch, Briefe, Berichte, Dokumente.* Bremen 1957, 55, states that there was no such a thing as a commission in the modern sense, but only talks between Talavera and Columbus. This opinion was aired as early as 1892: J. G. Magnabal, *Christope Colomb et L'Université de Salamanque.* Paris 1892, 88: 'Toutes les opinions d'Irving sont un peu suspectes'. Madariaga, 194, on the other hand, believes in formal meetings.

12   A. A. Ruddock, 'Columbus and Iceland: New Light on an Old Problem'. *Geographical Journal* 136 (1970), 177–189.

13   A. Davies, 'Columbus and King John'. *Brasilia* 5 (1950), 696–697.

14   Cf. W. H. Babcock, *Legendary Islands of the Atlantic. A Study in medieval Geography.* New York 1922 (American Geographical Society, Research Studies 8); O. Dreyer-Eimbcke, Island, Grönland und das nördliche Eismeer im Bild der Kartographie seit dem 10. Jahrhundert. Hamburg and Wiesbaden 1987 (Mitteilungen der Geographischen Gesellschaft in Hamburg. 77), 19–27.

15   F. Salentiny, *Aufstieg und Fall des portugiesischen Imperiums.* Vienna, Cologne and Graz 1977, 40f and 50f.

16   Cf. Babcock, *Legendary Islands;* for literary references to Atlantis see G. Gadow, *Der Atlantis-Streit.* Frankfurt 1973; G. Lanczokowski, *Die Inseln der Seligen und verwandte Vorstellungen.* Frankfurt 1986, 31ff; A. Manguel and G. Guadalupi, *Von Atlantis bis Utopia.* Munich 1981, 36f. The island of Antilia or Antiglia, which was said to be eponymous for the Antilles, is first shown on a map in 1424, mentioned by Toscanelli (1474) and also appearing on the Beheim globe (1492). Cf. Jacob, *Christoph Columbus,* 40; O. Muris, 'Der "Erdapfel" des Martin Behaim'. *Ibero-Amerikanisches Arkiv* 17 (1943/44), 49–64: 64, and E. G. Ravenstein, *Martin Behaim. His Life and his Globe.* London 1908, 77.

17   According to Granzotto, *Christoph Columbus,* 107, who, however, rather distorts St Augustine's teachings.

18   A title which was bestowed on the Spanish Kings by the Pope after the fall of Cordoba.

19   Madariaga, *Kolumbus,* 193ff; Granzotto, *Christoph Columbus,* 106f; Jacob, *Christoph Columbus,* 55.

20   From Columbus's journal of his third voyage; translation in Jacob, *Christoph Columbus,* 253.

Notes to Chapter Two

1   E. Grant, 'Cosmology', in *Science in the Middle Ages*, ed. D. C. Lindberg. Chicago and London 1978, 265–302: 268.

2   Grössing, 'Weltmodelle im antiken Griechenland', in *Mensch und Kosmos*, ed. W. Seipel. Linz 1990, 63.

3   Oppenheim, *Das astronomische Weltbild im Wandel der Zeit.* Part I. Leipzig, Berlin 3rd ed., 1920, 59–65.

4   For the corrections of the epicycle theory cf. below p. 14ff.

5   Seven times bigger: Macrobius; 8 times: Honorius of Autun, Wilhelm of Conches; 160 times: Konrad of Megenberg; 170 times: Roger Bacon, Albertus Magnus; for comments on these data, see G.-K. Bauer, *Sternkunde und Sterndeutung der Deutschen im 9.–14. Jahrhundert unter Ausschluß der reinen Fachwissenschaft.* Berlin 1937, 34f.

6   Strunz, *Geschichte der Naturwissenschaften im Mittelalter.* Stuttgart 1910, 34.

7   Not of course including those unknown to him in the southern hemisphere.

8   Konrad of Megenberg, *Die deutsche Sphaera*, ed. by F. B. Brévart. Tübingen 1980, 16.

9   E. Grant, *Das physikalische Weltbild des Mittelalters.* Aus dem Amerikanischen übersetzt von Jan Prelog. Zurich and Munich 1980, 126.

10 F. Fellmann, *Scholastik und kosmologische Reform.* Münster 1971, 39–45.

11 For medieval world maps, see below p. 41ff.

12 The latter kind is found in the illustrations to John of Sacro Bosco's *Liber de sphaera*, in particular in the translation of this work into Middle High German made by Konrad von Megenberg (cf. also note 34 below).

13 The list of medieval natural scientific works with illustrations of the diagram of the universe is long, starting with Bede's *De natura rerum*, including Lambert's *Liber floridus* and John of Sacro Bosco's *Liber de sphaera*, William's *Philosophia mundi*, Daniel's *Liber de naturis inferiorum et superiorum* and the late medieval *Ymago mundi* by Pierre d'Ailly.

14 Hildegard von Bingen, *Liber Scivias* (Stuttgart, Württemberg. Landesbibliothek MS. Hist. 415 fol, f 16; cf. J. Zahlten, *Creatio mundi.* Stuttgart 1979, 84f and Ills. 274–276).

15 Thomas Aquinus, *Summa theologica*, Quaestio LXVIII, Art. 4: *utrum sit unum coelum tantum* ('whether there is only one heaven').

16 Honorius of Autun, *Elucidarius* (*Lib.* I, 3).

17 Namely the angels, archangels, seraphims, cherumbims, thrones, powers, dominations. This is how it is in Pseudo-Dionysios Areiopagites about 500 AD who was a great influence on the concept of heavenly hierarchies in the Middle Ages. This careful classification of the spiritual heaven into nine spheres is found in Lambert of St Omer's *Liber floridus* from around 1120: A.Derolez (ed.), *Lamberti S. Avdomari canonici Liber floridus.* Gent 1968, 452.

18 Hartmann Schedel, *Liber Chronicarum.* Nuremberg 1493, Vv.

19 Cf. A. Piltz, *Die gelehrte Welt des Mittelalters.* Cologne and Vienna 1982, 117.

20 Cf. Zahlten, *Creatio mundi*, Ills. 269–270, 281–290, in particular 283.

21 E. Grant, *Cosmology*, 271.

22 Grant 269f.

23 Figure 32 below.

24 Concerning Arabic and Chinese astronomy cf. the numerous articles by W. Hartner,

partly quoted in the footnotes to W. Hartner, 'The Rôle of Observation in Ancient and medieval Astronomy'. *Journal for the History of Astronomy* 8 (1977), 1–11.

25 C. M. Botley, 'The Position of Supernova 1006 and the St Gallen Chronicle'. *Journal for the History of Astronomy* 7 (1976), 139f; U. Dall'Olmo: 'Latin Terminology Relating to Aurorae, Comets, Meteors and Novae'. *Journal for the History of Astronomy* 10 (1979), 25f.

26 Konrad von Megenberg, *Buch von der Natur*, 78.

27 Simek, Rudolf, *Altnordische Kosmographie. Studien und Quellen zu Weltbild und Weltbeschreibung in Norwegen und Island vom 12. bis zum 14. Jahrhundert.* Berlin and New York 1990, 81–83; Honorius uses the image just as does Walter of Metz, who used Honorius as his source; a similar image, but with different argumentation, is to be found in Alexander Neckham, *De naturis rerum* I, 9.

28 The last two examples are taken from G.-K. Bauer, *Sternkunde und Sterndeutung der Deutschen im 9.–14. Jahrhundert unter Ausschluß der reinen Fachwissenschaft.* Berlin 1937, 27.

29 Augsburg 1490; cf. Piltz, *Die gelehrte Welt des Mittelalters,* 116f.

30 Cf. Grant, *Das physikalische Weltbild des Mittelalters,* 21.

31 K. Sudhoff, 'Daniels von Morley Liber de naturis inferiorum et superiorum, nach der Handschrift Cod. Arundel 377 des Britischen Museums zum Abdruck gebracht'. *Archiv für die Geschichte der Naturwissenschaften und der Technik* 8 (1917), 1–40.

32 Namely London, The British Library, MS. Arundel 377 and Oxford, Corpus Christi College, MS. 95.

33 Cf. F. B. Brévart and Merso Folkerts, 'Johannes de Sacrobosco.' In *Die deutsche Literatur des Mittelalters. Verfasserlexikon.* 2nd ed., vol. 4, Berlin and New York 1983, cols. 731–736, 733; F. B. Brévart (ed.), *Das Puechlein von der Spera, Abbildung der gesamten Überlieferung, kritische Edition, Glossar.* Göppingen 1979 (Litterae. 68), 9f.

34 About Konrad of Megenberg in general cf. H. Ibach, *Leben und Schriften des Konrad von Megenberg.* Würzburg 1938; G. Hetzelein, *Konrad von Megenberg, der erste deutsche Naturhistoriker.* Nürnberg 1973; concerning his *Deutsche Sphaera*: J.-P. Deschler, *Die astronomische Terminologie Konrads von Megenberg. Ein Beitrag zu mittelalterlichen Fachprosa.* Berne and Frankfurt/M. 1977; F. B. Brévart, 'Zur Überlieferungsgeschichte der "Deutschen Sphaera" Konrads von Megenberg'. *Beiträge zur Geschichte der deutschen Sprache und Literatur* 102 (1980), 189–214; G. Steer, 'Konrad von Megenberg'. *Die Deutsche Literatur des Mittelalters. Verfasserlexikon.* 2nd ed., vol. 5, Berlin and New York 1985, 221–236. – The text of his *Deutsche Sphaera* has been edited twice: O. Matthaei (ed.): *Konrads von Megenberg Deutsche Sphaera aus der Münchener Handschrift.* Berlin 1912 (Deutsche Texte des Mittelalters 23); F. B. Brévart, *Konrad von Megenberg: Die Deutsche Sphaera.* Tübingen 1980 (Altdeutsche Textbibliothek 90).– For Konrad's other book on nature in the vernacular, the *Buch von den naturleichen Dingen,* see below Chapter 8.

35 Cf. Simek, 'Übersetzung kosmographischer Begriffe in altnordischen enzyklopädischen und geographischen Texten'. *Nordeuropa. Studien* 23 (1988), 96–103, 58; F. B. Brévart (ed.), *Das puechlein von der Spera, Abbildung der gesamten Überlieferung, kritische Edition, Glossar.* Göppingen 1979 (Litterae. 68); F. B. Brévart, 'Eine neue Übersetzung der lat. "Sphaera mundi" des Johannes von Sacrobosco'. *Zeitschrift für deutsches Altertum* 108 (1979), 57–65.

36 R. Simek, 'Die mittelhochdeutschen Übertragungen von Johannes von Sacroboscos *Liber de sphaera*. Zur Funktion der astronomischen Abbildungen in den Handschriften und Frühdrucken'. *Codices manuscripti* 13 (1987), 57–76, 58; F. Brévart (ed.), *Konrad Heinfogel: Sphaera materialis. Text und Kommentar.* Göppingen 1981, V–VIII.

37 Only a dozen manuscripts and three printed editions between 1508 and 1531; cf. L. Baur (ed.), *Die philosophischen Werke des Robert Grosseteste, Bischofs von Lincoln.* Münster 1912, 10.

38 Baur, 10–32; cf. Baur, 60*–64*; L. Thorndike, *A History of Magic and Experimental Science.* New York 1923, II, 629; L. Thorndike, *The* Sphere *of Sacrobosco and Its Commentators.* Chicago 1949, 24f; S. P. Marrone, 'Grosseteste, Robert', in *Dictionary of the Middle Ages* 6, New York 1985, 1f; R. W. Southern, *Robert Grosseteste. The Growth of an English Mind in medieval Europe.* Oxford 1986, 142–146.

39 Cf. Thorndike, *The* Sphere *of Sacrobosco*, 26–28.

40 Likewise in the works of Robertus Anglicus; cf. Thorndike, *The* Sphere *of Sacrobosco*, 194.

41 Cf. C. Kren, 'Astronomy', in *The Seven Liberal Arts in the Middle Ages*, ed. D. L. Wagner. Bloomington, Ind. 1983, 219–225.

42 H. Grössing, 'Weltmodelle im antiken Griechenland', 63f.

43 Cf. Oppenheim, *Das astronomische Weltbild*, 59ff; Grant, *Cosmology*, 280–284.

44 Cf. Kren, 223f.

45 Grössing, 66.

46 O. Pedersen, 'Astronomy', in *Science in the Middle Ages*, ed. David C. Lindberg. Chicago and London 1978, 303–337, 307.

47 H. R. Plant, M. Rowlands and R. Burkhart, *Die sogenannte "Mainauer Naturlehre" der Basler Hs. B VIII 27.* Göppingen 1972 (Litterae. 18).

48 Plant, 17.

49 Cf. Baur, *Die philosophischen Werke des Robert Grosseteste*, 11; similar in John of Sacrobosco and his commentators; cf. Thorndyke, *The* Sphere *of Sacrobosco*, 12.

50 For the numerous passages on the egg shape of the earth in Classical and medieval times cf. V. Stegemann, *Aus einem mittelalterlichen deutschen astronomisch-astrologischen Lehrbüchlein. Eine Untersuchung über Entstehung, Herkunft und Nachwirkung eines Kapitels über Planetenkinder.* Reichenberg 1944 (Prager deutsche Studien. 52); F. Lukas, 'Das Ei als kosmogonische Vorstellung'. *Zeitschrift des Vereins für Volkskunde* (Berlin) 4 (1894), 227–243; H. Liebeschütz, *Das allegorische Weltbild der heiligen Hildegard von Bingen.* Leipzig and Berlin 1930, reprint 1964 (Studien der Bibliothek Warburg. 16); P. Dronke, *Fabula. Explorations in the uses of myth in medieval Platonism.* Leiden and Cologne 1974; R. Simek, 'Die Kugelform der Erde im mittelhochdeutschen Schrifttum'. *Archiv für Kulturgeschichte* 70 (1988), 361–373.

51 More in Empedokles, as well as in Achilles' commentary on Aratus (Tatius Astronomus Achilles, *Introductio in Aratum* 4; c. AD 300) and in Damascus (5th/6th century).

52 According to Cassiodor (*Institutiones* II, 7,4); 1st half of the 6th century; cf. W. H. Stahl, R. Johnson and E. L. Burge, *Martianus Capella and the Seven Liberal Arts.* New York 1977, II, 26.

53 Martianus Capella at the beginning of the 5th century (*De nuptiis Philologiae et Mercurii* Lib. I, 68, ed. F. Eyssenhardt, Leipzig 1866, 20); Macrobius (4th century

AD) mentions the comparison in his little known *Saturnalia* (quoted by Dronke, 83).

54 *Per ovum totam caelestem sphaeram significat: per crocineum splendorem superum, per umorem albidum splendidatem aetheris et aeris significat, per solididatem interius terram significat* (whereby here the earth is identified with the yolk); the otherwise unedited passage is quoted after Dronke, 156.

55 et per hanc ovi speciem totus mundus significatur (C. E. Lutz (ed.), *Remigius of Auxerre: Commentum in Martianum Capellam*. Leiden 1962–1965, I, 177; cf. Dronke, 82.

56 PL 178, cols. 735f.

57 *Commentum in Macrobium* (printed in Dronke, 158).

58 Quoted after Zahlten, *Creatio mundi*, 149, note 160.

59 William of Conches and Honorius of Autun were, of course, the most important sources of this cosmic comparison: Through Honorius' *Imago mundi* the egg/cosmos comparison found its way into vernacular medieval literature. Vernacular adaptions of Honorius such as the French *Image du monde* by Walter of Metz (cf F. Fritsche, *Untersuchungen ueber die Quellen der Image du Monde des Walther von Metz*. Halle/S. 1880, 18f) use the comparison just as do a whole list of cosmographical passages in German speaking religious and astronomy works, whereby Honorius' comparison of the earth as the drop of fat in the yolk is almost always changed to become the comparison of the earth with the yolk itself.

60 F. Pfeiffer (ed.), *Berthold von Regensburg. Vollständige Ausgabe seiner Predigten*. Vienna 1862, I, 392.

61 Cf. dazu Y. Lefévre, *L'Elucidarium et les Lucidaires*. Paris 1954; K. Schorbach, *Studien über das deutsche Volksbuch Lucidarius*. Strasburg 1894; G. Glogner, *Der mittelhochdeutsche Lucidarius, eine mittelalterliche Summe*. Münster 1937.

62 H. Jellinghaus (ed.), *Das Buch Sidrach. Nach der Kopenhagener mittelniederdeutschen Handschrift v. J. 1479*. Tübingen 1904 (Bibliothek des Litterarischen Vereins in Stuttgart. 235), 110.

63 Cf. Bauer, *Sternkunde und Sterndeutung*, 15.

64 F. Heidlauf (ed.) *Lucidarius aus der Berliner Handschrift herausgegeben*. Berlin 1915 (Deutsche Texte des Mittelalters. 28), 8.

65 F. Pfeiffer (ed.), *Konrad von Megenberg, Das Buch der Natur*. Stuttgart 1861, reprint Hildesheim 1962, 78f.

66 PL 111, col. 262.

67 Grant, *Das physikalische Weltbild*, 69f.

68 Piltz, *Die gelehrte Welt des Mittelalters*, 117.

Notes to Chapter Three

1 Prause, *Niemand hat Kolumbus ausgelacht*, 50ff.

2 A. Norlind, *Das Problem des gegenseitigen Verhältnisses von Land und Wasser und seine Behandlung im Mittelalter*. Lund and Leipzig 1918 (Lunds Universitets Årsskrift. 14/1. Heft 12), 43.

3 G. Hamann, *Der Eintritt der südlichen Hemisphäre in die europäische Geschichte. Die*

Erschließung des Afrikaweges nach Asien vom Zeitalter Heinrichs des Seefahrers bis zu Vasco da Gama. Vienna 1968, 24–28.

4   The Portugese sailed round Cabo de Não in 1416; Cape Bojador, 70 nautical miles further south, under Gil Eanea in 1434; Cabo Blanco (300 miles further south) under Nuno Trisão in 1441; Cape Verde, the western point of Africa, (another 300 miles) under Dinis Dias in 1444. In 1461 Pedro de Sinta reached Cabo Mesurado, 500 sea miles still further south, near today's Monrovia. In 1470 a private expedition led by Fernão Gomes went a further 1000 nautical miles to Cape Three Points. Not far from here in 1482 King Juan II. had Fort São Jorge de Mina on the Gold Coast built which was to be extremely important in the future. In 1482 Diego Cão sailed up the river Congo and on his second expedition in 1485 possibly got as far as Walvis Bay. In 1488 Bartolomew Diaz finally rounded the southern tip of Africa; cf. Hamann, 49–350, and Salentiny, 37–64.

5   Hamann, 139–147, and Salentiny, 57ff.

6   C. M. Radding, *A World Made by Men. Cognition and Society, 400–1200.* Chapel Hill and London 1985, 70–73.

7   For example, J. G. Leithäuser, *Mappae mundi, die geistige Eroberung der Welt.* Berlin 1958.

8   See above, note 86.

9   F. Heidlauf, *Lucidarius,* 8.

10   H. Jellinghaus, *Das Buch Sidrach,* 111.

11   Cf. J. R. Shackelford, 'The Apple/candle illustration in "The King's Mirror" and the "South English Legendary" '. *Maal og Minne* 1984, 72–84, and Simek, *Altnordische Kosmographie,* 131–133.

12   Also P. E. Schramm, *Sphaira. Globus. Reichsapfel.* Stuttgart 1958.

13   O. Muris, 'Der "Erdapfel" des Martin Behaim'. *Ibero-Amerikanisches Archiv* 17 (1943/44), 49–64; Maury, Mytton, 'On Martin Behaim's Globe, and his Influence upon Geographical Science'. *Journal of the American Geographical Society of New York* 4 (1874), 432–452; E. G. Ravenstein, *Martin Behaim. His Life and his Globe.* London 1908; J. Löwenberg, *Geschichte der Geographischen Entdeckungsreisen.* Leipzig 1880, 447–458, with a coloured reproduction of the earth-apple.

14   Cf. L. Zögner, 'Martin Behaim und das vorkolumbianische Weltbild', in *Die Welt in Händen. Globus und Karte als Modell von Erde und Raum,* ed. L. Zögner. Berlin 1989, 43–50, 44.

15   M. Behland (ed.), *Die Dreikönigslegende des Johannes von Hildesheim.* Munich 1968, 194.

16   Quaestiones naturales IV, 11.

17   Naturalis Historia II, 70.

18   See Chapter 2, note 85.

19   *Naturalis historia* II, 164 and 178.

20   Plant, *Mainauer Naturlehre,* 17.

21   H. Stadler (ed.), *Albertus Magnus. De animalibus libri XXVI. Nach der Kölner Urschrift.* Münster 1916–20, book II.4.9–11.

22   Grant, *Das physikalische Weltbild,* 110.

23   A. Ruppel, *Die Erfindung der Buchdruckerkunst und die Entdeckung Amerikas.* Mainz 1948, 9.

24   See more about this in Chapter 4.

25   A. A. Ruddock, 177–189.

26 Even today it is still not clear whether John (or Jean de) Mandeville was a fugitive English nobleman or a barber-surgeon from Liége or even a third person. Literature dealing with his identity includes in particular M. Letts, *Sir John Mandeville. The Man and his Book*. London 1949; J. W. Bennett, *The Rediscovery of Sir John Mandeville*. New York 1954; for more recent scholarly literature, cf. E. Bremer, 'Mandeville, Jean de'. In *Die deutsche Literatur des Mittelalters. Verfasserlexikon*. 2nd ed., Berlin, New York 1985, v, cols. 1201–1214; C. K. Zacher, 'Mandeville's Travels'. In *Dictionary of the Middle Ages*. New York 1987, viii, 81f; M. B. Campbell, *The Witness and the Other World. Exotic European Travel Writing 400–1600*. Ithaca, London 1988, 122–161; and especially C. Deluz, *Le Livre de Jehan de Mandeville. Une 'Geographie' au XIVᵉ siècle*. Louvaine-la-Neuve 1988, which must be considered the standard work on Mandeville, and where the biographical problems are dealt with in chapter 1, 3–24.

27 See Chapter 5.

28 More about Marco Polo likewise in chapter 5.

29 H. v. Tscharner (ed.), *Der mittelhochdeutsche Marco Polo nach der Admonter Handschrift*. Berlin 1935, 50; Latin *in alto mare* 'on the high seas' could be translated as *in der tiefen des mêres*, but even this formulation presupposed the sphericity of the hydrosphere.

30 For the MHG text see E. J. Morrall (ed.), *Sir John Mandevilles Reisebeschreibung in deutscher Übersetzung von Michel Velser*. Berlin 1974, 36; for the ME text see P. Hamelius (ed.), *Mandeville's Travels. Translated from the French of Jean d'Outremeuse*. London etc. 1919, reprint 1960, 204.

31 I have recently argued the case touched upon in this section in greater detail in my paper: 'Die Form der Erde im Mittelalter und die Erfinder der Scheibengestalt', to be published soon in the conference papers of the Bayreuth conference 1995 of the Deutscher Mediävistenverband.

32 See Chapter 4.

Notes to Chapter Four

1 Salentiny, 72ff; Hamann, 345–347.

2 G. J. Marcus, *The Conquest of the North Atlantic*. Woodbridge 1980, 168f.

3 For these journeys and the French initiatives in America see F. Gewecke, *Wie die neue Welt in die alte kam*. Stuttgart 1986, 17 and 20–39.

4 Among these were the Greek historian Herodotus, who travelled to Egypt and Mesopotamia in the 5th century BC, Ktesias and somewhat later (in the 4th century BC) Megasthenes, whose works on their respective journeys to India are only preserved in extracts.

5 Apart from Egypt, especially the kingdom of Sheba in today's Yemen.

6 A certain Himilco is supposed to have reached the British Isles in the 5th century BC (Pliny, *Naturalis Historia* II, 169), and Pytheas sailed along the west coast of Europe as far as Scandinavia before 300 BC; his contemporaries, however, rejected his report as fabulous, but what is still extant of his writings through excerpts in Pliny (II, 187, and IV, 102) is generally correct.

7   Especially in the writings of St Augustine, who thus provided the Middle Ages with
    their line of thought (*De civitate Dei*, XVI, 9).

8   The list of goods transported by an Arabian caravan in 1411 includes pepper, ginger,
    nutmeg, cloves, cinammon, incense and brazil wood as the most important bur-
    dens cf. E. Ashtor, 'Europäischer Handel im spätmittelalterlichen Palästina'. In *Das
    Heilige Land im Mittelalter. Begegnungsraum zwischen Orient und Okzident.* ed.
    Wolfdietrich Fischer and Jürgen Scheider. Neustadt a. d. Aisch 1982, 107–126, 125;
    brazil wood was mainly used as a colouring agent.

9   See Chapter 5.

10 See Chapter 7.

11 See F. Kirnbauer and K. L. Schubert, *Die Sage vom Magnetberg.* Vienna 1957, and
    in much greater detail, C. Lecouteux, 'Die Sage vom Magnetberg', *Fabula* 25 (1984),
    35–65. The legend of the magnetic mountain occurs in the Alexander material, but
    is only occasionally referred to in encyclopedic literature and is missing in Solinus,
    Isidore and Honorius. The legend, which was first told in Europe by Ptolemy,
    reappears in the big encyclopedias of the 13th century (Vincent of Beauvais,
    Bartholomew Anglicus).

12 A literary history of medieval cosmographies remains yet to be written, cf. Simek,
    Altnordische Kosmographie, 150–154.

13 Such large maps were rare even in the Middle Ages. Nowadays only the Hereford
    map is still preserved intact. The Epstorf map perished in the Allied bombing of
    Hanover in 1943. There is only a fragment of the Cornish map still in existence. See
    the Appendix for more details.

14 For the following chapter on *mappae mundi* I have mainly used: R. Simek, 'Mappae
    mundi'. *Archiv der Geschichte der Naturwissenschaften* 22/23/24 (1988), 1061–1091;
    R. Simek, *Altnordische Kosmographie*, 31–74; D. Woodward, 'Medieval *Mappae-
    mundi*', in J. B. Harley and D. Woodward. *The History of Cartography.* Chicago and
    London 1987, I, 286–370.

15 M. de La Roncière and M. Mollat du Jourdin, *Portulane. Seekarten vom 13. bis zum
    17. Jahrhundert.* Munich 1984. There is only a single, privately owned copy of a
    Portulan chart of the North Sea and the Baltic known to date.

16 G. H. T. Kimble, *Geography in the Middle Ages.* London 1938, 182.

17 H. Kugler, 'Die Ebstorfer Weltkarte. Ein europäisches Weltbild im deutschen Mit-
    telalter'. *Zeitschrift für deutsches Altertum* 116 (1987), 1–29, 16.

18 *Septus est enim undique romphea flammea, id est muro igneo accinctus*: Isidore:
    Etymologiae XIV,3,2; and, *inadibilis hominibus, qui igneo muro usque ad coelum est
    cinctus*: Honorius of Autun, *De imagine mundi* I, 9.

19 V. H. de P. Cassidy, 'The Voyage of an Island'. *Speculum* 38 (1963), 595–602.

20 K. Miller, *Mappaemundi. Die ältesten Weltkarten.* Vol. 4, *Die Herfordkarte.* Stuttgart
    1896, 36f, and vol. 5, *Die Ebstorfkarte*, Stuttgart 1896, 52.

21 See Chapter 6.

22 Miller, iv, 27; Miller, v, 35.

23 Genesis 10,2; Ezekiel 38,1 to 39,29.

24 Hugo of St Victor: *loca in quibus res geste sunt* (quoted by A.-D. v. d. Brincken,
    '*Mappa mundi* und Chronographia: Studien zur *imago mundi* des abendländischen
    Mittelalters'. *Deutsches Archiv für Erforschung des Mittelalters* 24 (1968), 118–86,
    124 and A.-D. v.d.Brincken, ' "...ut describeretur universus orbis." Zur Universal-
    kartographie des Mittelalters'. *Miscellanea Mediaevalia* 7 (1970), 249–278, 255).

25 *Libya, id est Africa*: Isidore, *Etymologiae*, XIV,4,1.

26 Roger Bacon (see below) on the other hand did not describe western Europe at all, his reasoning being that it was unnecessary to describe things that are so close.

27 A Franconian verse cosmography from the 7th century which otherwise gives many names lists only Scithia, Alania, Dacia and Gotia (K. Strecker, *Der rythmus De Asia et de universi mundi rota*. Berlin 1909, 17); the MHG *Christherrechronik* (mainly based on Honorius) at least ennumerates Tenemarke, Sweden, and Norwêgen, as well es the islands Orchadês and Chilê (should read Thile = Thule): I. Zingerle (ed.), 'Eine Geographie aus dem dreizehnten Jahrhundert'. *Sitzungsberichte der Phil.-hist. Cl. der österr. Akademie der Wiss*. 50, 4 (1865), 371–448.

28 Miller, iv, 16–18; v, 24f.

29 Simek, *Altnordische Kosmographie*, 428–456.

30 Simek, *Altnordische Kosmographie*, 428–456, and Simek, 'Elusive Elysia, or: Which Way to Glæsisvellir?' In *Sagnaskemmtun. Studies Hermann Pálsson*, ed., R. Simek. Vienna 1986, 247–275.

31 Hamann, 93–103.

32 Prause, 63; Jacob, *Christoph Columbus*, 33f; S. E. Morison, *Admiral of the Ocean Sea. A Life of Christopher Columbus*. 6th ed., Boston 1954, 24f; Ruddock, 177–189.

33 Ruddock, 181–188.

34 IV *Esdras* 6,42.

35 O. F. Fritzsche, *Liber Apocryphi veteris testamenti graece*. Leipzig 1871, 603.

36 E. Wisotzki, *Die Vertheilung von Wasser und Land an der Erdoberfläche*. Königsberg 1879, 7f; A. Norlind, *Das Problem des gegenseitigen Verhältnisses von Land und Wasser und seine Behandlung im Mittelalter*. Lund, Leipzig 1918, 33; E. Grant, *A Source Book in medieval Science*. Cambridge, Mass. 1974, 630; Simek, *Altnordische Kosmographie*, 195; A. D. v.d. Brincken, 'Die Kugelgestalt der Erde in der Kartographie des Mittelalters'. *Archiv für Kulturgeschichte* 58 (1976) 77–95.

37 L. Salembier, *Petrus ab Alliaco*. Lille 1886; P. Tschackert, *Peter von Ailly*. Gotha 1877; L. Thorndike, *A History of Magic and Experimental Science*. New York 1934, iv, 101–113; E. Buron (ed.), *Ymago mundi de Pierre d'Ailly. Texte latin et traduction française des quatre traités cosmographiques de d'Ailly et des notes marginales de Christophe Colomb*. Paris 1930, I, 37–113.

38 *Ymago mundi*, Chapter VIII (Buron, I, 206–215).

39 This printed version with Columbus's annotations is now in Seville; cf. Grant, Source Book, 630.

40 Wisotzki, 7f; Norlind, 23.

41 For example Notker in his translation of Boethius (P. W. Tax (ed.), *Notker der Deutsche: Boethius, 'De consolatione Philosophiae'. Buch I/II*. Tübingen 1986, 96.

42 Isidore, *Etymologiae* XIV,5,17.

43 Clearly visible already on the maps of Beatus of Liebana, 9th century: Miller, *Die Weltkarte des Beatus (776 n. Chr.)*, Stuttgart 1895, I, 31, 35, 39.

44 *Ymago mundi*, chapter 7 (Buron, I, 198–204).

45 *Genesis* X.

46 St Augustine, *De civitate Dei* XVI, 9.

47 Hamann, 98–103.

48 S. Günther, *Die Lehre von der Erdrundung und Erdbewegung im Mittelalter bei den Occidentalen*. Halle/S. 1877, 3.

49 C. Kretschmer, *Die physische Erdkunde im christlichen Mittelalter*. Vienna 1889, 55.

50 *De perversa enim et iniqua doctrina, quae contra Deum et animam suam locutus est – si clarificatum fuerit, ita eum confiteri, quod alius mundus et alii homines sub terra sint seu sol et luna – hunc habito concilio ab ecclesia pelle,sacerdotii honore privatum.* (PL 89, col 946f).

51 V. I. J. Flint, 'Monsters and the Antipodes in the Early Middle Ages and Enlightenment'. *Viator* 15 (1984), 65–80, 66.

52 W. Hartmann (ed.), *Manegold von Lautenbach: Liber contra Wolfelmum.* Köln 1972, 51.

53 Cf. A. Hüttig, *Macrobius im Mittelalter. Ein Beitrag zur Rezeptionsgeschichte der Commentarii in Somnium Scipionis.* Frankfurt, Berne, New York and Paris 1990.

54 O. Zöckler, *Geschichte der Beziehungen zwischen Theologie und Naturwissenschaft mit besonderer Rücksicht auf Schöpfungsgeschichte.* Gütersloh 1877, I 340; the minutes of the trial are printed in: I. v. Döllinger (ed.), *Dokumente vornehmlich zur Geschichte der Valdesier und Katharer.* Munich 1890, 585–597.

55 Strunz, 102.

56 *Nonne enim et antipodes sub pedibus nostris esse dicuntur. Sitamen philosophice loqui volueris, non magis sunt sub pedibusnostris quam nos sub pedibus eorum. Sed numquid de primisparentibus descenderunt antipodes? Secundum Augustinum, nonsunt antipodes, sed doctrinrär causa autfigmenti ita dicisolet.* (Alexandri Neckam *De naturis rerum libri duo.* ed. T. Wright. London 1863, 159f.)

57 Kretschmer, 58f.

58 Wilhelm of Conches, *De philosophia mundi* IV, 3 (PL 172, col. 85f).

59 *Lamberti S. Avdomari canonici Liber Floridus,* ed. A. Derolez. Gent 1968, 189.

Notes to Chapter Five

1 See Chapter 4.

2 Original version: L. F. Benedetto, *Marco Polo: Il Milione.* Florence 1928; English version: H. Yule (ed.), *The Book of Sir Marco Polo.* Third ed., rev. by H. Cordier. London 1903; MHG version: H. v. Tscharner (ed.), *Der mittelhochdeutsche Marco Polo nach der Admonter Handschrift.* Berlin 1935.

3 See E. Burman, *The World Before Columbus 1100–1492.* London 1989, 89.

4 See H. E. Rübesamen (transl.), *Die Reisen des Venezianers Marco Polo.* Munich 1969, 10f.

5 See note 26 in Chapter Four.

6 Karl May (1842–1912) was one of the most prolific German authors of the 19th century. He excelled in wild and romantic novels, usually set in the Near East, North Africa, China and particularly North America, although he only left his native Saxony, where he was repeatedly imprisoned for theft and fraud, for one journey to the Near East, Ceylon, Malaysia and Sumatra in 1899–1900. Karl May is still a household name to every schoolboy in German-speaking countries, and he has left an important legacy by perpetuating the picture of the noble North American Indian. Therefore, whilst in English-speaking countries, the cowboys are generally considered to be the heroes, in German-speaking countries the Indians enjoy this status, due to Karl May's virtually single-handed efforts.

7 Among his main sources were the *Legenda aurea* and various texts about Alexander

the Great, the works of Eugesippus, Bede, Orosius, the travel journals of William of Boldensele, Johann of Würzburg, Odoric of Pordenone and William of Tripolis, apart from the *Etymologiae* by Isidore of Seville, the encyclopedias *Speculum naturale* and *Speculum historiale* by Vincent of Beauvais, and the *Trésor* by Brunetto Latini as well as the *Otia imperialia* by Gervase of Tilbury, the *Book Sidrak* and the *Historia Hierosolimitana* by Jacques de Vitry. An extremely exact list of his sources can be found in Deluz, in the tables given in the appendix.

8   The number of manuscripts preserved of Mandeville's Travels is given by Deluz (371–382) as 233, of which fifty-six are in Latin, sixty-three in German, forty-seven in French, thirty-three in English, thirteen in Italian, ten in Dutch, seven in Czech, four in Danish and three in Old Welsh.

9   German versions appeared in Basle and Augsburg in 1481, Latin in Strasburg in 1484, Dutch in Gouda in 1475, English in London in 1499, French in Lyon in 1508, Spanish in Valencia in 1521, a number of Italian in Milan in 1480, Bologne in 1488, Venice in 1491, and Florence in 1492.

10   Campbell, *The Witness and the Other World*, 126.

11   See the last section of this Chapter.

12   From the *Legenda aurea*, cf. Deluz 58 and 430ff.

13   John of Sacrobosco, *Liber de sphaera*; cf. Deluz, 58.

14   N. Ohler, *Reisen im Mittelalter*. Munich 1986, 399f.

15   Burman, 66f; G. D. Painter, 'The Tartar Relation'. In R. A. Skelton, T. E. Marston and G. D. Painter, *The Vinland Map and the Tartar Relation*. New Haven and London 1965, 34f.

16   Painter, 34–39. The relevant edition is now: *Giovanni di Piano di Carpini: Storia dei Mongoli*. Edizione critica del testo latino a cura di E. Menestò, traduzione italiana a cura di M. C. Lungarotti, e note di P. Daffinà. Introduzione di L. Petech, studi storico-filologici di C. Leonardi, M. C. Lungarotti, E. Menestò. Spoleto 1989; cf. C. R. Beazley, *The Texts and Versions of John de Piano Carpini and William de Rubruquis*. London 1903; F. Risch (ed. and transl.), *Johann de Plano Carpini*. Leipzig 1930; C. Dawson, *The Mongol Missions*. London 1955.

17   A. van den Wyngaert, *Itinera et relationes fratrum minorum saeculi XIII et XIV.* Quaracchi and Florence 1929 (Sinica Franciscana. 1), 164–332, 290–297; Burman, 83–86.

18   Burman, 85.

19   Campbell, *The Witness and the Other World*, 112–121.

20   The MHG version, preserved in four manuscripts, has been edited by G. Strasman, *Konrad Steckels deutsche Übertragung der Reise nach China des Odorico von Pordenone*. Berlin 1968 (Texte des späten Mittelalters und der frühen Neuzeit. 20); the Latin text by H. Yule, *Cathay and the Way Thither*, London 1866, reprint 1913–16, appendix I, i–xliii; and by Wyngaert I, 413–495.

21   Wyngaert I, 453; cf. Burman, 54f.

22   Si essin vleysch allit tyr, sundir menschin vleysch essin si allir libist: H. v. Tscharner, *Der mittelhochdeutsche Marco Polo*. Berlin 1935, 55.

23   For these and other strange races of peoples see Chapter 7.

24   Honorius, *De imagine mundi*, I, 11; Thomas of Cantimpré, *Liber de natura rerum*, III, 5, 2; Gervasius of Tilbury, *Otia imperialia* II, 3; Tscharner, *Der mittelhochdeutsche Marco Polo*, 56.

25   Deluz, 475.

26 For some more or less serious concepts concerning the ends of the earth, see R. Kaiser, *Der Zaun am Ende der Welt.* Frankfurt 1989.

27 Kaiser, 26f.

28 *Und da von sprich ich daz er über erd und wasser gefaren waz also daz er die erden umb gegangen hett und waz wider kumen in sin land. Er wist sin aber nit und kert sich wider umb, und den weg den er waz kumen zogt er wider und verlor manig tagwaid. Da von sprich ich daz man wol mag umb und umb die welt faren.* (Morall, *Sir John Mandevilles Reisebeschreibung,* 36).

29 A. Zorzi, *Marco Polo.* Munich 1986, 194.

30 Tscharner, *Der mittelhochdeutsche Marco Polo,* 44–46.

31 Zorzi, 194.

32 Tscharner, *Der mittelhochdeutsche Marco Polo,* 50–54.

33 Zorzi, 243–247.

34 H. Gregor, *Das Indienbild des Abendlandes bis zum Ende des 13. Jahrhunderts.* Vienna 1964, 15f.

35 Gervase of Tilbury, *Otia imperialia* II, 3; Vinzenz of Beauvais, *Speculum historiale* XXXI, 10.

36 Miller: *Mappae mundi,* Stuttgart 1898, VI, 31f.

37 A. Cunningham, *The Ancient Geography of India.* New enlarged ed. Varanasi 1975, 1–8.

38 C. Bercovici, 'Prolegomenes a l'étude de l'Inde au XIIIème Siécle'. In *Voyage, quête, pèlerinage dans la littérature et la civilisation médiévale.* Aix-en-Provence, Paris 1976 (Sénefiance 2), 221–234.

39 Morall, *Sir John Mandevilles Reisebeschreibung,* 165–167.

40 Morall, 153.

41 Morall, 151.

42 V. Langmantel (ed.), *Hans Schiltbergers Reisebuch nach der Nürnberger Handschrift herausgegeben.* Tübingen 1885; other editions are based on early imprints rather than on manuscripts (F. Neumann, Munich 1859; E. Geck, Wiesbaden 1969); modern German translation by U. Schlemmer, *Johannes Schiltberger. Als Sklave im Osmannischen Reich und bei den Tartaren 1394–1427.* Stuttgart 1983.

43 For travellers to Palestine see Chapter 6 below.

44 Langmantel, 84–97.

45 Tscharner, 52.

46 Tscharner, 55.

47 Campbell, 87f.

48 For pilgrim guides, see Chapter 6 below.

49 Even if this respect of authority often happened unconsciously and a similarly sub-conscious reconciliation of rational experience and the authorities frequently has to be assumed. See R. L. Poole, *Illustrations of the History of medieval Thought and Learning.* 2nd ed., London 1920, 4; C. H. Haskins, *The Renaissance of the Twelfth Century.* Cambridge, Mass. 1927, reprinted New York 1957, Cambridge, Mass. 1971, 342ff.

50 Isidore, *Etymologiae* XIV, 5, 17; Honorius, *De imagine mundi* I, 6.

51 H. A. R. Gibb (ed.), *Ibn Battuta: Travels.* London 1971. Ibn Battúta, *Travels in Asia and Africa 1325–1354.* London 1983 (excerpts only). H. D. Leicht (ed.), *Ibn Battuta: Reisen ans Ende der Welt. Das größte Abenteuer des Mittelalters 1325–1353.* Darmstadt 1985; cf. Burman, 117–130.

52 Translation in T. Wright, *Early Travels in Palestine*. London 1848; cf. Burman, 43–47.

53 In the late Middle Ages this detour via the Sinai peninsular, the St Catherine monastery on Mount Sinai, Alexandria and Cairo was already considered to be the main route; cf. for example Hans Tucher and Sebald Rieter 1479, Paul Walther 1481, Felix Fabri 1483, Bernhard of Breydenbach 1483–1484 and Arnold of Harff 1496–1499.

54 The former concept is iconographically realised on the Ebstorf map, the latter in Lambert of St Omer's *Liber floridus*.

55 Identical with Old Cairo, actually P'i-Hapinon, a place near Cairo, nowadays called Deir-Babilun or Babiljun, whose name was confused with Babylon which ultimately led to this second Babylon.

56 As could be found in Livy and Sallust.

57 Isidore, *Etymologiae*, chapters IX and XII.

58 Animals are dealt with in Pliny, *Naturalis Historia*, in Books VIII–XI. In Solinus' *Collectanea rerum memorabilium* animals are spread out according to geographical distribution.

59 F. Lauchert, *Geschichte des Physiologus*. Straßburg 1889, reprint 1974; N. Henkel, *Studien zum Physiologus im Mittelalter*, Tübingen 1976; C. Schröder, 'Physiologus'. In *Die deutsche Literatur des Mittelalters. Verfasserlexikon*. 2nd ed., vol 7, Berlin and New York 1988, vii, cols. 620–634.

60 N. Henkel and C. Hünemörder, 'Bestiarium, -ius, Bestiarien'. In *Lexikon des Mittelalters*, Munich and Zurich 1980, I, cols. 2072–2074; B. Rowland, 'Bestiary'. In *Dictionary of the Middle Ages*, vol. 2, New York 1983, 203–207; W. B. Clark and M. T. McMunn (ed.): *Beasts and Birds of the Middle Ages. The Bestiary and its Legacy*. Philadelphia 1989.

61 Miller, *Mappae mundi*, V. *Die Ebstorfkarte*. Stuttgart 1896, 1–5 and 71; B. Hahn-Woerle, *Die Ebstorfer Weltkarte*. Ebstorf o.J.

62 Hahn-Woerle, 45.

63 Miller, *Mappae mundi*, IV, *Die Herefordkarte*. Stuttgart 1896, 37.

64 Isidore, *Etymologiae* XII, 2, 14f.

65 The dislike which elephants are supposed to have of mice (or actually against their smell) had been referred to by Pliny (*Naturalis Historia* VIII, 10,30) but not, however, in the medieval *Physiologus* literature (cf. Henkel, 177–9), although it reappears in modern folklore. For illustrations of elephants in the Middle Ages cf. G. C. Druce, 'The Elephant in medieval Legend and Art'. *Archaeological Journal* 76 (1919), 1–73; K. Lassacher, *Der Elefant in der mittelalterlichen Literatur*. Vienna 1988.

66 T. H. White, *The Book of Beasts*. Gloucester 1984, 14–51.

67 See White; H. Schöpf, *Fabeltiere*. Graz 1988; D. J. McMillan, 'The Phoenix', in M. South (ed.): *Mythical and Fabulous Creatures. A Source Book and Research Guide*. New York, Westport, Conn. and London 1987, 59–74; P. Lum, *Fabulous Beasts*. London 1952; B. Holbek, and Iørn Piø, *Fabeldyr og Sagnfolk*. Copenhagen 1967, 2nd ed., 1979.

68 See the more recent collections of articles on the relationship of medieval man to the animal world and to fabulous animals in particular: *L'uomo di fronte al mondo animale nell'alto medioevo*. 7–13 aprile 1983, 2 vols. Spoleto 1984; Harf-Lancner, L. (ed.), *Metamorphose et bestiaire fantastique au Moyen Age*. Paris 1985; *Le monde animal et ses Representations au Moyen-Age (XIe–XVe siècles)*. Toulouse 1985.

69 O. Brenner, *Nord- und Mitteleuropa in den Schriften der Alten bis zum Auftreten der Cimbern und Teutonen*. Munich 1877, 29–34. See Pliny, *Naturalis Historia* II, 187.

70 Brenner, 25f and 34–61.

71 Simek, *Altnordische Kosmographie*, 209f.

72 One reason for this detail is that both of the largest known medieval world maps come from Ebstorf in North Germany and Hereford in England.

73 A.-D. v. d. Brincken, 'Mappa mundi und Chronographia', 163.

74 Cassidy, 595; Dreyer-Eimbcke, 4.

75 For detail see G. Ehrismann, *Geschichte der deutschen Literatur*. Munich 1922, II,i, 231–234.

76 C. Hofmann, 'Über das Lebermeer'. *Sitzungsberichte der Königlich Bayerischen Akademie der Wissenschaften*, Phil.-hist. Cl. 2 (1865), 1–19, 4.

77 K. Weinhold, 'Die Polargegenden Europas nach den Vorstellungen des deutschen Mittelalters'. *Sitzungsberichte der phil.-hist. Cl. d. Kaiserl. Akademie der Wissenschaften Wien* 68 (1871), 783–808, 793f; Hofmann, 4; J. L. Lowes, 'The Dry Sea and the Carrenare'. *Modern Philology* 3 (1905), 1–46; M. Letts, Malcolm, 'The Liver Sea'. *Notes and Queries* 191 (1946), 47–49.

78 See Hofmann, 11, with older literature.

79 Dicuil, *Liber de mensura orbis terrae* VII, 11–15.

80 Isidore (*Etymologiae* XIV, 6, 4) calls it *pigrum et concretum*.

81 Adam of Bremen, *Gesta Hammaburgensis Ecclesiae Pontificum*, 4, 34, Scholion 150: *Magister Adam Bremensis: Gesta Hammaburgensis Ecclesiae Pontificum*. In *Quellen des 9. und 11. Jahrhunderts zur Geschichte der Hamburgischen Kirche und des Reiches*. Darmstadt 1973, 137–503, 482f; cf. Lowes, 44.

82 See Chapter 6.

83 See Chapter 4.

84 Martianus Capella, *De nuptiis Philologiae et Mercurii* VIII, 876ff.

85 Ad illud quod obicitur de auctoritate Alfragani et Ptholomei, qui ponunt primum clima incipere citra equinoctialem, dico quod ista ratio non cogit, tum quia ultimum clima, scilicet septimum, parum continet de Anglia, non duas dietas, tamen non sequitur quod Anglia non sit habitabilis, eo quod non diviserunt philosophi tunc temporis terras nisi habitabilis famosas, tum quia non erat terra habitata tunc temporis vel non venerat rumor apud nos. Et, ut breviter dicam, non diviserunt terram habitabilem solum sed inhabitatam publice et famose et ad quam erat accessus liber et recessus. (L. Thorndike, *The Sphere of Sacrobosco*, 192).

86 The first paragraph tends to vary quite drastically even within the Latin tradition. The version here is translated from F. Zarncke, 'Der Priester Johannes'. *Abhandlungen der philologisch-historischen Classe der königlich-sächsischen Gesellschaft der Wissenschaften* 7 (1879), 909.

87 See Chapter 7 below.

88 For the sandy sea, mentioned also by Mandeville and beforehand by Odorico (Wyngaert I, 419; Strasman, 47), see Lowes, 4–19, who identifies it with the Chinese desert of Lop Nor in Sinkiang.

89 Quare sublimitas nostra digniori quam presbiteratus nomine nuncupari se non permittat, non debet prudentia tua admirari. Plures enim in curia nostra ministeriales hebemus, qui digniori nomine et officio, quantum ad ecclesiasticam dignitatem spectat, et etiam maiori quam nos in divinis officiis praediti sunt. Dapifer enim noster primas est et rex, oicinera noster archiepiscopus et rex, camerarius

noster episcopus et rex, marescalcus noster rex et archimandrita, princeps co-
corum rex et et abbas. Et icirco altitudo nostra non est passa se nominari eisdem
nominibus aut ipsis ordinibus insigniri, quibus curia nostra plena esse videtur, et
ideo minori nomine et inferiori gradu propter humilitatem magis elegit nuncupari. (Zarncke, 923f).

90   E. D. Ross, *Prester John and the Empire of Ethiopia.* In *Travel and Travellers of the
Middle Ages,* ed. A. P.Newton. New York 1926, 3rd impression London 1968,
174–194; V. Slessarev, *Prester John: The Letter and the Legend.* Minneapolis 1959,
41–47.

91   L. Olschki, *Storia Letteraria della Scoperte Geografiche. Studi e Ricerche.* Firenze
1937, 209.

92   L. Olschki, 'Der Brief des Presbyters Johannes'. *Historische Zeitschrift* 144 (1931),
1–14; C. E. Nowell, 'The Historical Prester John'. *Speculum* 28 (1953), 437.

93   Slessarev, 5.

94   M. Gosman, *La Lettre du Prêtre Jean. Les versions en ancien français et en ancien
occitan. Textes et commentaires.* Groningen 1982, 50–117.

95   Zarncke, 877–908.

96   I.e, up to 1500. Slessarev, 64, talks of 14 early prints of the French version alone,
the earliest being from 1488.

97   Olschki, 'Der Brief', 10ff, who puts its success mainly down to the Utopian element
of the letter.

98   Johannes de Hese, *Itinerarium.* In G. Oppert, *Der Presbyter Johannes in Sage und
Geschichte.* Berlin 1864, 180–93; cf. Zarncke, 2nd part, 1883, 159–171.

99   M. Behland, *Die Dreikönigslegende des Johannes von Hildesheim.* München 1968;
cf. Zarncke, 154–159.

100 See Zarncke, 128–154.

101 Both Nowell, 435–445, and Gosmann, 23–31, discuss older research and reach the
same conclusions as Slessarev, 80–92, namely that only a combination of various
theories can explain the genesis of Prester John; nothing new about Prester John's
letter in K. Zatloukal, 'India – ein idealer Staat im "Jüngeren Titurel" '. *Strukturen
und Interpretationen.* Vienna 1974, 401–445, while K. Helleiner, 'Prester John's
Letter'. *The Phoenix* 13 (1959), 47–57, discusses the political dimensions of the
letter, especially its alleged anti-Byzantine stanze.

102 Reported in the anonymous *De adventu patriarchae Indorum ad Urbem sub Calixto
papa secundo* and in a letter by Abbot Odo of Rheims (1118–1151) about the same
visit; see Slessarev, 9–25. Other theories link them with Syrian Christians of
Malabar.

103 See Oppert; R. Hennig, 'Das Christentum im mittelalterlichen Asien und sein
Einfluss auf die Sage vom "Priester Johannes" '. *Historische Vierteljahrsschrift* 29
(1935), 234–252; referred to by Nowell, 436 and 439, and Gosman, 24f.

104 Once *Iohannes* [. . .] *rex et sacerdos,* shortly afterwards *Presbyter Iohannes;* cf.
Zarncke, 1st part, 1879, 848.

105 C. Marinescu, 'Le Prêtre Jean. Son Pays. Explication de son Nom'. *Bulletin de la
Section Historique de l'Academie Roumaine* 10 (1923), 73–112; mentioned by
Nowell, 437f, and Gosman, 24f.

106 For example, John of Mandeville (Morall, 144 and 145f), Marco Polo (Tscharner,
15f and 20); John of Plano Carpini (Giovanni di Pian di Carpini, *Storia dei
Mongoli,* 259); Wilhelm of Rubruk (Wyngaert, 240).

107   Sometimes his empire was considered to be on the upper reaches of the river
      Congo, sometimes on the East African coast in Mozambique: Salentiny, 59 and 71;
      Hamann, 66, 175f, 272f and 397.

Notes to Chapter Six

1   Madariaga, 207–209.
2   Madariaga, 207.
3   Irving, 53f.
4   A list of references from Flavius Josephus, Jerome and from Arkulf's pilgrim report
     (written down in the 7th century by the Scottish abbot Adamnan) besides passages
     from the High Middle Ages (Petrus venerabilis, Gervasius of Tilbury) is given by
     W. Müller, *Die heilige Stadt. Roma quadrata, himmlisches Jerusalem und die Mythe
     vom Weltnabel.* Stuttgart 1961, 53f; R. Konrad, 'Das himmlische und das irdische
     Jerusalem im mittelalterlichen Denken. Mystische Vorstellung und geschichtliche
     Wirklichkeit', in *Speculum Historiale. J. Spörl aus Anlaß seines 60. Geburtstages,* ed.
     C. Bauer, L. Boehm and M. Müller. Freiburg and Munich 1965, 523–540.
5   On most T–O maps (see J.-G. Arentzen, *Imago mundi cartographica.* Munich 1984,
     S. 217–220), even the big ones from Ebstorf and Hereford (see Miller, *Mappae
     mundi,* IV–V, Stuttgart 1896).
6   Isidore, *Etymologiae* XIV, 3, 21 (as in Vincent of Beauvais, *Speculum historiale* I, 67)
     calls Jerusalem the umbilicus of Judea, but not of the world.
7   See R. Röhricht and H. Meisner, 'Ein niederheinischer bericht über den orient'.
     Zeitschrift für deutsche Philologie 19 (1887), 8.
8   E.g. Adamnan (7th century: P. Geyer, *Itinera Hierosolymitana saeculi IV–VIII.*
     Prague, Vienna and Leipzig 1898 (CSEL 39), 219–297), who calls Jerusalem verba-
     tim *umbilicus mundi;* Venerable Bede, *De locis sanctis* (8th century: PL 94, cols.
     1179–1190); *Anonymus Mercati* (12th century: K. N. Ciggaar, *Byzance et L`An-
     gleterre.* Leiden 1976, 125f); Nikulás of Munkathverá (12th century, Icelandic:
     Simek, *Altnordische Kosmographie,* 264–280).
9   R. Simek, 'Hierusalem civitas famosissima. Die erhaltenen Fassungen des mittel-
     alterlichen *Situs Jerusalem* (mit Abbildungen zur gesamten handschriftlichen Über-
     lieferung)'. *Codices Manuscripti* 15 (1989), 1–40.
10   Breviarius de Hieroslyma, translated in H. Donner, *Pilgerfahrt ins Heilige Land. Die
     ältesten Berichte christlicher Palästinapilger (4.-7. Jahrhundert).* Stuttgart 1979,
     232–239.
11   Theoderich, Guide to the Holy Land. Translated by Aubrey Stewart. Second edition
     with new introduction, notes and bibliography by Ronald G. Musto. New York
     1986.
12   Burchard de Monte Sion: *Descriptio terrae sanctae,* ed. W. A. Neumann, 1880.
13   See C. Hippler, *Die Reise nach Jerusalem. Untersuchungen zu den Quellen, zum Inhalt
     und zur literarischen Struktur der Pilgerberichte des Spätmittelalters.* Frankfurt,
     Berne and New York 1987, 139f, without, however, naming any actual texts.
14   Treated in some detail by U. Ganz-Blättler, *Andacht und Abenteuer. Berichte
     europäischer Jerusalem- und Santiago-Pilger (1320-1520).* Tübingen 1990, 103–106.
15   H. Busse, 'Vom Felsendom zum Templum Domini', in *Das Heilige Land im*

Mittelalter. Begegnungsraum zwischen Orient und Okzident, ed. Wolfdietrich Fischer and Jürgen Scheider. Neustadt an der Aisch 1982, 19–32.

16   J. Hill, 'From Rome to Jerusalem: An Icelandic Itinerary of the Mid-Twelfth Century'. *Harvard Theological Review* 76 (1983), 175–203, 192.

17   Itinerarium Burdigalense, in Donner, 57.

18   Donner, 60f.

19   Donner, 199–218.

20   H. Kellenbenz, 'Die Südosteuroparoute der deutschen Kreuzfahrer', in *Das Heilige Land im Mittelalter. Begegnungsraum zwischen Orient und Okzident,* ed. W. Fischer and J. Scheider. Neustadt a. d. Aisch 1982, 95–106.

21   H.-J. Lepszy, 'Die Reiseberichte des Mittelalters und der Reformationszeit'. Diss. Hamburg 1952, 168.

22   See Hill, 195.

23   Eusebius, *Vita Constantini,* III, 42.

24   E. M. Jung-Inglessis, *Romfahrt durch zwei Jahrtausende.* Bozen 1978, 6.

25   For the numerous reasons to go on a pilgrimage in the Middle Ages see Ohler, 82–105. For pilgrimages in general see Lepszy, 16–23 and 110–181. For further literature see P. J. Brenner, *Der Reisebericht in der deutschen Literatur. Ein Forschungsüberblick als Vorstudie zu einer Gattungsgeschichte.* Tübingen 1990, 41–79.

26   See Donner, 36–68 (with German translation); Lepszy, 112.

27   English translation in Wright, *Early Travel in Palestine,* 1–12, and J. Wilkinson, *Jerusalem Pilgrims Before the Crusades.* Warminster 1977, 93–116; German translation in Donner, 332–421, with additional literatur, 331.

28   Lepszy, 113f; Wright, 13–22.

29   See J. v. Newald, 'Der Heilige Koloman'. *Die Kultur* 13 (1912), 281–292.

30   Burman, 24–41.

31   Wright, 31ff.

32   P. Riant, *Expéditions et pèlerinages des Scandinaves en Terre Sainte au temps des Croisades.* Paris 1865; B. Z. Kedar and Chr. Westergård-Nielsen, 'Icelanders in the Crusader Kingdom of Jerusalem: A Twelfth-Century Account'. *Mediaeval Scandinavia* 11 (1978/9), 193–211.

33   Riant, 303–338.

34   Simek, *Altnordische Kosmographie,* 478–490 (with German translation of the itinerary).

35   Burman, 43–47.

36   R. Röhricht and H. Meissner, *Deutsche Pilgerreisen nach dem Heiligen Land.* Berlin 1880, 4.

37   Cf. the list of pilgrims in Röhricht and Meissner, 463–546.

38   Lepszy, 119.

39   Simek, *Altnordische Kosmographie,* 490.

40   Hippler, 49f.

41   F. P. Magoun, 'The Rome of two Northern Pilgrims: Archbishop Sigeric of Canterbury and Abbot Nikolás of Munkathverá'. *Harvard Theological Review* 33 (1940), 277–289.

42   Mirabilia Urbis Romae. The Marvels of Rome, or a picture of the Golden City, an English Version of the Mediaeval Guidebook. ed. and Transl. F. M. Nichols. London 1889. 2nd edition, with new introduction, gazetteer and bibliography by E. Gardiner. New York 1986, 3–46.

43 For pilgrims to Rome and their description of the Eternal City, see J. Zettinger, *Die Berichte über Rompilger aus dem Frankenreiche bis zum Jahre 800*. Rom 1900; Müller, *Die heilige Stadt*; J. Jung, 'Das Itinerar des Erzbischofs Sigeric von Canterbury und die Strasse von Rom über Siena nach Luca'. *Mittheilungen des Instituts für Österreichische Geschichtsforschung* 25 (1904), 1–90; H. Jordan, *Topographie der Stadt Rom im Altertum*. Berlin 1871–1907; H. Bloch, 'Der Autor der "Graphia aureae urbis Romae' ". *Deutsches Archiv für Erforschung des Mittelalters* 40 (1984), 55–175.

44 G. Walser, *Die Einsiedler Inschriftensammlung und der Pilgerführer durch Rom (Codex Einsidlensis 326). Facsimile, Umschrift, Übersetzung und Kommentar.* Stuttgart 1987, 143–211; the *Mirabilia Urbis Romae* mentioned date to the middle of the 12th century.

45 K. Herbers, *Der Jakobsweg. Mit einem mittelalterlichen Pilgerführer unterwegs nach Santiago de Compostella*. Tübingen 1986; R. Plötz, 'Deutsche Pilger nach Santiago de Compostella bis zur Neuzeit'. In *Deutsche Jakobspilger und ihre Berichte*, ed. K. Herbers. Tübingen 1988, 1–27; Ganz-Blättler, 10.

46 See K. Herbers, *Der Jakobuskult des 12. Jahrhunderts und der* Liber Sancti Jacobi. Wiesbaden 1984; German precis of the *Liber Sti. Jacobi* in Ohler, 282–298.

47 The return home of the Icelander Björn Einarson (c. 1350–1415), who did not only reach Greenland, but also travelled three times to Rome and once each to Jerusalem, Santiago and Canterbury, was even mentioned in the Icelandic annal to the year 1406 (see Simek, *Altnordische Kosmographie*, 295f).

48 For Jerusalem as the centre of earth see the sources mentioned at the beginning of this chapter; cf. also Müller, *Die heilige Stadt*; Konrad, 'Das himmlische und das irdische Jerusalem im mittelalterlichen Denken', 523–540; F. Niehoff, Umbilicus mundi – Der Nabel der Welt. In *Ornamenta Ecclesiae. Kunst und Künstler der Romanik in Köln*. III, Cologne 1985, 53–72; Simek, 'Hierusalem civitas famosissima', 1ff.

49 Geyer, 219–297; in German translation in Donner, 353.

50 See Chapter 3.

Notes to Chapter Seven

1 See W. Neuber, *Fremde Welt im europäischen Horizont. Zur Topik der deutschen Amerika-Reiseberichte der Frühen Neuzeit*. Berlin 1991; E. Luchesi, 'Von den 'Wilden/Nacketen/Grimmigen Menschfresser Leuthen/in der Newen welt America gelegen'. Hans Staden und die Popularität der 'Kannibalen' im 16. Jahrhundert'. *Mythen der neuen Welt*, ed. K.-H. Kohl. Berlin 1982, 71–74.

2 W. Neuber, 'Imago und Pictura. Zur Topik des Sinn-Bilds im Spannungsfeld von Ars Memorativa und Emblematik (am Paradigma des 'Indianers')', in *Text und Bild, Bild und Text*, ed. W. Harms. Stuttgart 1990, 245–261.

3 Apart from Staden, for example: *Underweisung und uszulegen der Cartha Marina*. Straßburg 1530 (cf. H. Honour, 'Wissenschaft und Exotismus', in K.-H. Kohl, *Mythen der neuen Welt*. Berlin 1982, 22–47); Th. de Bry, *America* (part 3 and 4). Frankfurt 1593–1594 (cf. B. Bucher, 'Die Phantasien der Eroberer', in K.-H. Kohl, *Mythen der neuen Welt*. Berlin 1982, 75–91).

4 A very useful list of such letters and broadsheets relating to the discovery of America

from the 15th and 16th century can be found W. Neuber, *Fremde Welt*; as an example it may be sufficient to quote the title of the German edition (pre-1522) of the report on the first and third journey of Christopher Columbus: *Ein Schöne Newe zeytung so Kayserlich Mayestet auß India yetz nemlich zukommen seind. Gar hüpsch von den Newen ynseln, vnd von yrem sitten gar kurtzweylig züleesen.*

5   U. Bitterli, *Die Wilden und die Zivilisierten. Grundzüge einer Geistes- und Kulturgeschichte der europäisch-überseeischen Begegnung.* Paperback ed. Munich 1982, 91.

6   Isidore, *Etymologiae*, IX, 2, 129–132; Vincent of Beauvais, *Speculum historiale*, I, 68.

7   A. R. Anderson, *Alexander's Gate, Gog and Magog, and the inclosed Nations.* Cambridge, Mass. 1932; for the medieval German reception, see C. Lecouteux, *Les Monstres dans la litterature allemande du Moyen Age*, Göppingen 1982, I, 293f.

8   See M. Panoff and M. Perrin, *Taschenwörterbuch der Ethnologie.* 2nd ed. Berlin 1982, 155.

9   Solinus, *Collectanea rerum memorabilium* 32, 4 and 52, 22; Honorius of Autun, *De imagine mundi*, I, 11; Lambertus Audumarensis, *Liber floridus* 53r; Thomas Cantimpratenis, *Liber de natura rerum* III, 5, 2; Konrad of Megenberg, *Das Buch der Natur* (ed. Pfeiffer, 489).

10   Quoted from an Old Icelandic text on fabulous races: cf. Simek, *Altnordische Kosmographie*, 468.

11   Morall, 124.

12   Tscharner, 55f.

13   Tscharner, 52.

14   W. Neuber, "garriebat philomena". Die erste Columbus-Reise und ihre narrative Tradierung in Deutschland bis zum Jahr 1600', *Columbus zwischen zwei Welten. Historische und literarische Wertungen aus fünf Jahrhunderten.* Titus Heydenreich (ed.), Frankfurt/M. 1992, 125–142.

15   M. Fracan, *Newe unbekannthe Lande*, 1508; cf. Neuber, *Fremde Welt*; F. Kluge, *Deutsches Etymologisches Wörterbuch*, 22nd ed. Berlin and New York 1989, 352. A strangle anachronistic view of 'Kannibalismus und Fremdheit' may be found in F. Gewecke, *Wie die neue Welt in die alte kam.* Stuttgart 1986, 231–239.

16   Although he never went to India himself; the book, like all others by Ctesias, is lost, but was used in the Greek *Bibliotheka*, written by the theologian Photios in the 9th century, and we thus have some extracts form it; cf. J. B. Friedman, *The Monstrous Races in medieval Art and Thought.* Cambridge, Mass. and London 1981, 5, and R. Shafer, 'Unmasking Ktesias' Dog-headed People'. *Historia* 13 (1964), 491–503.

17   Friedman, 6.

18   H. Hosten, 'The Mouthless Indians of Megasthenes'. *Journal and Proceedings of the Asiatic Society of Bengal.* New Series 8 (1912), 291–301; a list of references is included in Lecouteux, vol. 2, 12f.

19   Friedman, 15.

20   R. Hennig, 'Der kulturhistorische Hintergrund der Geschichte vom Kampf zwischen Pygmäen und Kranichen'. *Rheinisches Museum für Philologie* N.S. 81 (1932), 20–24.

21   Friedman, 27.

22   The matter of Alexander was used in the 4th century by Julius Valerius (*Res gestae Alexandri Macedonis*). It was then popularised by a shortened version made in the 9th century ('Zacher Epitome'), and in the 10th century by the arch-presbyter Leo (*Nativitas et victoria Alexandri Magni*), in the Middle Ages it was mainly used in

the version called *Historia de preliis* (11th century); see G. Cary, *The medieval Alexander*, ed. D. J. A. Ross. Cambridge 1956, 9ff.

23 C. Marvin (ed.), *Galteri de Castellione: Alexandreis*. Padua 1978.

24 H. Buntz, *Die deutsche Alexanderdichtung des Mittelalters*. Stuttgart 1973.

25 Gen 10,2; Ez 38,1ff; Apoc 20,7.

26 Pliny the Younger, Epist. VI.16, and Friedman, 7.

27 See Chapter 3.

28 *C. Ivlii Solini Collectanea rervm memorabilivm*. Itervm recensvit Th. Mommsen. Berlin 1895.

29 The three manuscripts of the Latin/OE *Wonders of the East* are described by P. A. Gibb, *Wonders of the East: A Critical Edition and Commentary*. Duke Univ. 1977, 6–9 and 200–204 (continental parallels); for the Old Norse lists there is far richer manuscript material, see Simek, *Altnordische Kosmographie*, 229–249, and R. Simek, 'Wunder des Nordens. Einfoetingar, Hornfinnar, Hundingjar und Verwandte', in *triuwe. Studien zur Sprachgeschichte und Literaturwissenschaft. Gedächtnisbuch für Elfriede Stutz*, ed. K.-F. Kraft, E.-M. Lill and U. Schwab. Heidelberg 1992 (Heidelberger Bibliotheksschriften. 47), 69–90.

30 See R. Simek, 'Elusive Elysia, or: Which Way to Glæsisvellir?' In *Sagnaskemmtun. Studies Hermann Pálsson*, ed. R. Simek. Vienna 1986, 247–275.

31 Simek, 'Wunder des Nordens'.

32 See Isidore, *Etymologiae* IX, 2; Martianus Capella, *De nuptiis Philologiae et Mercurii* VI (ed. F. Eyssenhardt, 227ff).

33 Honorius of Autun, *De imago mundi* XI and XXXIII.

34 Hrabanus Maurus, *De universo* XII, 4.

35 Miller, *Mappae mundi*, IV, 45.

36 Miller, V, 59-62 and 74.

37 Harley, J. B. and David Woodward, *The History of Cartography*. I. *Cartography in Prehistoric, Ancient, and medieval Europe and in the Mediterranean*. Chicago and London 1987, plate 14.

38 Harley and Woodward, 350.

39 This Sciopode is still found on the copies from Paris (Bibl. Nat. Cod. lat. n. aqu. 1366) and from Burgo de Osma in Castilia (cf. Miller, I, 11f and V, plates 2 and 3.

40 See Chapter 3.

41 R. Wittkower, 'Marvels of the East, a study in the history of monsters', *Journal of the Warburg and Courtauld Institute* (1942), 159–197, 167f.

42 Isidore, *Etymologiae* IX, 2; similar to Hrabanus Maurus, *De universo* XVI, 2, who leaves out the actual teratological chapters from Isidore.

43 Martianvs Capella (ed. Eyssenhardt), 233; English translation in W. H. Stahl, R. Johnson and E. L. Burge, *Martianus Capella and the Seven Liberal Arts*, New York 1977, 2, 252. Very similar in Lambert von St Omer, who has compiled a chapter on fabulous races from various sources, of which only Martianus is explicitly quoted in the title of the section: *Marcianvs Felix Capella De Gentibvs Diversis Et Monstris* (A. Derolez, *Lamberti Liber floridus*, 101–3 = MS Ghent, UB 92, fol. 50r–51r).

44 Isidore, *Etymologiae*, XI, 3 (*De portentis*).

45 Konrad von Megenberg, *Buch der Natur*, ed. Pfeiffer, 486; cf. Lecouteux, *Les monstres*, I, 217ff; C. Lecouteux, 'Konrad von Megenberg: "Von den Wundermenschen" '. *Etudes germaniques* 37 (1982), 290–304, 297ff. Konrad's book on nature was very popular and there were six printed versions before 1500.

46 Gen. IV, 15; see Friedman, 31.

47 Augustine, *De civitate Dei* XIV, 8.

48 *De portentis. 1. Portenta esse ait Varro, quae contra naturam nata videntur; sed non sunt contra naturam, quia divina voluntate fiunt, cum voluntas Creatoris cujusque conditae rei natura sit. Unde et ipse gentiles Deum modo Naturam, modo Deum appellant. 2. Portentum ergo fit non contra naturam, sed contra quam est nota natura.* (Isidore, *Etymologiae* XI, 3).

49 Isidore's *portenta*, which included fabulous races as well as comets. Differently Nicolas Oresme: *quod sequitur est quod monstrum in una villa vel patria, si accidat, non significat ibi fore malum et cetera* (*De causis mirabilium* 3, 719f; B. Hansen (ed.), *Nicolas Oresme and the Marvels of Nature.* Toronto 1985, 246).

50 *De causis mirabilium* 3, 471ff: Hansen, 228.

51 *Exemplum et gratia exempli: dic quod in generatione hominis ista se sequuntur: primo est sperma, 2⁰ est ut fungus terre, 3⁰ ut animal quasi non figuratum ut narrat Aristoteles in 7 animalium quod est quoddam quod dubium est utrum sit planta vel animal et cetera, 4⁰ ut symeus, 5⁰ ut pigmeus, 6⁰ est homo perfectus et cetera.* (*De causis mirabilium* 3, 592ff: Hansen, 238).

52 See H. W. Janson, *Apes and Ape Lore.* London 1952, 88ff.

53 *Simia autem habens caput canis, vultus quidem similis est cani, sed totum residuum corpus maius est fortius quam canis: et haec sunt quae in Mappa mundi canini homines vocantur. Facies enim illarum symiarum similes sunt faciebus canum* (*De animalibus libri XXVI* 2.1.4: ed. Stadler, 247).

54 'Cynocephali et ipsi sunt e numeri simiarum' (*Collectanea rerum memorabilium* 27, 58: ed. Mommsen, 128).

55 *In hoc latifundio et inter Egyptum et Ethyopiam et Libiam sunt genera simiarum silvestria, quorum primum genus generaliter simias dicimus, secundum genus cirofitici, tertium cynocefali, quartum synges, quintum satiri, sextum fauni dicuntur.* (Miller, *Mappae mundi*, V, 61).

56 K. Smits, *Die frühmittelhochdeutsche Wiener Genesis.* Berlin 1972, 134–137; cf. Friedman, 93.

57 Even for a theologian such as the Franciscan prior Alexander of Hales in 13th-century Paris the sinfulness of mankind was the reason for deformities: *Summa Theologica*, ed. B. Marrani, Florence 1928, 576.

58 *De animalibus libri* XXVI.

59 Cap. XVI: *De mirabilibus Indie* (Edmond Buron (ed.), *Ymago mundi de Pierre d'Ailly.* Paris 1930, I, 264–269).

60 Buron, 264 and 266.

61 See Hosten, 291–301.

62 *Naturalis Historia* V, 8.

63 See Hosten, 291ff.

64 Plinius, *Naturalis Historia* VI, 35; Solinus, *Collectanea rerum memorabilium* 17, 2; Isidore; Thomas von Cantimpré.

65 Bragmani: Pliny, *Naturalis Historia* (Bragmanae) VI, 64; Gymnosophists: *op. cit.* VII, 22.

66 See Friedman, 168ff.

67 Maritimi: Plinius, *Naturalis Historia*, VI, 194.

68 Solinus, *Collectanea rerum memorabilium* 30, 6.

69 See Lecouteux, *Les Monstres*, II, 117f; Illustration in Friedman, 17, Ill. 9.

70 Troglodytes ('cave dwellers'), originally Trogodytai, are repeatedly mentioned in Pliny (*Naturalis Historia* V, 8; VI, 28; VI, 29; VI, 30) and Vincent of Beauvais, *Speculum naturale* XXXII, 130.

71 See Thomas of Cantimpré, *De natura rerum* III, 5, 30; Walter of Metz, *Image du Monde*, 134; Vincent of Beauvais, *Speculum naturale* XXXI, 120. Numerous other references in encyclopedic literature. About hermaphrodites and androgynism in general, see H. Baumann, *Das doppelte Geschlecht. Ethnologische Studien zur Bisexualität in Ritus und Mythos*. Berlin 1955.

72 Tscharner, *Mittelhochdeutscher Marco Polo*, 31 and 33; see Friedman, 21f, who does not give his sources. There is as yet no research on the background to this custom.

73 Passing mention could be made here of such beings as E.T., Alf, Alien, and Gremlins to name but a few of the other partly humanoid monsters of science-fiction novels and films who daily storm our living rooms and who would all qualify under the medieval definition of 'fabulous people'. Their similarity to humans, but with physical or social deficiencies, exotic origin, belonging to a race with similar characteristics (that is, not freak births) and also frequently superiority over normal people in one limited area likens them to the medieval races.

74 On the delicate subject of belief in fabulous races in the Middle Ages, see C. Gerhardt, 'Gab es im Mittelalter Fabelwesen?' *Wirkendes Wort* (1988), 156–171.

75 The concept of giants could easily have originated from the description of extremely large African races (such as the Watussi), the Amycteres from the cosmetic lip stretching of the African Ubangi and the Panoti from various Polynesian and Central African races who have similar traditions respecting ear decoration.

76 The most important informant of fabulous races in medieval encyclopedias was Honorius of Autun who obviously used Solinus directly in his *Imago mundi* and then reworked his findings together with those from St Augustine and Isidore. Honorius's work was translated into a French rhymed version by Walter of Metz (F. Fritsche, *Untersuchungen ueber die Quellen der Image du Monde des Walther von Metz*. Halle/S. 1880). Naturally enough fabulous peoples are also found in the voluminous *Speculum historiale* by Vincent of Beauvais (I, 92). Vernacular versions were also made of the natural historical encyclopedia *De natura rerum* by Thomas of Cantimpré, including a French one and Konrad of Megenberg's Middle High German one.

77 Like the versified chronicle by Rudolf von Ems and the closely related *Christherrechronik*; cf. O. Doberentz, 'Die Erd-und Völkerkunde in der Weltchronik des Rudolf von Hohen-Ems'. *Zeitschrift für deutsche Philologie* 12 (1881), 257–301, 387–454 and 13 (1882), 29–57, 165–223; R. Simek, 'Die Wundervölker in der Weltchronik des Rudolf von Ems und der Christherrechronik'. *Österreichische Zeitschrift für Volkskunde* XLIII/92 (1989), 37–44.

Notes to Chapter Eight

1 O. Dunn and J. E. Kelley, Jr. (ed.), *The* Diario *of Christopher Columbus's First Voyage to America 1492–1493. Abstracted by Fray Bartholomé de las Casas. Transcribed and Translated into English, with Notes and a Concordance of the Spanish*. Norman and London 1989, 38f.

2   Dunn and Kelley, 30–33.

3   R. J. Forbes, *Studies in Ancient Technology*. Leiden 1966, VII, 10–37.

4   E. Kölbing, 'Geistliche Auslegung von Schiff und Regenbogen'. *Zeitschrift für deutsches Altertum* 23 (1878), 258–261; L. Larsson, 'Nochmals Schiff und Regenbogen'. *Zeitschrift für deutsches Altertum* 33 (1891), 244–248.

5   Grant, *Das physikalische Weltbild des Mittelalters*, 40ff and S. 90f.

6   M. Schramm, 'Roger Bacons Begriff vom Naturgesetz'. In *Die Renaissance der Wissenschaften im 12. Jahrhundert*, ed. P. Weimar. Zurich and Munich 1981, 197–209.

7   Strunz, 97.

8   P. H. Blair, *The World of Bede*. Cambridge 1990, 261.

9   See Forbes, 10–37.

10 D. C. Lindberg, 'The Science of Optics'. In *Science in the Middle Ages*, ed. D. C. Lindberg. Chicago and London 1978, 338–368; D. C. Lindberg, *Auge und Licht im Mittelalter. Die Entwicklung der Optik von Alkindi bis Kepler*. Frankfurt 1987, who unfortunately ignores the common connections between astronomic and optical theories in the Middle Ages.

11 The transference of Greek and Arabic knowledge to Europe is shown (for example in medicine) by H. Schipperges, *Die Rezeption arabisch-griechischer Medizin und ihr Einfluß auf die abendländische Heilkunde*, in P. Weimar (ed.), *Die Renaissance der Wissenschaften im 12. Jahrhundert*. Zurich and Munich 1981, 173–196, 194, note 26.

12 Grant, *Das physikalische Weltbild des Mittelalters*, 69f.

13 Simek, *Altnordische Kosmographie*, 101, using the Old Icelandic manuscript *Hauksbók* (early 14th century).

14 For example Isidore, *Etymolgiae* XIII, 3 and *De natura rerum* XI, 1 (PL 83, cols. 979f); Beda, *De natura rerum* 4 (PL 90, cols. 195ff); Honorius of Autun, *De imagine mundi* I, 3 (PL 111, cols. 262); William of Conches, *De philosophia mundi* I, 21 (PL 172, cols. 121).

15 See the previously mentioned *Mainauer Naturlehre*, a MHG treatise mainly dealing with computistics and only preserved in a single manuscript from the 14th century, which presents a very clear and concise theory of the four elements at the beginning: Plant, 5f and 17f.

16 Dealt with above in chapter 5.

17 Burnett, *Pseudo-Bede*, 20–22; cf. D. Gottschall, 'Sternschnuppen und Altweibersommer. Zu "De mundi constitutione", einem naturwissenschaftlichen Traktat des 12. Jahrhunderts aus der süddeutschen Provinz'. *Zeitschrift für deutsches Altertum* 119 (1990), 154–162.

18 For example Anaxagoras and Democritus of Abdera; see Forbes, *Studies in Ancient Technology*, VII, 40–47.

19 Forbes, 22.

20 Grant, *Das physikalische Weltbild*, 124f.

21 Based on the *Liber de natura rerum* by Thomas Cantimpratensis, ed. H. Boese. Berlin and New York 1973.

22 Konrad von Megenberg, *Buch von der Natur*, ed. Pfeiffer, 107–113.

23 For earthquakes in the Middle Ages see G. Dragon, *Quand la terre tremble*. Paris 1981 and J. Vogt, 'Historische Seismologie – Einige Anmerkungen über Quellen für Seismologen'. *Frühneuzeit-Info* 1 (1990), 17–22.

24 Avicennae 'De congelatione et conglutinatione lapidum'; being sections of the

Kitâb al-shifâ. The Latin and Arabic Texts. ed. with an English translation by E. J. Holmyard and D. C. Mandeville. Paris 1927; cf. Grant, *Das physikalische Weltbild*, 124f.

25 Cf. R. A. Koch, 'Die aktualistische Bedeutung der Vulkanexperimente des Albertus Magnus'. *Abhandlungen des Staatlichen Museums für Mineralogie und Geologie zu Dresden* 11 (1966), 307–314.

26 Forbes, 52ff.

27 Isidore, *Etymologiae* XIV, 6, 32 and XIV 8, 14; with direct reference to Aristotle in Arnoldus Saxo, *Liber in naturalibus* I, 4, 17 (E. Stange (ed.), *Die Enzyklopädie des Arnoldus Saxo, zum ersten Mal nach einem Erfurter Codex herausgegeben.* (Königliches Gymnasium zu Erfurt. Beilage zum Jahresbericht 1904/05, 1905/06, 1906/07), 40).

28 L. Thorndike, A History of Magic and Experimental Science. IV, 414ff.

29 S. Jenks, 'Astrometeorology in the Middle Ages'. *Isis* 74 (1983), 185–210.

30 Jenks, 193ff.

31 D. Harmenig, 'Bauernpraktik', in *Lexikon des Mittelalters.* Munich and Zurich 1980, I, cols. 1621f; G. Eis (ed.), *Wahrsagetexte des späten Mittelalters. Aus Handschriften und Inkunabeln.* Berlin 1956.

32 Konrad of Megenberg, ed. Pfeiffer, 95f.

33 De mundi celestis terrestrisque constitutione, ed. Burnett, 26.

34 Burnett, 26.

35 Konrad of Megenberg, ed. Pfeiffer, 81.

36 Konrad of Megenberg, ed. Pfeiffer, 82.

37 Thomas Cantimpratensis, *Liber de natura rerum*, ed. Boese, 381.

38 Konrad of Megenberg, ed. Pfeiffer, 83.

39 Thorndike, *A History of Magic and Experimental Science.* II, 580.

40 Pliny, *Naturalis Historia* II, 162; see Forbes, 33f.

41 Bede, *De natura rerum* XXXIV and XXXV (PL 90, cols. 253f); Thomas of Cantimpré, *Liber de natura rerum* XVI, 3–4, ed. Boese, 380f; *De mundi celestis terrestrisque constitutione*, ed. Burnett, 26–28; Konrad of Megenberg, ed. Pfeiffer, 86 and 84; William of Conches, *De philosophia mundi* III, 8 (PL 172, cols. 77).

42 De mundi celestis terrestrisque constitutione, ed. Burnett, 26–28; Konrad von Megenberg, ed. Pfeiffer, 86 and 84; William of Conches, *De philosophia mundi* III, 8 (PL 172, col. 77).

43 De mundi celestis terrestrisque constitutione, ed. Burnett, 30.

44 Konrad of Megenberg, ed. Pfeiffer, 77.

45 Gottschall, 158–161, dealing with Konrad's sources.

46 Mainauer Naturlehre, ed. Plant, 17; Alexander Neckham, *De naturis rerum* II, 14: *Alexandri Neckam De naturis rerum libri duo*, ed. by Th. Wright. London 1863, 135f.

47 De naturis rerum II, 49, ed. Wright, 159.

48 For the relation between globe and hydrosphere, see S. Günther, *Die Lehre von der Erdrundung,* 10ff, and S. Günther, *Aeltere und neuere Hypothesen über die chronische Versetzung des Erdschwerpunktes durch Wassermassen.* Halle 1878, 129–164.

49 Johannes Burdidanus, *De coelo et mundo* II, 7 (English translation in Grant, *A Source Book in medieval Science,* 621–624).

50 Günther, *Aeltere und neuere Hypothesen,* 146–154.

51 B. Hansen, *Nicole Oresme and the Marvels of Nature. A Study of his* De causis mirabilium *with Critical Edition, Translation and Commentary.* Toronto 1985, 392;

for the physical theories of Nicolas Oresme cf. J. D. North, 'Intimations of Cosmic Unity? Fourteenth century Views on Celestial and Sub-lunar Motion'. In *Nicolas Oresme. Tradition et innovation chez un intellectuel du XIVe siècle. Etudes recueillies et éditées par P. Souffrin et A. Ph. Segonds.* Paris 1988, 45–55.

52 Bede, *De natura rerum* XXXIX (PL 90, cols. 258–260); Thomas of Cantimpré: *Liber de natura rerum* XIX, 4, ed. Boese, 409; *De mundi celestis terrestrisque constitutione,* ed. Burnett, 24.

53 De mundi celestis terrestrisque constitutione, ed. Burnett, 24.

54 The two currents turning north hit each other, and that impact might be the reason for the tides: *De mundi celestis terrestrisque constitutione,* ed. Burnett, 24.

55 William of Conches, *De philosophia mundi* III, 8 (PL 172, col. 80).

56 Athanasius Kircher, *Mundus Subterraneus* I, 86, 147ff (cf. Thorndike, *A History of Magic and Experimental Science,* VII, 572).

57 Adam von Bremen, *Gesta Hammaburgensis Ecclesiae Pontificum,* 4, 39: *Magister Adam Bremensis: Gesta Hammaburgensis Ecclesiae Pontificum,* 490f.

58 H. de Boor, *Die deutsche Literatur von Karl dem Großen bis zum Beginn der Höfischen Dichtung.* 8th ed. Munich 1971, 153f.

59 Bede, *De natura rerum* XXVI (PL 90, cols. 246f); similar in William of Conches, *De philosophia mundi* III, 15 (PL 172, cols 81f).

60 De mundi celestis terrestrisque constitutione, ed. Burnett, 30.

61 ed. Burnett, 30.

62 Etymologiae XIII, 8.

63 De natura rerum XXVIII (PL 90, cols. 249f).

64 Thomas of Cantimpré, *Liber de natura rerum* XVIII, 2, ed. Boese, 396; Konrad of Megenberg, ed. Pfeiffer, 91.

65 Thomas von Cantimpré: *Liber de natura rerum,* XVIII, 2, ed. Boese, 396; *De mundi celestis terrestrisque constitutione,* ed. Burnett, 30.

66 Konrad of Megenberg, ed. Pfeiffer, 91.

67 Konrad of Megenberg, ed. Pfeiffer, 91.

68 Konrad of Megenberg, ed. Pfeiffer, 97–100.

69 Mentioned in the Old Norse *Hauksbók* (F. Jónsson (ed.), *Hauksbok.* København 1916, 174f.

70 For the *Physiologus* and the bestiaries see Chapter 5 above.

71 Bede, *De natura rerum* XXXI (PL 90, col. 252); similarly, *De mundi celestis terrestrisque constitutione,* ed. Burnett, 32, but the colours given here are green, grey, blue and red.

72 One of the most talented scholars of the 14th century, Nicole Oresme dealt with refraction and optics in his book on miracles (*De causis mirabilium*), because he knew, that certain optical phenomena were considered to be miraculous by his contemperaries. For Nicole Oresme's scholarship cf. E. Grant, 'Nicole Oresme on Certitude in Science and Pseudo-Science'. In *Nicolas Oresme. Tradition et innovation chez un intellectuel du XIVe siècle. Etudes recueillies et éditées par P. Souffrin et A. Ph. Segonds.* Paris 1988, 31–43.

73 Isidore, *Etymologiae* III, 71, 3; Bede, *De natura rerum* 11; Honorius of Autun, *De imagine mundi* I, 70; William of Conches, *De philosophia mundi* II, 12; Thomas of Cantimpré: *De natura rerum* XVIII, 3.

74 Thorndike, *A History of Magic and Experimental Science*. II, 320; for Michael Scotus cf. Thorndike, *The Sphere of Sacro Bosco and its Commentators*, 21–23.

75 U. Dall'Olmo, 'Latin Terminology Relating to Aurorae, Comets, Meteors and Novae'. *Journal for the History of Astronomy* 10 (1979), 10–27.

76 Konrad of Megenberg, ed. Pfeiffer, 78.

77 Dall'Olmo, 23, remarks on the term not being used in Latin texts of the Middle Ages; the MHG was not known to him.

78 Bauer, *Sternkunde und Sterndeutung*, 51ff.

79 De imagine mundi III, 13: *Quod cometa non sit stella* (PL 172, col. 80).

80 H. Pruckner, *Studien zu den astrologischen Schriften des Heinrich von Langenstein*. Leipzig 1933, 25.

81 An English translation of the Latin text by Albertus Magnus is to be found in Grant, *A Source Book in medieval Science*, 539–547.

82 Thorndike, *A History of Magic and Experimental Science*. IV, 83.

83 Thorndike, *A History of Magic and Experimental Science*. IV, 414ff; Hansen, *Nicole Oresme*, 59, note 30, and 191f, note 30.

Notes to Chapter Nine

1 Admittedly, Willem Jansz landed in Australia in 1605, Dirk Hartog in 1616, Tasman (who found New Zealand in 1642/3) in 1644, Dampier in 1688 and Cook in 1770, but it took three hundred years before Australia was recognised as a continental land-mass.

2 P. M. de Anghiera, *De Orbe Novo*. Sevilla 1511.

3 Jacob, *Christoph Columbus*, 327f.

4 Salentiny, 90; Hamann, *Der Eintritt der südlichen Hemisphäre*, 347.

5 Salentiny, 84.

6 Jacob, 327f.

7 Hamann, 363–417.

8 Salentiny, 72ff.

9 Salentiny, 77.

10 Gewecke, 41.

11 Gewecke, 42f, relying on E. J. Hamilton, *American Treasure and the Price Revolution in Spain 1501–1650*. 2nd ed., Cambridge, Mass. 1934, 34ff.

12 O. Peschel, *Die Theilung der Erde unter Papst Alexander VI. und Julius II*. Leipzig 1871, 14–17; E. Staedler, 'Die "donatio Alexandrina" und die "divisio mundi" von 1493'. *Archiv für katholisches Kirchenrecht* 117 (1937), 363–402; Hamann, 370–378.

13 Salentiny, 93ff.

14 Hartmann Schedel, *Liber chronicarum*, f. XIIv–XIIIr.

15 See Gewecke, Ill. 3 and 4.

16 See Gewecke, Ill. 5.

17 E. Zinner, *Entstehung und Ausbreitung der copernicanischen Lehre*. 2nd ed., Munich 1988, 181f.

18 H. Grössing, 'Die Kopernikanische Wende', in W. Seipel (ed.), *Mensch und Kosmos*. Linz 1990, 78–80.

19 Grössing, 80f.

20 Grant, *Das physikalische Weltbild*, 114–120.

21 G. Hamann and H. Grössing (ed.), *Der Weg der Naturwissenschaften von Johannes von Gmunden zu Johannes Kepler*. Wien 1988 (Sitzungsberichte der österr. Akademie der Wiss., phil.-hist. Kl. 364).

22 S. Arrhenius, *Die Vorstellung vom Weltgebäude im Wandel der Zeiten*. Leipzig 1908, 73.

23 His second law was that an imaginary line between the planet and the sun swept across equal areas of space in an equal time, regardless of how far the planet was from the sun; and his third, that the square of the time a planet takes to orbit the sun is proportional to the cube of the planet's distance from the sun. What this all meant was that only one single distance had to be calculated for the whole solar system and all the other distances could be computed with measurements of time; cf. Hamann and Grössing, 81.

24 E. McMullin, 'Introduction. Galileo, Man of Science', in *Galileo, Man of Science*. Princeton Junction, New Jersey 1988, 20f; W. Hartner, 'Galileo's Contribution to Astronomy', in *Galileo, Man of Science*. Princeton Junction, New Jersey 1988, 182ff.

25 H. Grössing, 'Galilei und Kepler oder Theologie gegen Naturwissenschaft', in W. Seipel (ed.), *Mensch und Kosmos*. Linz 1990, 114f.

26 W. Brandmüller, 'Das Ende einer Affäre'. *30Tage* 1/3 (1991), 54–59.

27 Konrad von Megenberg, ed. Pfeiffer, 78.

Notes to Appendix

1 Cf. Miller, *Mappae mundi*, IV, 4.

2 M. Jancey, *Mappa mundi. The Map of the World in Hereford Cathedral*. Hereford 1987, 1f.

3 See Chapters 4 and 7 above.

4 For illustrations of the labyrinth in the Middle Ages cf. F. Weissengruber, 'Labyrinthus. Hic habitat Minotaurus'. In *Festschrift zum 400jährigen Jubiläum des humanist. Gymnasiums in Linz*, Linz 1952, 127–147; P. Santarcangeli, *Il libro dei labirinti*. Florence 1967; H. Birkhan, 'Laborintus – labor intus'. In *Festschrift für R. Pittioni*, Wien 1976, 423–154; R. Simek, 'Völundar hús – Domus Daedali. Labyrinths in Old Norse manuscripts'. In *Twenty-Eight Papers presented to H. Bekker-Nielsen on the Occasion of his Sixtieth Birthday 28 April 1993*. Odense 1993, 323–368; and, most comprehensively, H. Kern, *Labyrinthe*. Munich 1982.

5 Cf. Miller, *Mappae mundi*, IV, 18.

INDEX